Shadow Work for the Soul

"*Shadow Work for the Soul* is practical, experiential, and will be of great assistance to individuals seeking self-realization."

~ **Peter J. Smith,** M.D.

"Mary is down-to-earth and an excellent conceptualizer of complex ideas. She can put into words things that seem ineffable. I highly recommend her work on self-inquiry and the shadow."

~ **Lawrence Wan,** acupuncturist

"I find myself a bit lost for words in terms of what depths Mary's work has taken me to and what it has given me. For me, Mary captures the grit and backbone of shadow work. The essential essence of something gifted to us with respect and understanding."

~ **Kim Leyland,** shamanic teacher and practitioner

"This book is extraordinary—each paragraph is just bursting with information and insight. It is a culmination of Mary's vast knowledge that no one else could have ever written."

~ **Kathy Tajik,** entrepreneur, CEO of Tajik Home

SHADOW WORK FOR THE SOUL

Seeing Beauty in the Dark

Mary Mueller Shutan

FINDHORN PRESS

Findhorn Press
One Park Street
Rochester, Vermont 05767
www.findhornpress.com

Findhorn Press is a division of Inner Traditions International

Disclaimer

The information in this book is given in good faith and intended for information only. Neither author nor publisher can be held liable by any person for any loss or damage whatsoever which may arise from the use of this book or any of the information therein.

A CIP record for this title is available from the Library of Congress

ISBN 979-8-88850-014-9 (print)
ISBN 979-8-88850-015-6 (ebook)

Printed and bound in the United States by Lake Book Manufacturing, LLC

10 9 8 7 6 5 4 3 2 1

Edited by Jane Ellen Combelic
Text design and layout by Anna-Kristina Larsson
This book was typeset in Garamond and DIN Next

To send correspondence to the author of this book, mail a first-class letter to the author c/o Inner Traditions • Bear & Company, One Park Street, Rochester, VT 05767, USA and we will forward the communication, or contact the author directly at **www.maryshutan.com**.

Scan the QR code and save 25% at InnerTraditions.com. Browse over 2,000 titles on spirituality, the occult, ancient mysteries, new science, holistic health, and natural medicine.

Contents

Introduction   7

Part 1
Meeting the Shadow

1 Understanding the Shadow   13
2 The Self and the Ego   24
3 Defense Mechanisms of the Ego   37
4 The Benefits of Shadow Work   58
5 Helpful Tools   64

Part 2
Working with the Shadow

6 Developing Emotional Intelligence   81
7 Emotional Intelligence Tools   99
8 The World as Mirror   109
9 Understanding Our Play   125
10 Casting Roles   142
11 Recrafting Our Narrative   159

Part 3
Collective Shadows

12 Archetypal Figures   177
13 Animus and Anima   190
14 Loops   201
15 Understanding Collective Shadows   217

Part 4
Embracing the Other
(Essays and Contradictions)

16	Embracing Our Full Continuum	239
17	The Power of Being Ordinary	244
18	The Myth of Perfection	246
19	Moving beyond Forgiveness	249
20	Rediscovering the Child Self	257
21	Releasing the Shame of the Body	259
22	Recapturing Voice	263
23	Engaging the Deep Wild	267
24	Our Online Shadows	274
25	Fear of Death, Fear of Life	278
	Afterword: Seeing the Beauty in the Dark	283
	Further Reading	286
	About the Author	288

Introduction

*P*icture a beautiful small lake or pond. As you sit next to it your shoulders move down from your ears and your breath slows down as you relax. You can now feel the stones and sand beneath where you sit and you see the small sparkles on the surface of the water. You feel totally present in this moment.

In this present moment your perspective shifts. You can see the light and beauty of the world. Your personal troubles seem lessened; you feel like a part of the world, a part of something much larger than yourself.

This practice is mindfulness and it is an important and well-known meditation method.

Now picture yourself being able to gradually see beneath the surface of the water with increasing depth. Below the surface you start to see the pain you carry, the conflicts that still play out in your mind and in your heart.

When you look even deeper you contact the emotions that you have held within, the traumas that have not been resolved, and the words that have been left unsaid.

In each of our lives there have been situations that have caused us soul-level damage. We have made choices regarding who we are and how we carry ourselves in this world due to this damage. We see reality through a filter of this pain. We have defended and shielded ourselves against experiencing the same types of pain again.

As we peer beneath the surface of this water, what we carry within ourselves surfaces. What is unknown becomes known, and what has become lost along the way becomes clear.

As we gaze further and further under the surface, what we see changes. We can now see how we have shut ourselves down, abandoned parts of ourselves in order to fit into our families, communities, school systems, and society.

As we look within the shadowy depths of the water, we can see the basic conflicts of our existence. Feelings of inadequacy, of unworthiness, and of being unlovable come into our awareness.

An essential loneliness arises when we reach the bottom of this lake. We are each lonely souls in our own way. We feel disconnected from ourselves, from one another, from the earth and sky, and from the divine. We are disconnected from the feminine and the body, as well as from the emotional, creative, intuitive, instinctual, and soulful aspects of our being.

Looking under the surface of this lake is shadow work, which allows us to descend to the depths of our being. In traversing such depths, we regain our soul and become authentically aligned with our unique essence. Such work lets us strip away our pain, heal conflicts, and to recognize that we deserve love and regard simply for being human.

It is by accepting each and every part of ourselves, no matter how dark, that we develop the emotional intelligence and self-realization to totally and completely fall in love with ourselves and the world again. We are not alone, and never have been. Realizing this takes time, but the journey is well worth it.

Shadow work requires a certain amount of courage. On its surface it is quite simple—it requires us to see what isn't working in our lives and to ask ourselves some basic questions. Answering these questions requires a type of radical honesty that is truly both life-changing and life-affirming.

Other parts of shadow work involve inwardly questioning our beliefs and understandings about ourselves and the world. When we are willing to question what we think and believe, an open mind will lead to an open heart.

Self-inquiry is a form of meditation that allows us to ask ourselves questions and to seek an honest response from deep within. It is the work of self-realization, and a large part of shadow work.

We can ask ourselves the same question many times and as more of our shadow comes into the light, our answers will change. We will recognize that seeing what is within ourselves, knowing our own pain and suffering, does not create more suffering. Suffering is created by what we push away, ignore, deny, and repress.

When we finally confront ourselves, we can see even the scariest or most alienated aspects of our being with compassion. It is by accepting even the darkest aspects of ourselves, by truly witnessing and feeling the suffering that we attempt to shove aside again and again, that we can be free from the fears and conflicts that define our existence.

The purpose of shadow work is not to become beings of light, but to revel in the dark. We can become a fully human being—accepting and allowing every aspect of ourselves to become a part of us again. Without our darkness we are only half a person, living a half-lived life. Our darkness is where our passions lie, where we can experience the beauty of our human bodies and take pleasure in our sensate experiences. By doing shadow work we can release the primal shame of the body and embrace ourselves exactly as we are.

Shadow work is one of the most direct paths to self-realization. It leads us to the end of conflict within the self, and gives us the ability to work through the suffering that we carry. If we only knew how much latent power we have, how much ability we have to change our mentalities, our whole way of being in the world could change. We experience ourselves as such limited beings because we have lost or given away so much of who we truly are. There is such freedom in recognizing and restoring our full vitality and possibility.

It is a paradox that exploring our depths and embracing our shadows allows us to find our light. We each have a unique essence; something we bring to the world that is solely ours. In this essence we find purpose and meaning which allows us to ultimately be of service to ourselves as well as others by finally being fully and completely ourselves.

Part 1

Meeting the Shadow

One does not become enlightened by imagining figures of light,
but by making the darkness conscious.

Until you make the unconscious conscious,
it will direct your life and you will call it fate.

C.G. Jung

Chapter 1

Understanding the Shadow

The shadow is most simply defined as what we do not know about ourselves. Our shadows are composed of all of the parts of ourselves that we have rejected, denied, or repressed. In psychological terms, we can refer to the shadow as the entirety of the subconscious: that which is dark, hidden, and not directly known by us.

The shadow is composed of all the parts of our personality that we have not integrated into our current self-concept—who we know ourselves to be. What we have made shadow can just as easily be our joy and enthusiasm for living as it can be our negative emotions, prior traumas, or the instinctual, animalistic parts of ourselves.

When we make something shadow, we cut it off from our conscious awareness. Parts of our personality become hidden to us. With this severing of ourselves comes a decrease in vitality: we suffer from this energy loss. This can result in a decrease in physical energy, or a lessened ability to experience joy and enthusiasm for life. It most often results in a feeling of something missing on a soul level and an understanding that we are not living our lives in a manner that is authentic to who we truly are or who we wish to be.

We cut off aspects of ourselves to appease our family, society, and the world. Poet Robert Bly called this "the long bag we drag behind us"—that bag filled with every single last bit of ourselves that we have learned is wrong, bad, or that we cannot show the world for fear of reprisal.

We learn to wear masks to hide who we truly are, because we find that parts of ourselves do not meet the approval of our parents or community. Our personal shadow is primarily composed of the parts of ourselves that we do not like to acknowledge because we view them as undesirable.

In our childhood home we form the baseline of our being. From the perspective of a child, our home is the entirety of the universe. We develop beliefs and understandings about what reality is, how it operates, and who we should be based on the beliefs, understandings, and behaviors of our parents or caregivers.

We are unable to consider that the few people we associate with in our childhood home do not represent the entirety of the world, and so we carry our early impressions out into the world as if they do. Many of us are stuck in patterns of infantile relating as adults, still living out the patterns and behaviors we learned in our childhood homes.

We all have a primal need to receive love and support from our parents. Our survival as a child depends on being nurtured and cared for properly. Other animals may be able to walk and receive nurturing in an independent way reasonably quickly but humans are totally dependent on their caregivers for extended periods of time.

In a healthy home, we would receive unconditional love, acceptance, and nurturing from our parents. That nurturing would be physical, emotional, and spiritual. We would receive proper nutrients and caring attention, we would feel safe in expressing our emotions openly, and we would feel wanted and cherished. The felt absence of one of these factors can dramatically impact how a child develops their basic understandings of reality. For example, a child who is neglected emotionally or physically can end up believing that nobody supports them in adulthood; they feel they cannot ask for help. A feeling of being unwanted, or not loved for who we are, can create an understanding that follows us throughout our lives that nobody wants us or loves us.

Additionally, in a healthy home our parents would offer us support and they would model healthy boundaries. Without a sense of safety or with parents who are emotionally dysregulated we will struggle to develop a healthy self-concept. We will not pass through the stages of childhood development in a way that would allow us to emerge as a confident, emotionally healthy adult. We cannot develop emotional intelligence if our parents do not model that same intelligence to us.

We learn how to be in the world based on the modeling of our mothers, fathers, or caregivers. They show us what is right, how to behave, and they imprint in us ideas regarding who we should be. We see their way of being in the world and mirror it. In doing this we cut off parts of our personality that do not resemble our parents. We assume that this modeling is what we should follow, and that other facets of our personality that are not shared by our parents are incorrect.

On a deeper level, we desire to be approved of and cared for; emulating a type of "sameness" as our parents ensures our basic survival. We are more likely to be taken care of if we synchronize with our parents' personalities and moods.

Parents often have wishes and desires for who they want their children to be. This can be a mother wanting a daughter who dances ballet just like her, or a father wanting a daughter who is seen as adorable and praiseworthy in order for him to gain acceptance by proxy from others.

They will most significantly have an internal sense of morality, a sense of what is right and wrong, that drives their parenting. This can be quite explicit, such as raising their children in a specific religious or spiritual tradition. It may also involve telling a child who they will be when they grow up, for example repeatedly telling a child that they need to go into business just like their mother did.

This sense of right or wrong is most often demonstrated through punishments, admonitions, shaming, and "jokes" that are repeated throughout the childhood. For example, a big one while growing up for me was "children should be seen and not heard." When parents tell their children this, they are teaching them to hide their exuberance, their curiosity, and their voice. In a naturally extroverted or talkative child this will turn into a larger shadow than it will in a naturally introverted or quiet child.

Through implicit or less obvious modeling we learn that parts of ourselves are not considered "good" enough by the parental figures and we make them shadow. For example, a child is born as a result of a brief relationship and his single father secretly hates the fact that his son resembles his ex-lover. The son learns that all of the parts of himself that resemble his birth mother are "bad" and so he makes them shadow.

A child with natural aptitude as an artist may grow up in a family of fellow artists. She would not need to make her artistic talent shadow; in fact, it is likely to thrive with the support of her family. Or she might grow up in a family of scientists who are more than willing to love and nurture her artistic talent. However, she may grow up in a family of engineers where she learns either explicitly or implicitly that being an artist is "bad" because it is dissimilar to the rest of the family.

A child who is different from her parents in personality or interests will make more parts of herself shadow. This may happen through outright punishment or shaming, or it may come from seeking approval on a subtler level. The child may completely cut off her artistic ability, only allowing herself as an adult to express her interest in art by watching reality shows about other creatives and vicariously experiencing that part of herself. She more likely will find herself as an adult stuck and struggling to find her artistic voice and expression. She may envision several art projects that she can simply never get started. This is because inwardly she feels conflicted about accepting and acting on her talent because to do so would go against the programming she received as a child that that part of her was "wrong." Or she will encounter her creativity differently, perhaps through cooking, an activity that society and her parents consider more appropriate.

More commonly we learn what is considered "good" based on our parents' understanding of normality. Everything our parents tell us to do—from what types of toys we should play with, to what we should wear, to how we should behave when company is around—creates an impression on us. We sever off the "bad" parts of ourselves in order to gain approval and acceptance and be considered "good" by our parents.

By the end of our childhoods, we are left with a faint sliver of who we once were. We have made large parts of ourselves shadow. Our need to receive love and approval is so significant that as children we lack the consciousness to consider if what our parents think of as "good" is really something that we agree with and want to take on as our own value system.

As adults we have the capacity to clearly see what sort of patterning occurred in our childhood home and we can learn how to react and heal in our adult capacity. From an adult perspective we can realize that no part of us was ever "bad" or "wrong" and we can reintegrate the parts of ourselves that we once needed to make shadow in order to survive.

The Longer Bag

When we are growing up the dominant aspects of our personality emerge. These become fixed. If you were to ask friends to describe you in three words, they will likely name the known and fixed aspects of your personality.

Over time we learn that these fixed aspects are who we are. We make them dominant, care for them, attend to them, and make other aspects of our personality shadow. For example, a teenager has a natural aptitude for English and reading. Her mother was a teacher and so her mother encourages these interests and prods her to be a teacher exactly like her. But this teenager is also interested in math, unlike her mother. The mother gently discourages this interest, even making fun of her daughter for wanting to join a math club.

While the daughter's interest in literature is always more apparent, her interest in math is also a part of her. Over time she learns to make the math part of herself shadow so as to make the literature part of herself more dominant and fixed. Now when people think of her as an adult, they think of her as "literary" and they do not see the math parts of her at all.

We all have parts of ourselves that are more dominant than others. In doing shadow work, we can reclaim the different parts of ourselves, and we can also discover new ones. Simply because a man was never an athlete as a child does not mean that he cannot go to the gym as an adult. Joining a gym would allow a large part of himself—the archetypal athlete—to become an acknowledged part even though previously he didn't identify with any sort of physical exercise.

Usually our ideas around ourselves are so fixated on a small spectrum of who we are that we deny other aspects of self. This is because in our self-concept we find it difficult to consider that we can be both a librarian who enjoys cats and reading books on a rainy Saturday as well as a woman who loves dancing at a loud club on a Sunday.

We truly know only a small portion of our possibility as human beings. We have been told who we are from our parents, our community, and the world. We have been shown what is possible through our schools and how we see others live.

We start to become defined by labels at such an early age; what we excel in, what we are not good at become fixed parts of our personality that constrict our way of being for the rest of our lives. We learn to fear the unknown, the Other, and so gradually we distance ourselves from anything that we have defined as "not-me." For example, "I am good at art and not good at math, so I do not bother to learn anything about finances or accounting."

This gets more complicated as we further contend with the shadow. For example, if a father is a doctor, he wants his children to also be doctors, despite their aptitude or interest. This has an even more complicated shadow, as the role of "doctor" can be considered socially and culturally successful. So a child deciding to become a teacher or a musician instead of a doctor may have to deal with both family and cultural shadows that define their chosen career as not being worthwhile.

We are also taught from an early age to perpetuate a state of separation from those we define as Other. As a child we rarely consider the Other and see little division between people. But as we grow and learn from our parents, communities, and schools, we learn to separate and hate others based on our differences. As we will cover in later chapters, these separations are projections of inner divisions. By reintegrating them into ourselves we can see the humanity in others, rather than what separates us.

Some of what is shadow can be considered "shadows of light." These are the parts of ourselves like our beauty, ingenuity, and charisma that we have hidden. They may also be a part of our shadow because we never expressed them as a conscious part of our personality. Shadow work allows us to embrace all parts of ourselves—the light and the dark.

Many of us attend school at the age of six, where we learn more rules, adopt more models to follow, and are given more opportunities to see what is wrong, inappropriate, or must be denied for us to fit in, and thus, to survive.

As we become teenagers our modeling moves to our peers and what they consider right and wrong. We become immersed in societal, cultural, and larger mythic models (movies, television, news, social media) which also model to us who we should be and what qualities are most desirable.

We also experience trauma, which causes survival mechanisms and biological impulses to kick in. We then erect a series of ego-based defenses so that we do not experience that trauma again. Beliefs emerge as a result of the trauma—beliefs about ourselves and the nature of the world. Who we are and what we know about the world is filtered through the lens of that trauma. We make shadow the parts of ourselves that are overwhelmed and that lack the proper resources to deal with the trauma.

Over time our wholeness, our radiance, gets cut down more and more. Our shadows grow larger and larger. We lose our vitality and our enthusiasm for life. We lose access to who we truly are, because who we truly are is our uniqueness, those divine attributes and the sum of our personal history that flow through us and allow us to bring something different to the world.

Our models teach us to prize sameness. Our schools in particular do this, but many parents worry about wanting their child to have a "normal" childhood. This concept of normalcy will most often be defined and imposed by parents and educational institutions, instead of what would actually be considered healthy for the individual child's needs.

On a more complex level, we come into this world with aspects of ourselves already shadow. Our ancestors experienced trauma just as we did; we carry this unhealed trauma within ourselves and live it out in our present lives. We can also experience trauma or lack of connection with our mothers *in utero,* or experience trauma in past lives. We enter the world with aspects of ourselves already dulled or cut off.

Additionally, when and where we are born makes a huge energetic impact on who we are and what we make shadow. Consider someone born in the midst of a World War—imagine the fear and pain and difficulty of that and the parts of themselves that may become shadow as a result. Out of fear and pain and struggle we have to cast aspects of ourselves aside simply to survive, to make it through.

Robert Bly says that we spend our lives until about age twenty putting things into "the long bag we carry behind us" (making them shadow) and that we then spend the rest of our lives attempting to pull them back out again.

As adults we often think of ourselves as being incapable of change. There is an irony to this as who we are is continually in a process of change; we just may not be aware of it. As we grow older, our ideas about ourselves and what life is become more fixed. At any age we can recognize that many aspects of ourselves that we thought of as our personality are actually derived from trauma and social conditioning. They are who we needed to be to ensure our survival. Yet we can discover, as philosopher Alan Watts did, that "we are under no obligation to be the same person we were five minutes ago."

Emotions and the Shadow

When we do not fully experience our emotions, we become cut off from them and they become shadow. They become rulers over us; over time they create a backlog in our body. They also become magnified and distorted. When we experience anger, we no longer only experience righteous anger (justified anger in the present moment) but all of the anger that lies unprocessed and unheard within ourselves. It is typical for us to have storehouses of unresolved past emotions buried within.

For those with particularly large shadows, looking within causes a tsunami of unprocessed emotions. When we are completely separated from our shadows, we are unable to talk about or acknowledge any of our emotions.

We live in a society that is slowly grappling with emotional intelligence and the ability to consciously know what we are experiencing. Picture yourself as a clear blue sky, and emotions as weather patterns passing through. By facing our emotions, we can recognize that no matter the weather, it will change in time.

Until we learn to face our emotions, we allow them to rule over us—and they are often such cruel rulers. We often get stuck in emotional patterns that result from unhealed parts of ourselves and unprocessed emotions. By allowing ourselves to feel, we can embody every single emotion. Any negative emotions can be fully felt safely and with the understanding that no emotion that we carry is bad. It is—or was—an entirely appropriate emotion to feel.

When we truly allow ourselves to feel, we come more fully into our bodies. We come more into our light, our joy, and a place of love for ourselves and others. Emotions can simply flow through us. There is a paradox in knowing that the depths of our sorrow reveal the greatest feelings of love. Eventually we find that our anger and hatred—once embraced—reveal joy and happiness. We cannot embody our light until we know our darkness. It is only through knowing the dark side of our emotionality that we can find the light.

Shadow work is the process of reintegrating the parts of ourselves that were lost or cut off from our self-concept. In our work with the shadow, it is important to understand that our shadows contain both darkness and light, positivity and negativity. Darkness contains the nurturing wisdom of the body. Our shadows have their own innate intelligence. Shadows are not "bad" or "evil"; they are simply facets of ourselves that have not yet experienced the light of conscious awareness.

In addition to our personal shadows, we also have collective shadows. Our personal shadows are composed of the parts of ourselves that we have cut off from our consciousness in order to gain the approval, acceptance, and love of our families and society. Our collective shadows (discussed further in later chapters) contain the shadows of the world: those of our communities, religious/spiritual traditions, collective history, and the sum of many individual shadows coming together.

Working through the personal and collective shadows, we find our instinctual responses. When we have taken back all of our personal and collective shadows, we find ourselves in direct contact with the drives and responses that give us our power, pleasure, and full potentiality as human beings.

Our shadows, once fully integrated, are our humanity. To discover our darkness is to become fully and completely human, to come into our bodies, our senses, and know our soul. To discover our light is to find our joy, beauty, and enthusiasm for living. When our darkness and light combine, they form the "dark light" of a fully realized human being.

The power of shadow work is that it involves many layers of healing. At first, we take back the parts of ourselves that have been lost to us. By doing so we become more and more of who we truly are. We then discover that our emotions are something that can be deeply felt, and when we feel even the darkest of emotions, joy and enthusiasm for living emerge. We can then move to the deepest layer of reclaiming our shadow, when our shadows have become a part of us wholly. This is a reclaiming of our instinctual selves, of our bodies, and of the power and life force that we have separated from by denying the dark half of ourselves.

When we begin shadow work we are bringing our shadows out into the light: examining them, understanding them, and integrating them into our self-concept. It is through doing so that we can eventually get to a point where we are totally comfortable in the dark. By embodying our darkness we can connect with our intuition, creativity, and passion. Eventually shadow work leads to an ability to simply live our lives and to accept all that is. Our darkness can remain as is, and we can remain as we are, instead of continually needing to be understood, changed, or fixed. We no longer need to be special, superior, or inferior. We can simply be an imperfect human, worthy of being loved and accepted exactly as we are.

The end result of shadow work is like being at the bottom of the ocean, feeling the comforting stillness and darkness that is present there. From the bottom of the ocean, we can experience ourselves as the entirety of the ocean, including the surface waves and currents. We do not become separate from our emotions or any other part of ourselves. We simply experience them from a different vantage point. We see others as a part of ourselves, and a part of that same ocean, instead of viewing anyone or anything as separate or other. When we can anchor into our bodies, truly accepting (and forgiving) ourselves for being human, and thus imperfect, we can let go of shadow work, and in fact any type of seeking, and simply live our lives. This is the possibility, and beauty, of fully integrating our shadow.

On this deeper level, working with the shadow means contending with the fact that we have energetically split our head from our body, prizing the mind and its logic. The physical body is the domain of feeling, of knowing, of intuition, and of Eros. All that is life affirming is contained within the physical form.

Shadow work is a process of re-engaging with the dismissed body, emotions, and parts of self to see ourselves as both darkness and light. If we are living only in the light, we are living a half-life, if that. If we are living only in the darkness, we lose sight of hope and meaning. It is by marrying the darkness and the light within ourselves that we become a fully realized human being.

Hidden in our shadows is the vitality and vibrancy of soul that many of us have not experienced since childhood, if ever. To once again see ourselves and the world as filled with magic and vibrancy is the greatest gift of shadow work. Ultimately our shadows grant us greater and greater freedom to simply be as we are. Shadow work removes the armor that we have put on, releases the masks that we wear, and connects us back to our bodies and to the world.

Chapter 2

The Self and the Ego

*T*o truly understand how the shadow works we first need to understand our goal. The Self is who we are in our wholeness; it is the result of a fully integrated shadow. Most of us are not there yet but we have an awareness of what that Self might be. We might experience faint glimmers of it when we feel truly alive and in the moment. We might also feel a sense of emptiness and longing for who we truly are.

Through shadow work we can directly remedy this emptiness by doing two things: by seeing the parts of ourselves that we have projected onto the world and onto others, and by engaging in the individuation process. When we take back our projections we reclaim all of the shadow part of ourselves that we have lost. Through individuation we discover what we think, feel, and want for ourselves, separately from what others think and want for us. We learn to hear our own inner callings and to know fully who we are as a person.

When the Self has taken back all of its projections from the outer world and has completed the process of individuation, we no longer seek approval and love outside ourselves in order to feel okay inside. We know who we are, what we like, and what we think (separate from what our families, society, popular culture, and the media want us to think). In others, we see humanity rather than feeling competition, jealousy, or hatred.

This state can be considered the end of inner division. Most of us have inner wars waging continually. These are conflicts within the self;

basic divisions within us that have yet to find healing. This is often portrayed in popular culture as our inner angel sitting on one shoulder and our inner devil sitting on the other. Or we might think of it as our inner critic (the part of us that is continually criticizing, bullying, and talking down to us) battling the part of us that is compassionate and kind towards ourselves.

Most of the time there is more nuance than this, as we have a variety of inner struggles that we may not see with clarity. They may not have clear direction, an obvious solution, or anything that can be strictly divided into "good" or "bad." They are conflicts that emerge because there is no clear right or wrong. These "this or that" divisions within ourselves make up the bulk of what separates us from the Self.

Understanding the Ego

To understand the shadow, we also need to understand how the ego operates. While there are many differing discussions regarding what the ego is, for the purposes of shadow work the ego is considered the operating system of the mind. It is not bad, or something to be gotten rid of. It is like a computer program, calibrating our reality.

Our ego works with material in our consciousness to organize the conceptual framework for our reality. Anything shadow, or cut off, will not be part of this organized reality.

We see our reality through a series of filters. If we did not have this filtering system, we would be continually overloaded with stimuli. Our ego's role is to organize and offer us reality as we know it. Its primary focus is to keep reality stable. This function is similar to how the immune system works in our bodies: it lets in what is known and rejects what is unknown in order to maintain a state of stability and health.

We can also call this the ego-mind— in this sense ego and mind are synonymous—and its function is to operate based on what is already known to us. We are inundated with so much information (sensation, emotions, data) every day that we need to process in some way or another. The ego-mind does this, creating files and folders so that it doesn't need to expend time and energy on what we already know.

Our commute to work may be so familiar to us that we no longer need to consciously think about it. It is an automatic habit; we have done it so many times that it is routine. This becomes problematic when we consider habits that are deeply ingrained to the point that they can lead us to get stuck in a rut, or even become self-destructive.

If every time you feel sad and lonely you eat a bag of cookies, that established "program" may offer you temporary relief but fail to provide any long-term solution. It may also be ingrained to the point of becoming automatic. Put more simply, you may find yourself reaching for that bag of cookies every time you need to feel safe and nurtured without realizing you are doing it.

On a larger level, our ego's filing system may reject or ignore what is not already known to it. The ego-mind protects us by keeping out threats—anything that is unknown or does not fit into its already established program. This results in dehumanizing other people, or not allowing ourselves to consider new information outside of what is already known by us to be "truth."

We need a strong, healthy, and flexible ego. A stable one that has a solid handle on reality but that can also allow in new information and integrate it.

The healthy ego-mind provides flexibility, evolution, and a true knowing of Self. It does this from the innate understanding that in order to keep a boundary (our individual sense of self) strong and safe, we need resilience. This only comes with some degree of flexibility and ability to adapt to the reality of new conditions. Think of how a strong stable tree also has the flexibility to bend in the wind. If our egos are too static, they defend themselves more fiercely against what is considered Other or unknown.

Our egos can be quite small, only allowing in a fraction of reality. They also can be a healthy bubble that surrounds us, allowing us to see more of reality but still retain an individual sense of identity. Those who lack ego integrity will not have this bubble, and they will have difficulty differentiating their individual personality from their environment (and the people in that environment). Those who have a large, inflexible bubble around them are those who we commonly refer to as having a "big ego." They are typically individuals who believe that the world is centered around them and who think that their opinions and insights matter more than those of others.

If our egos are healthy, they undergo a variety of stages of growth and easily assimilate new information. This largely occurs when we are young; when we are younger our minds are more open. As we are educated our minds are more willing to take in the insights of others. As we grow older, we become entrenched in habits. We have interfaced with the world, our families, our communities, and popular culture to the extent that we have developed a more static understanding of reality.

The ego-mind has several purposes in its organization. First, it provides a clear framework for what reality is. Second, it develops our individual identity. These are both created out of the stories and beliefs we are told about the world and about who we need to become to survive in the world. What we have made shadow, or do not know about ourselves, creates an absence around which our ego-mind organizes itself. For example, if we have cut off joy in our childhood because our parents told us that we were "too much too often," we will no longer consider ourselves as being joyous in adulthood. We are also unlikely to see the joy present in the world. When we do shadow work, our egos can change and shift to reorganize around a reality in which we can see the joy in ourselves as well as the joy in the world again.

Ego Death

We like to think of ourselves as static beings, but really, we are always in a state of flow. We experience small changes to our ego-mind in each moment of our lives. The ego is never "destroyed" but does experience a death-rebirth cycle. This is only a temporary reorganization wherein integration and reorientation to a new homeostasis occurs.

Our ego can experience small momentary changes of life without any issues—for example, we decide to turn left instead of right on a street, or we decide to have an egg for breakfast instead of our usual cereal. These small fluctuations rarely change our self-concept, so we largely remain unaware of them.

We also have experiences that result in moderate or larger changes in our ego's operating system. Throughout our lives we experience many ego "deaths": these are changes in our operating system and subsequent identity, that are large enough for us to notice them. We may even struggle with them.

If we consider our lives to be a book, a small ego death may be like going from one word to the next. This is unlikely to be noticed or reacted to. It can be integrated without issues. We then move on from one sentence to the next. Depending on how stable our egos are, this may result in a reaction, or it may not. It may simply be incorporated into a healthy ego system with no issues. We then move on to another chapter, or even to another section of the book. These larger experiences result in an ego death that we often struggle with.

When we have experiences that show us how little control we have, they result in an ego death. This is a perspective shift in which we experience an alteration of our relationship to ourselves and to the world. These shifts typically happen at the larger junctions of life: birth, sex, death, divorce, marriage, moving, and transition from one phase of our life to another (such as from adolescence to adulthood).

The phrase "dark night of the soul" was first coined by St. John of the Cross. It describes a period of lost faith, disorientation, and darkness. In this darkness, he recognized that there is profound ability for growth. It is not in the daylight and what is known and orderly that we take our greatest leaps of faith; it is when we feel the Earth fall from beneath our feet and we no longer know what to believe or how to operate. Consider this to be like the ego updating to a new operating system—it will be down for a bit while it is rebooting. This period can create confusion, depression, and disorientation for people unless they are aware of what is occurring.

It is typical for people to experience a large ego death when their ordinary everyday awareness and habitual routines become interrupted. A focus on larger and more primary needs is necessary. Some good examples of this are a cancer diagnosis, the death of a loved one, or the birth of a child. All of these experiences expand our perspective and engender a new way of being.

Sometimes perspective shifts can be temporary. We can have an incredible vacation that vastly changes our perspective of the world and of ourselves and then go back home to our routines. Our ego-mind goes back to the safety of its prior baseline.

Sometimes individuals get stuck in ego death because they do not recognize that it is a metaphorical death, rather than a literal one. A part of themselves that they previously knew, a belief that they once held, or the way that they once saw the world has died. This creates a liminal space in which it is easy to become stagnant. We can get stuck between one doorway and the next, between one way of being and another.

We are many things at once, all at different places. We are at once a child self and an adult self, a part of us still with our ancestors and genetic history, a part fully in the present moment and many parts of ourselves still stuck in the past. To fully move forward and recalibrate requires grieving for the former self and allowing for that self to fully die. In this way, we can move out of the past and our stagnant liminal spaces and fully move on to a new chapter of our lives.

Ego Inflation

It is incredibly common for the ego to become inflated. This is a simple defense mechanism that shields us from knowing more than the ego is ready to become aware of.

Every teacher, practitioner, and customer-service professional has met plenty of people who suffer from ego inflation. They believe that they are better than you, or know more than you, even though evidence may prove entirely contrary to this fact. The first way that ego inflation presents is a situation in which someone has so little information that they simply do not know what they do not know.

There certainly can be an inner well of inferiority and self-hatred that creates the need to pretend to be superior. However, much of ego inflation stems from common ignorance—someone lacks awareness of the limitations of their knowledge. They construct a shield, a defense system, to deflect any information that may threaten to reveal what they do not know.

For example, Elizabeth reads a book that includes words and insights that are outside of her current knowledge. A person with a healthy ego might look up the meaning of the words or research the concepts in order to understand them better. Since she has an inflated ego, she writes a review talking about how stupid and awful the author is (basic projection), and for good measure, she adds a bunch of slurs defaming the author. Her ego is preventing her from feeling inner negative feelings regarding herself or from grappling with new concepts that would threaten her ego. Instead, she pushes all of the self-hatred that arises within her onto the author. This way, the author is the villain, and she remains the victim. This allows for her ego to remain "as is."

Another example is Vinnie, an architect who is told by his boss that his design for a home needs work. Instead of accepting the criticism and asking his boss how he can improve, he reacts from a place of inflated ego. He thinks that his unique genius is never understood. He then goes home and vents to his wife about how terrible his boss is and how under-appreciated he feels.

In some individuals there may be an open door (see Chapter Five, Helpful Tools) but in others the ego has created a solid defense mechanism that shields it from ever being able to interface with any information that would create change. It frequently uses a victim complex to do this.

The Buddhist teacher Chögyam Trungpa's work on spiritual materialism points to this phenomenon quite well. He states: "The ego can convert anything to its own use, even spirituality. Ego is constantly attempting to acquire and apply the teachings of spirituality for its own benefit. The teachings are treated as an external thing . . . a philosophy we try to imitate. We do not actually want to identify with or become the teachings. We go through the motions, make the appropriate gestures, but we really do not want to sacrifice any part of our life. We become skillful actors, and while playing deaf and dumb to the real meanings, we find some comfort in pretending to follow the path."

While this is easy to point out in others on spiritual and religious paths, it can happen within any role. When I worked as a bartender, we looked down on the bartenders at a neighboring bar. They largely served beer and we had cocktails and served better food. We can develop an inflated ego as a result of our material possessions, beauty products, social media likes or followers, careers, vacations, relationships. We can have an inflated ego regarding our role as mother, father, student, teacher, or employee. For this inflation to subside and for the ego to come into a healthier state we need to examine why our ego "hooks in" to that feeling of superiority.

Spiritual Bypass

It is quite easy to utilize spiritual concepts to look away from the body and the world. The concept of "spiritual bypass" was first introduced by John Welwood, a psychologist who noted that meditation and other practices can be used to avoid facing our unresolved pain and difficulties. Spiritual practices should allow us to develop tools to live our lives more fully and to ground ourselves in our bodies. If a person is not doing this and they are instead using spirituality as an escape from reality, it is spiritual bypassing.

Common popular methods of spiritual bypassing include telling ourselves that we should be beyond emotions, such as anger. Another is believing that we are enlightened, superior, or different in some way, in order to avoid dealing with our insecurities and other personal issues.

This can be seen frequently when people believe that they are somehow responsible for their pain or disease. An understanding that "only people of a certain vibration" can get sick, means by definition that the "higher vibration" person is morally superior to the person who becomes ill. The person in pain or dealing with trauma is never "good enough" as long as they struggle with physical or mental pain.

Such simplistic beliefs create a lack of basic empathy. These feelings regarding superiority emerge from fear and an understandable desire for simplicity, order, and control. When we fully integrate with our shadows, we can understand the chaos of existence: good people who do everything "right" get sick, morally bankrupt people get rich, and people without talent get record deals.

Spiritual bypassing allows us to separate from our shadows and avoid dealing with the nuance of existence. We may believe that we have much more control over our bodies and our lives than we truly do. Sometimes suffering is simply unfortunate, and to accept this brings grace in the pain of existence. To move beyond simplistic cause and effect is to experience nuance and the grey area of reality in which all of us live.

Habits

Our brains are like roads. Over time we pave paths because we regularly utilize them: it is a road we have gone down again and again. Following the paved road means continually making the same decisions and taking the same actions in our lives. Often we follow the roads paved by our wounds rather than roads that would be healthy or helpful for us. Out of habit we move in the direction of imbalance. Over time it becomes much easier for us to follow the paved road than to forge a new one.

In shadow work it is helpful to recognize that our minds follow paved roads out of habit. We may be miserable or understand that our choices and attitudes towards life are not helpful to us, but we know what to expect on that paved road. Over time other roads darken and disappear entirely if we are too strict in following our routines.

Shadow work creates the capacity to have more options available to us in our lives. Having many roads open allows us to create change in our lives and to choose what is best for us. In time we may find that a side road becomes a main road. We may also find that a super-highway has been traveled so many times that we know exactly where that road ends and so we decide to choose another option.

Sometimes people have found tremendous healing within themselves but have not broken their old habits. We can develop good self-esteem, self-worth, and freedom from childhood patterns but we may still treat ourselves poorly out of habit. Knowing that we can change our habits and create new roads in our brains and lives gives us permission to change. We can also offer ourselves the grace to realize that new habits take time to develop. A road is not paved in a single day. Simple and small changes in habits done regularly can help us to pave new roads and move away from habitual behaviors that are creating harm.

The Princess and the Dragon

We do not grow absolutely, chronologically. We grow
sometimes in one dimension, and not in another; unevenly.
We grow partially. We are relative. We are mature in one
realm, childish in another. The past, present and future mingle
and pull us backward, forward, or fix us in the present.
We are made up of layers, cells, constellations.

Anaïs Nin

We like to think of ourselves as one cohesive, congruent being, but we are really composed of parts. Some parts of our personality are stronger or more dominant than others. We can be many things at once. A quiet, demure, and apologetic aspect of ourselves and a raging vendetta aspect of ourselves can create a war within—or at least a great deal of confusion.

We can be one person to a friend and an entirely different person to our parents or our lover. A child might inherit an intensity of personality from one parent and the fragility of temperament from another. All of these sides live within each of us. Ideally they are congruent, or get along. But often they may be at odds with one another, or have different needs and agendas.

To do shadow work is to come to peace with the fact that we are many things at once. We learn to embrace all aspects of ourselves, rather than deny the parts of our personality that we deem personally or socially unfortunate. Each part of ourselves that we do not love and accept becomes an enemy to us. To know ourselves in our totality, to embrace our dichotomies, allows us to choose how we live our lives and who we want to be. If we embrace our warrior and our peacemaker, making peace becomes a choice. Without embracing our warrior, being a peacemaker turns into being an unwilling doormat. We are unable to choose peace unless we can also choose violence or war.

It is the strongest in us that can be vulnerable, and the most secure in us that can let go of caring what others think about us. When any part of us is healthy and whole, it naturally expresses its opposite. Joy requires the contrast of grief and rage, otherwise it is incomplete. Many of us miss out on the experience of happiness and peace in our lives because we cannot accept chaos and uncertainty. By embracing all parts of ourselves—our full continuum of expression—we have conscious options on how we act and who we choose to be. If we do not integrate all aspects of ourselves, we will be stuck in a cycle of reactivity where choices are made for us.

There are also parts of ourselves that have stagnated in their development. Within us we carry an army of inner children. These children did not have the opportunity to appropriately process trauma or move through all of the stages of physical, mental-emotional, and spiritual development. In this way we can be both an adult who pays taxes, works, and cares for children, and simultaneously be an angry toddler who throws a tantrum each time he doesn't get his way.

Trauma can best be defined as the effect of an event that is too overwhelming for us to process at the time that it occurs. The purpose of this work is not to remove the stories we have carried, or to erase the trauma we have experienced, but to operate in an adult capacity regarding what we have experienced. To see it through the rearview mirror, so to speak. When we see with the wisdom of an adult, we realize that the trauma is in the past. This is much different from being psychically and emotionally stuck in the age at which we experienced the trauma.

As adults we have different resources and a different power structure than when we were children. We can make choices, including leaving a situation, which we could not as a child. As an adult, we are no longer powerless to the whims and issues of our parents and family.

The same thing is true of our former selves. If we experienced a sexual assault at age twenty-five and are now forty, we are now a different person with greater knowledge and capacities to handle the traumatic event. Recognizing this can allow our inner child to grow up and be integrated into our current selves.

Our inner child has a fierce need to protect itself. It is frozen in time and in its circumstances. We may desire to heal that inner child, but until we fully allow that part of ourselves to be seen and heard, it will retaliate against us, sabotaging our efforts to move forward in our lives.

For example, a man was told to suppress his feelings as a child, frequently being told to "man up" when he did show any emotion. He learned to repress all of his feelings, and as an adult he has difficulty being emotionally available to his partner. He is now a man divided: a part of him desires to be vulnerable and to be known on a deep level. Another part of him defends and even punishes himself when he opens up to others. His inner critical voice tells him how weak and pathetic he is for sharing his emotions. When he does show his vulnerability, he then spirals, drinking heavily to numb the feelings arising. A part of him desperately wants and needs others close, and another part pushes them away.

This type of split is common in trauma. We can refer to it as the "inner child" and the "fierce protector." It can also be referred to mythologically as the "princess and the dragon." The part of ourselves that has experienced trauma has also experienced power loss; it feels small, inferior, unloved, and unworthy. It rightfully feels victimized, and often has large emotions that are too overwhelming to feel. This part can be considered the princess, or the inner child.

To safeguard this part of ourselves, the dragon appears, the fierce protector that will keep the overwhelming contents of the trauma safe. This protector often shields itself by claiming superiority. This superiority then results in not needing anyone and feeling a type of alienation that allows the inner child to remain profoundly alone in their pain.

The inner child remains blind to the fact that others have experienced this type of pain because they are so protected and isolated by the dragon. This strategy may have been necessary at the time of the trauma, but the princess-dragon split persists over time. The isolated inner child remains stuck in the mythology of the princess and the dragon even though months or even decades have passed, and it no longer serves the current adult.

We create mythologies for ourselves as both a protective strategy and a coping mechanism. The beliefs of the isolated princess are that she is inferior, unworthy, and unlovable, and there is something wrong with her. The dragon then shields and protects her by creating grandiose beliefs that the inner child is special and magical and chosen and different from everyone in a way that she will one day show the world.

Understanding this split of mind shows us a major protective mechanism of the ego. Integrating the princess means resolving the trauma. This resolution comes from validating the child and whatever they are feeling. We have a primary need to be seen and heard; allowing the righteous pain of the inner child to surface is necessary for healing. The wound needs to be exposed to heal, and the inner child needs to be treated with the grace and dignity she deserves.

We were told as children that many of the things that we knew on a visceral, primal level to be true were wrong. When we discover that we were, in fact, right, our inner child can feel justified in what she felt and knew.

When our inner princess is able to tell our story and realizes that the emotions that we feel can be resolved in a different, more adult manner, we can release the emotionality involved with the originating trauma. The dragon no longer needs to protect the princess as the current adult self can face the emotions of the inner child. Our inner child then no longer needs to purposefully stagnate in the behaviors and beliefs that perpetuate the trauma. We can move out of a state of victimhood and power loss and into a state of understanding that whatever we experienced was terrible and should not have happened.

The resolution of the princess-dragon split means the return of innocence and joy that were lost to trauma. We not only hold on to the emotional overwhelm and circumstances of trauma within our bodies but also hold back the light that we once contained. By resolving our trauma and healing the princess-dragon splits in our mind, we can realize that deep change is possible. With this awareness comes hope and the return of inner light.

Chapter 3

Defense Mechanisms of the Ego

*T*he ego is our conscious interface with reality. It is ultimately a protective mechanism that allows us to experience our identity and reality as orderly, consistent, and safe. If we have "ego integrity," our ego-minds identify who we are, where we begin and end. Think of this as a bubble or a cell wall. One of the results of self-realization work is individuation, which gives us the ability to differentiate ourselves from others.

If this bubble is not present or does not maintain its integrity, we may merge with everything around us. We will be unable to distinguish who we are as an individual separate from who our neighbor is, or our mother. If our bubble is too thick, we will not absorb new information or ideas, resulting in a rigid self-concept.

When we have shadow parts—the rejected aspects of ourselves that we have cast out into the world—our ego will not have the healthy solidity that it needs. We will react to what we have rejected in ourselves when we see it in others; we will continually seek approval, love, and validation from the outside world. As we integrate these shadow parts and take our projections back, our ego becomes healthier. We can know who we are more fully. We can experience self-worth and self-love and a feeling of being at home in our bodies, ending the search for these things outside ourselves.

Our ego filters the information it receives. Information that is considered too threatening, overwhelming, stressful, or shameful will be rejected by the ego. We will defend against it through a variety of mechanisms discussed in this chapter, including "denial" and "projection."

When we are able to clearly see how the ego works to defend and protect itself, we can more consciously participate in its decision-making. For example, we may decide that repressing an overwhelming amount of stress due to an ongoing work situation is the appropriate response. Or we may decide that wearing a mask around family is the right thing to do. Deciding to utilize these mechanisms consciously is far different from using them automatically, without our conscious awareness and participation.

Denial

Denial is one of our most primitive responses to stress. If something is too overwhelming or difficult to incorporate into our conscious awareness, we deny its reality.

Denial is a protective response that prevents us from accepting anything that is too painful or shameful. It shields us from any information that would shift our conceptualization of reality or our self-concept too radically.

Denial is rarely a conscious defense; we commonly reject anything that we have not experienced personally. This mentality allows us to feel safety within our worldview, and to reject and deny anything that causes us to feel uncertainty and a lack of control. Those with healthy ego mechanisms can accept the reality of others as truth even if it is disparate from their personal experiences of this world. The protective ego, which desires a simple reality and is propagated by fear, will feel threatened by anything that differs from its own experiences.

We live in a world of moral opposites; what we are against we oppose and deny. Anything that causes our self-concept to feel unworthy, unloved, or unappreciated creates a need for denial.

If we encounter something that threatens our worldview, we can pass through varying stages of denial. We may simply not see it or register it at all. We may consciously reject it. Rejection requires noticing and being actively opposed to the information. If something creates too much danger to our self-concept, we will not only reject it but we will also attack the source of the information. This allows us to project our negative reactions onto a person or situation, so we do not need to contend with them within.

For example, Kara goes on a first date with someone. Later she wonders why she is not called back for a second date, as she had a good time and was attracted to him. She hears back from the friend who set her up and he says that her date thought that she was cute but that he wants to be in a relationship with someone more accomplished and financially secure. Instead of dealing with the disappointment and embarrassment that she feels, she engages in denial and projects her bad inner feelings onto him. She now decides that he is materialistic and just looking for someone to take care of him. She says this to her friend and then she sends him a nasty message telling him these things. She posts a vague quote on social media about how people out for money cannot love. This all prevents her from processing any negative feedback regarding herself.

Instead of the situation being one in which they are simply not compatible, it has now turned into a situation in which she has been wronged and is the moral victor, and he is someone to villainize.

On some level, she registers that she is hurt but she is not yet able to actively sit with those hurt feelings. Instead, she uses denial, deflection, and projection so that she does not have to consciously come to terms with her hurt feelings.

Intellectualization

Intellectualization is a natural and healthy method of integrating information. We must know something on a conceptual level before we can live it out on a bodily level.

We all have experienced events that we intellectually know have happened, but they do not feel as if they are quite real. We haven't fully admitted to ourselves that painful or overwhelming events have occurred. This form of compartmentalization is quite common, but it prevents us from fully integrating our life experiences. When we are able to emerge from denial into a state of full acceptance, these events become a part of our lived experience, rather than experiences that remain in a state of abstract realization or intellectual conceptualization.

Until we fully absorb our experiences on a bodily level, intellectualization makes us aware of the fact of our experiences, but we do not feel their impact emotionally or physically. For example, after a death we may be fully aware that someone has died, but because we must move on with our daily lives we do not yet have the time or emotional capacity to truly feel what we have experienced. So we do not feel the depths of our grief.

Similarly, Edwin understands spiritual concepts on an intellectual level but does not yet live them out in his life. If he were to embody his spiritual knowledge, he would need to come to terms with the fact that he dislikes his job, has several problematic friendships, and suffers from inner self-hatred and feelings of worthlessness. He is not yet at the point where he can directly face all of this; intellectualization helps him to think about spiritual concepts that he might put into action, when he is ready, in the future.

We often know things to be true long before we act on them. This allows us time for mental digestion and planning for action. Often, we get stuck in a contemplative phase for long periods of time before acting, and in those cases, it is helpful to inquire about what is causing us to stagnate. Typically, it is because an inner child has developed an unhealthy coping mechanism. For example, our plans to eat better will get sabotaged each time our inner teenager feels overwhelmed and eats a lot of pizza.

Intellectualization is also used as a mechanism of defense and separation. Our words do not match our actions; our minds are not in line with our bodies. This split separates the head from the body and creates a scenario in which we use thinking to separate from feeling.

When information is embodied, our thoughts and actions are aligned. We do what we say and we are who we say we are. When our thoughts and actions are out of sync, we will become hypocritical; we judge and condemn others for lacking virtues that we do not demonstrate ourselves.

Rationalization is a form of intellectual defense. It seeks to preserve the "logical" mind and its ideas without fully considering feelings and emotional needs. For example, we may rationalize that we have not yet exercised today and so exercising tomorrow is a good plan; tomorrow comes and we rationalize using the same thought. By rationalizing, we are attempting to justify our behavior and emotional reactions with thoughts that seem logical or "right."

Josef is an addict who blames his childhood for his addiction. He even says to his therapist, "My mother should be paying for these sessions." This may be true but this rationalization keeps him from taking responsibility for his addiction and working through his childhood emotions. By blaming his "narcissistic" mother, he doesn't take ownership of his adult situation and so remains in a state of perpetual childhood.

Intellectualization can be utilized as a way of anesthetizing ourselves against reality. Disassociation can be a part of this process, allowing us to escape from a reality that may be too painful to bear.

Disassociation

It is now considered normal in our culture to be in a trance-like state, continually distracted and unable to concentrate on anything but for a short period of time. Some amount of disassociation from our bodies and our lives can be healthy. This healthy form of disassociation is done purposefully and with complete awareness. We may love watching movies or reading books because they expand our worldview and expose us to beauty. It is also healthy at times to be able to consciously separate ourselves from our lives. When we utilize disassociation as a conscious tool, we offer ourselves space to reorient, breathe, relax; we can then go back to our lives with renewed ability to handle the daily stresses of life.

If we are doing this in a healthy way, these behaviors are life-affirming and bring us joy. They allow us to reset so that we can once again face the world. If done in an unhealthy way, we utilize them to escape reality and what we are feeling.

Disassociation is a coping mechanism in response to high levels of stress and trauma. The skill of disassociation is learned from life circumstances.

There are moments when removing awareness from bodily sensations is totally appropriate. If we are being eaten by a lion, any part of our consciousness that can escape will do so. During abuse or any type

41

of traumatic experience, it is right for part of our energy to leave. For example, a child who is continually picked on by her mother learns to "zone out" so as not to hear her mother's constant criticisms. A man who lives in a household where his wife is physically abusing him learns to completely separate himself from his emotions and thoughts; if he shows any emotion during these interactions his wife will use those as a reason to scream at him or punch him.

In cases of abuse, disassociation provides protection and separation so that emotions do not surface. Our bodies are the present moment, and when we are fully embodied, we are fully feeling. When we do not want to feel, we can disassociate from our bodies and the present moment. This type of disassociation is key to understanding many addictions, including video games, internet, and television.

Disassociation occurs in a continuum, from feeling spacey to being completely out of body. Most often, people report this out-of-body feeling as being behind or beside themselves. In more intense forms of disassociation, we may become so separated from ourselves that we lose awareness of moments in time; we have no memory of what happened to us.

Blankness is another form of disassociation. This is a "freeze" response that offers protection from a traumatic situation that you're not able to process at the time. Blankness keeps us from acknowledging what is going on, or the full extent of what is going on. This diminishes a painful reality and keeps us from reacting emotionally. For example, Devon needs to give a speech at work, which he is quite nervous about. He is not a natural public speaker. He goes "blank" and does not remember much of the speech. In a more extreme example, a mother opens the door and sees her boyfriend abusing her daughter. Instead of registering this, she simply closes the door.

Clara is confused when Eliza ends their friendship. Eliza calls her toxic and cites numerous examples of when Clara was not there for her, or when she was negative or downright nasty towards her. Clara does not remember any of these instances—she has "blanked" them from her memory. We have an innate need to think of ourselves as good people; we blank our faults or aspects of ourselves that we dislike so as to keep our image of ourselves as a "good person."

We have often disassociated partially or fully at an early age and so we do not know what it feels like to be in the body, or in the present moment. Anyone in our modern culture can use methods of coming more into their body, such as grounding, developing present-moment awareness, exercising, and in-person interactions.

With shadow work we are not seeking to completely rid ourselves of any behavior but rather to become consciously aware of that behavior. Someone deciding to relax and take a break from their lives to read a book or watch a movie for conscious escapism is much different than someone watching endless hours of television without awareness because they cannot bear to live their lives.

Knowing what disassociation is, why it occurs, and why we may reach for disassociation as a way to separate ourselves from reality can allow us to come more firmly into our bodies and to face the reasons why we feel the need to escape from our bodies and our lives in the first place.

Fantasy

We can escape reality by fantasizing about how our lives or our world could be different. We can also use fantasy in a healthy manner—to dream, to hope, and to imagine. We can open wide to reality being different from the confines that we experience in our daily lives. Fantasy allows us to take a break from an often brutal world and to reset and recharge so that we can face it afresh.

When we use it as a defense mechanism, fantasy puts us into an idealized position that conflicts with reality. We imagine that we are secretly the "chosen one," the center of the universe, in our own private *Truman Show.* "My father didn't abandon me, he is secretly a part of a top-secret military organization." "If only people knew how special, talented, and magical I truly am!"

One useful skill is stepping back to ask: "Is this connecting or disconnecting?" This question will differentiate between helpful fantasy, which allows us to dream and hope for a better future, and fantasy that causes us to alienate ourselves from others.

Unfortunately, in the modern world it is easy to find communities that consolidate fantasy and harmful mythologies instead of learning tools to cope with reality and inner pain. It is only when we look towards our inner pain, and what lies at the root of our fantasies, that we can heal that pain.

Avoidance

When something becomes painful, we may avoid it. This can be quite conscious, such as avoiding a spouse who is angry. When we do not have the capacity to deal with something, we may simply avoid it. Avoidance is a common defense mechanism when we are stressed or overwhelmed.

Becoming aware of our tendency to avoid feelings or difficulties can show us how often we utilize this mechanism. As with all mechanisms, it can be used in a healthy and conscious way. This gives us choices. For example, if we are too overwhelmed, it may be time for a break, not time to clean our whole living space.

Shutting Down and Numbing

Both shutting down and numbing can be a part of disassociation, but they may also be separate mechanisms. Shutting down may also be a part of masking (see next category).

When we learn that who we are will be punished, mocked, or rejected by others, we learn to shut down. We become robots, operating only on the surface of interaction. We learn to hide or become invisible because to show ourselves would mean reprisal. We may learn to shut down because we feel like a burden to those around us, simply by existing. If you are someone who apologizes constantly to others for simple things, it is likely that you have been taught that your mere existence is a burden to those around you; so you learned to shut down a significant part of yourself.

There is a reason why we hide who we are from friends, family, colleagues, or classmates. It is because we have learned that to close ourselves off will keep us out of trouble. Revealing our true selves is only asking for problems.

It is natural to be a different self when we are around friends versus family members, or at work versus at home. Different parts of ourselves naturally come forward in these situations while others take a back seat. We do not need to share the entirety of ourselves with anyone who asks.

But when we shut down it is because we decided at an early age to make a significant part of ourselves shadow. We have cut off a large chunk of ourselves merely to survive. This creates significant inner conflict—a feeling that we are sitting at the sidelines of our lives rather than living. We cannot live fully when a significant part of who we are is shadow. Restoring the parts of ourselves that we have shut down is essential for feeling confident and experiencing self-worth. We can find others who love and appreciate us for exactly who we are—those people may just not be your parents or the people at work or school.

Numbing is the first step in shutting down. If you ever find yourself saying "okay" a lot or checking out of conversations because you know that your participation would create conflict, you are numbing yourself. Frequently, we do this because to respond fully and emotionally might cause the other person to heighten their own emotional response. We learn to numb so that we can avoid experiencing the onslaught of their emotions. The last thing we want is to feed into any drama that they are likely to create or to create an emotional situation that we may not yet be equipped to handle.

Masking

When we learn that we cannot show the world who we truly are, we put on a mask. We learn to wear a mask as a defense mechanism in order to survive a specific social situation. This is typically a response to being punished or shamed in the past for showing what we truly were feeling.

We wear masks in a variety of situations. At work we may wear a mask of seriousness, with our children a mask of enthusiasm. A depressive may wear a mask of intense cheerfulness to not show others their inner suffering.

Masking can be considered healthy. Who we are should shift based on the nature of our environment. We are intersecting with people and the environment we are stepping into. We would want to bring out a different part of us to a funeral than to a party. In its detrimental form, masking becomes permanent and subconscious; we appear the way that others have told us to be. It is a way to seem "normal" to the world. This can create a massive internal struggle between who we pretend to be and who we truly are. It is exhausting to mask. Often, an internal voice wonders why we cannot simply be ourselves.

Our modern world is built for extroverts and neurotypical individuals; those who end up masking the most are frequently introverts and neurodivergents. This comes at a cost, as wearing a mask means neglecting our needs and wants in order to appear "normal" for others.

Wearing makeup is a form of masking that can be unhealthy or healthy. It may shield us from the world, or it may reveal who we truly are through our artistry.

As with any of our defense mechanisms, we can learn to consciously wield masking as a tool. We may decide to wear a mask of competency and confidence even though inside we feel like an imposter. Wearing a mask to a holiday event with family can prevent intrusive questions or upsetting criticisms.

Regression

When we regress, we move into an earlier stage of development. When you get angry you may throw a temper tantrum like a two-year-old or cry like an infant. Patterns in regression can point to a need for healing at that age, which will be more fully explored in Chapter Five, "Helpful Tools." If we always regress to a sullen teenager or have a pattern of reacting like a tiny five-year-old dictator, that points to an inner child that needs healing and better skills to handle their emotional reactions.

Repression

A tool like repression is a more moderate form of denial. In this case, we do not cut something out from our awareness completely, rather we stuff it into a sort of box within ourselves. When thoughts and emotions arise that we do not wish to identify with, we put them into this box. For example, Paulo has angry, resentful, and even occasionally violent thoughts regarding his boss, who treats him poorly. He cannot act on these impulses, and to admit how much resentment he feels would mean facing the toxicity of his work environment. So instead he represses the thoughts and impulses that arise. In this way, repression is often a thought, emotion, or impulse that is followed by a quick decision on the part of our ego to shut it down and pack it away.

We also will repress memories that are too much for us to handle. In our older life, these can show up as fears that we cannot identify logically. For example, a child is terrified of a dentist who was rough with her as a child. She represses the memories, but as an adult she experiences a magnified fear of going to the dentist. She knows that not many people enjoy going to the dentist but she also knows that most people will not shake and shut down while in the dental chair.

We can also hold on to objects to repress emotions. Shira lost her daughter Maria at the age of sixteen. Although ten years have passed, Shira has kept her daughter's room the same. Clearing out the room or even changing anything about the room would cause Shira to face her unprocessed grief.

Shielding and Armoring

When our heart gets broken, we armor ourselves against further pain. Instead of having a heart that is open and vulnerable with the world, we have a heart that is guarded and shielded against re-experiencing that same pain.

The armoring that we wear in our bodies is for good reason: we are injured. Like a psychic cast, we wear the energies of past emotional and spiritual pain. Yet our shielding and armoring comes at a high cost— our connection to ourselves and to one another. If our heart is shielded, we may be protected against others using our vulnerabilities against us, but we will also be unable to fully open ourselves up to love others.

Any area of our body can be subject to the sort of psychic and emotional injuries that we experience. We feel as if we must get through, and how we get through is by placing armor on ourselves to do battle with the outer world. Each piece of armor may allow us to get through a particularly rough time. But over time, that armor remains and accumulates.

We often shield ourselves through our beliefs. We tell stories to ourselves to justify our beliefs and perpetuate trauma. "Women don't like nice guys," says a man who feels awkward around women, to soothe his isolation and pain. "They don't like me because I am too good for them," says a woman who cannot see that she pushes others away in her pain.

By recognizing how we shield ourselves, we can see the pain that is creating the belief in the first place. Any belief that we repeat to ourselves and to others is worthy of examination. If we know something to be true regarding ourselves, we do not need to repeatedly tell ourselves or the world about it. If we are telling ourselves and the world a belief repeatedly, we are attempting to convince ourselves that it is true.

If we do not question our beliefs, we experience cognitive dissonance: our thoughts and ideals regarding ourselves do not match up with what is happening in reality. This can happen while encountering others, such as someone believing that they are incredibly special but finding that others treat them like a normal human being. It can also be experienced internally, such as someone exercising and being excited about their healthy new lifestyle while simultaneously drinking to excess every night.

Inconsistency between our thoughts and our actions creates conflict within ourselves. If we smoke, we may compartmentalize our behavior. One part of us will know that it is unhealthy to smoke, but that part will be repressed and in conflict with the part of us that is smoking. It is by looking at these divisions within ourselves that we come out of conflict and see ourselves and reality more clearly.

Manipulation

Lying and manipulating are behaviors that emerge because we have learned that we cannot simply speak our truth and have it be taken seriously. There is a need for bargaining, manipulation, lying, and "negging"—utilizing backhanded compliments—to get others to take care of our basic needs or wants.

We may have learned to talk down to someone with low self-esteem because we know that they will respond to it. Those with healthy self-esteem will not accept our insults, and the backhanded compliments and passive-aggressive shaming will not work. If we have healthy self-esteem, being called an idiot will be seen as silly or untrue. If we struggle with self-esteem, we may wonder if what they have said is true.

Gaslighting is a more severe form of manipulation that involves distorting reality to confuse and alienate the victim. This can be an abuser calling their victim crazy or saying that they deserve the abuse. Over time, the victim will feel like they are at fault and they should apologize to their abuser.

In severe cases, abusers shift what is considered "true" to the extent that the victim completely severs any relationship to their own inner truth. They have repressed their own sense of morality and inner knowing in order to remain in the thrall of the abuser. Many children who have experienced gaslighting are not aware that what they experienced was not normal or healthy. Adults in abusive relationships will not leave, in part because the abuser has made them feel powerless and isolated. The abuser is in such control of the narrative that it may take considerable time for the victim to move away from the relationship. It may take even longer for the victim to see with clarity just how much abuse took place.

In less severe cases, we manipulate others every day to fit our own conceptual understanding of reality. We put them in a role, and if they step out of it, we subconsciously direct them back into that role. We seek to keep others within the framework of our understanding of reality, because questioning that reality would result in some type of deconstruction of the ego-mind.

Distraction

We distract ourselves because our reality is stressful, and we feel a need to escape. This is a milder form of defense in which we are aware of our stress or overwhelm but we purposefully engage in an activity that allows us to put our attention elsewhere.

Deflection and Displacement

When we experience an unwanted thought or feeling that we cannot express due to a power dynamic, we may displace that impulse onto a substitute. We cannot get mad at our boss, or our parent, because they hold more power than us, but what we can do is get mad at our spouse, pet, or child.

In this way, we attempt to express our feelings towards the substitute object, or a person who has less power than we do. This is why so many people treat customer service representatives so terribly. This is also why someone may punch a wall. Their displaced negative thoughts and feelings are directed towards someone or something that cannot fight back.

Deflection is one of the most common mechanisms the ego uses when it is criticized or blamed. Instead of accepting that blame or being accountable for our own actions, we lash out against the accuser or "scapegoat" another person. Thus we attempt to lessen our guilt and avoid negative consequences. People who cannot take accountability for themselves may gaslight others into believing that they are at fault instead.

Patrice wakes up her husband Thomas on a Saturday morning. She is upset because it is noon, and she has been up since eight a.m. with the children. He spends his nights gaming while she takes full responsibility for their children as well as her husband's needs. Instead of thanking her for waking him up, Thomas becomes angry and calls her dramatic. She is exhausted from playing the role of "mother" to her husband and children with no time to herself. She has shut down her own needs, wants, and emotional reactions in order to avoid fueling his anger and creating an argument, in which he will give her the silent treatment. He has deflected both his adult responsibility as well as his tendency to overreact onto her.

Deflection involves attacking or blaming another person instead of reconciling our own faults. This can involve hiding one's own mistakes and pushing the blame onto someone else, like a colleague at work blaming you for something that he did. This is also common in family dynamics, such as a sibling blaming or scapegoating a specific family member so that they do not have to look at their own issues.

This also can involve abdicating any responsibility whatsoever, like a group member in a school project expecting credit without doing any of the work. It also can be something as simple as laughing to deflect from an embarrassing mistake you have made, or utilizing self-deprecating humor or sarcasm.

At some point, the person who deflects has learned that they need to make people think that they are perfect or better than they are. They cannot admit their mistakes or allow others to think negatively about them, because to experience this would be a crushing blow to an ego that has repressed negative feelings regarding the self.

In certain cases, deflection can also be an attempt at ego inflation. An example is an employee who wants his boss to think highly of him, so he always jokes about "Josh" who screws up all the time.

Once we take responsibility for ourselves, our need to deflect lessens or ceases entirely. We can instead note when we are to blame and take accountability and we can reject blame when someone is attempting to deflect their own issues onto us.

Projection

Whenever you are about to find fault with someone, ask yourself the following question: What fault of mine most nearly resembles the one I am about to criticize?

Marcus Aurelius

When we make something shadow, we cut that part of ourselves off, shoving it out of our conscious mind and away from our self-concept. We then push those rejected parts of ourselves onto others.

When we recognize the traits that we have made shadow, in other people, we subconsciously react to them with negative emotions, like anger or disgust. We condemn others for qualities that lie unrecognized within ourselves. We populate our unlived lives onto other people and become furious at them for living them out.

Projection allows us to deny or repress information or aspects of ourselves that would be too difficult to integrate. Projection is a defense mechanism. We do not feel ready to skillfully, in an adult capacity, interface with information that goes against our conditioning and our pain patterns.

When we project, we experience a degree of power loss. We have given away parts of our power to another. We project outwards our approval and self-worth so that it can be reflected back to us. We expect others to show us that we are worthy, lovable, and acceptable.

Projection is the main mechanism that we explore in shadow work because we can so readily see what we have cut off by how we react to others. At its healthiest, projection allows us to observe aspects of ourselves from a safe distance. In a power dynamic, the observer holds the power; in this way we can relate to a part of ourselves outwardly without the pressure to integrate it. There is a reason why many people gravitate towards watching crime documentaries and horror movies: they let us observe the darkest aspects of our nature from a safe distance.

Part of the dynamic of making something shadow is placing our shadows onto individual people (and the world, as we will discuss later) so that we can observe them. It is much harder to observe a conflict within ourselves. If we push our inner divisions and conflicts outwards—onto other people—we have a better chance of resolving them. That is, if we have the consciousness, to recognize that we are not seeing people as they are, but instead seeing them as we need them to be.

When we project, we tend to cast people into roles (see Chapter Ten). We assume that the world and the people in it are only as we see them. We do not recognize that there is a difference between what we need other people and the world to be and what other people and the world actually are. As psychoanalyst Carl Jung stated, "In this way everyone creates for himself a series of more or less imaginary relationships based essentially on projection."

In some ways it is healthy to project. If we did not project, we would not have many of the bonds and relationships that we have in our lives.

Our projections connect us to others. The people to whom we connect the most are our own projected selves—people who have had similar experiences of the world as we have. We can see ourselves most directly in the people that surround us. Their struggles, suffering, and joys are our own reflected. It is by seeing ourselves in this way that we can connect deeply with the humanity of others, as well as our own humanity.

When we are able to utilize projection in a healthy way, we bond with others. We can form friendships, neighborhoods, communities, and a world in which we see our similarities, rather than our differences. By doing shadow work we can move from unhealthy projections—projections that show our own inner divisions outwards—into healthy projections, which is the ability to see the best parts of ourselves reflected back to us.

However, some people find that when they take their projections back, the mutual compatibility in a relationship suffers. For example, in "trauma bonding," people who are suffering the same defense mechanisms against reality find companionship in one another. This is because they have formed similar identities and reactions to the world due to the trauma that they have experienced. When one of those individuals finds better ways to manage their trauma and has a healthier, fuller version of reality, the friendship is likely to suffer. They no longer live in the same reality.

This can also happen in intimate relationships. We typically loop (see Chapter Fourteen) through the same experiences we had as children, especially in our relationships with our parents. We find our mother or father in our partner and live out the wounds and relationship patterning of our parents. When we take our projections back and work to heal the inner child that suffered as a result of our upbringing, we no longer need to repeat the same patterns. We no longer need to project the mother or father figure onto our partner.

There are three basic types of projection: simple projection, direct projection, and indirect projection.

Simple Projection

This is the projection of our undifferentiated stress and suffering onto a safe target. For example, a woman who is stressed from work visits a news site and projects her work stress through hate-filled comments onto others in the comments section. A woman grieving her father's death gets angry at a retail clerk because she cannot find the correct size blouse for her. A man screams at a waiter for not bringing the pepper to him for his eggs.

While we have a right to feel mildly irritated at the inconveniences of life, we may unleash our suffering onto a target that is safe—one that has less power than we do. Simple projection is like a release valve; it feels temporarily good to push that suffering outwards and to make another suffer. But it doesn't last. The person who projects in this way ends up with an even thicker shadow, and a greater need to take out their suffering on others.

Direct Projection

We can also place our shadow parts more specifically onto other individuals. This is a "direct projection." We project onto another person a part of ourselves that we have cut off or denied.

A man projects his inner wealth onto "financial gurus" on social media. A woman is obsessed with watching shows that feature physical prowess because she is not physically fit. Another woman obsesses about other women's bodies and how flat their stomachs are because she hates her own body, especially her stomach.

We also project our unlived lives and our expectations onto others. A mother who was never able to take dancing lessons as a young child forces her children to dance. A father who is a successful baker expects his eldest son to take up the family business.

Although we project onto everyone, we tend to project the most onto the people closest to us. Our spouses, children, relatives, and friends wear the weight of our projections and the expectations that arise out of those projections. In them we can see up close the largest parts of our shadow.

We tend to project the parts of ourselves that we identify with least onto safe but foreign targets: celebrities, public figures, athletes, and politicians. Our hatred and pain can easily find a target with a pop star; we can easily project the beauty, charisma, and wealth we deny in ourselves onto someone on social media.

When our projections are not grounded in reality, they can easily become obsessions. We may fixate on a specific celebrity or public figure, turning our projections into delusions. In this way, we dehumanize the public figure, making them "more (or less) than human."

Our entire consumer culture is propelled by our shadows. We spend money to vicariously experience the shadows we will not allow into our daily lives. We buy a pair of sneakers to feel acceptable and trendy. We watch television, which projects our unlived life back to us. We project onto food our desire for comfort and nurturing.

Indirect Projection

Indirect projection occurs when we project a part of ourselves that we cannot identify with at all. For example, Brad is a teacher who complains online frequently about "New Agers." Everyone to him is a narcissist, just like his mother. He does not realize that his teachings are directly from New Age ideologies. As a child he was not able to develop his self-identity fully because his mother was a narcissist. Brad has a rightfully angry inner child that is obsessed with narcissists in his adult reality because he is stuck at the stage of development where his identity should have formed.

This is an indirect projection: it reflects back to him what he cannot be. To heal this part of himself he would need to look at his anger and recognize that he sees his mother in all of these projections. He would then need to identify with what he lost: he was unable to be selfish or to be the center of attention as a child.

In time, Brad can come into contact with healthy selfishness within himself, and learn to express his own needs and wants. He may even move on to direct projection: recognizing that there is a part of him, unexpressed, that is a bit narcissistic. If he were to do this, his obsession with narcissism would wane, and he could recognize that he can move on from his childhood.

We often start with indirect projections because it is easy to identify people who are doing or saying things that we cannot see within ourselves. In time, we move on to direct projections, where we eventually see every quality within ourselves.

In upcoming chapters, we will learn how to more fully identify, retrieve, and integrate our shadows. In doing so, we can learn to take our power back and become more fully ourselves. We can find our self-worth within, instead of continually seeking to prove ourselves worthy to the world.

Transmutation and Integration

The defense mechanisms discussed earlier in this chapter arise from the extreme intelligence of the ego-mind. When reality is too much to bear, we shield ourselves from it. Reality may simply be too overwhelming for us to process in the present moment and we need a protective mechanism (the ego) to ensure that we can simply survive.

Part of shadow work is noticing these defense mechanisms in ourselves and others. Frequently we feel safer noticing them in others first, but ultimately looking within at what defense mechanisms we use most often helps us to make conscious choices. But it is important to not shame or bully ourselves when we notice any of these mechanisms in ourselves. Being aware of our ego-mind is the first step in a natural process of reclaiming our shadow.

For example, there is a reason why you avoid conflict. In the future you may still decide to avoid conflict, but that is a choice in a wide range of choices. In that same situation, you may decide to punch someone in the face, to talk things through, to go out and exercise to alleviate emotional energy, or to avoid the situation. The difference is in the conscious choice.

Many of our defense mechanisms can be considered maladaptive. This means that they do not bring us closer to a state of navigating a situation in a skilled manner. When we make our defense mechanisms conscious, we recognize that we always run away from our issues. In noticing this, we may begin to question why we are running. Eventually we may naturally recognize that we do not want to hide or give someone the "silent treatment" because we do not want to communicate our anger or hurt to them. We may make a different decision.

More adaptive and healthier defense mechanisms include "integration" and "transmutation." Integration involves processing the emotions in the present moment and strategically making a conscious decision about how to act to achieve the desired outcome. This requires emotional intelligence (see Chapter Six) as well as skills to be able to face reality.

While it may sound counterintuitive, having the skill to face reality may mean making a conscious choice to deny reality for a while, such as watching a movie or daydreaming on your couch. Then when you are ready, you can face the reality of an overwhelming situation bit by bit. Facing reality may also mean stopping yourself from disassociating so that you are fully present in a difficult conversation.

With integration we process whatever is arising in our system in a healthy way. That said, much of shadow work is dealing with mechanisms and emotions that we chose when we were much younger. Seeing our defense mechanisms, recognizing their reasons for being, and then moving into an adult-level consciousness allows us to release our past decision-making patterns, while validating our past emotions. This allows us to integrate our past selves and to make different choices in our adult life.

Transmutation is an option that allows us to adapt to our situation. If you are furiously angry at your boss at work, you cannot scream at her or punch her. Both of those would not be good choices and would cause you to lose your job. But you can consciously decide to take that screaming energy and go out for a walk, or vent to a friend about her. Both of these options transmute the energy, releasing it in a healthy manner by transforming it.

If we feel deep grief or depression, watching a sad movie may be the correct choice to transmute that energy. By deeply feeling into sadness, it changes. We may also watch a comedian to uplift ourselves or walk in nature to feel a part of the wider world. How we decide to adapt and transmute what we are feeling is an individual choice, depending on what we need at the time.

Both transmutation and integration help us process what we are feeling in a healthy and conscious manner. As we notice our other defense mechanisms and bring them into consciousness, we can begin on the path of making healthier choices in our lives.

Chapter 4

The Benefits of Shadow Work

*As far as we can discern, the sole purpose of human existence is
to kindle a light in the darkness of mere being.*

Carl Jung

We often deny, repress, and ignore the darkest aspects of our nature, but it is in embracing those aspects of ourselves that we find healing. Our darkness shows us the path to our light. We cannot become light without claiming our darkness—reclaiming every single bit of ourselves that we have lost or cut off in order to survive.

This work fosters an essential aliveness in us; it builds a bridge to the wildness that we have left behind. In that wildness lie our passions, the emotionality that links us to this world and to each other. Our true power lies in the most base, animalistic aspects of ourselves. It is in our bodies, not in our thoughts, that we find the power that not only gives us life but that also bestows upon us the ability to create and re-create ourselves.

What we have cut off or made shadow within ourselves steals large parts of our vitality. By reclaiming our shadows, we can restore the vitality that we have lost. We experience more enthusiasm for life.

We cut off so much of ourselves in order to gain acceptance and forgiveness for who we truly are. We feel ashamed of our physical body, because we have learned that our natural eroticism and presence in our physical forms is something to abandon or despise.

Shadow work reconnects us with our bodies and with the full continuum of feeling within ourselves. Our emotions are not a source of shame, or something to be turned into what we personally or culturally define as "good." Emotions are a wellspring of passion and vitality that continually offers us a life filled with soul-making endeavors.

When we make something shadow it rules our lives without our conscious recognition. We unconsciously react and feel powerless to our emotional reactions. When we take back our shadows, both our internal nature and the way that we relate to the world change for the better.

When we look to the outer world and take back our projections, we find that we are less angered by the world. We grow calmer and we express more equanimity and empathy to those around us. We can see the humanity in one another instead of seeing others through our negative projections.

Situations which we once thought were overwhelming cease to be looming terrors. We see them as simply the normal ups-and-downs of existence. Our lives are meant to include feelings of depression, joy, happiness, grief, loss, suffering, and bliss, if we allow them. This is the duality and the paradox of existence: sorrow contains joy; and happiness, a sliver of darkness. Within the full continuum of our emotions each pole reveals its opposite. Feeling the darkness of despair eventually brings hope and meaning. Without feeling our depths, we cannot experience our heights—bliss, ecstasy, peace, and happiness. By fully feeling our darkest emotions, we open ourselves up to joy.

As we proceed along this path, we find ourselves less inconvenienced by the normal fluctuations of existence. The Universe becomes less "for or against us" and more ambivalent. In this understanding we discover an inner strength that we once projected outwards onto others. We experience a new outlook on life as we regain our shadows. We find guidance as we start to trust again in the intuitive and feeling aspects of existence.

When we take back our shadows, we no longer see ourselves as singularly good and others as bad. We no longer view ourselves as the ultimate victim of our own existence. We have good and bad parts, as does our neighbor, and in recognizing this we can see ourselves in one another. Instead of division, we can see the nuance of humanity in one another.

When we do this work well, we develop a more stable personality and complete the individuation process. When we take back our projections, we know our likes and dislikes, free from the likes and dislikes of others. We no longer like or dislike things because our neighbor does, or because a pop star does. We freely know what we think and feel; we own our personal opinions.

This work reconnects us with our bodies. Our bodies are the present moment. When we are in our bodies, we can live our lives more fully and joyously. We are no longer in the past, or thinking of the future. We are in the now. Through embodiment we can experience pleasure and the ability to connect with our senses, seeing the beauty and light of the world. Our projections of darkness color the world with negativity; taking back our shadows helps us find the inner goodness and light of the world, as well as the goodness and light within ourselves.

We can stop seeing the world as an endless competition, one in which we expend so much energy judging ourselves and others as either superior or inferior. Taking that energy back gives us the ability to find within ourselves the approval and love we sought outside. We no longer focus on superiority or inferiority when we realize that we do not need to be anything other than what we are to receive love.

We all are worthy of receiving love simply because we are human, not because of anything that we may accomplish. If we move beyond the pain of what has caused us to feel unlovable, unworthy, and alienated from our natural connections, we no longer externalize our suffering in the outer world. We are intended to be connected to ourselves, to one another, to earth, sky, and the divine. These connections are all still within us, we have disconnected from them and they form the largest aspects of our shadow.

In accepting our humanity, we give up the need to be perfect. To be human is to be imperfect. We can take back all of the energy that we have spent attempting to be perfect in order for the world to accept us. We realize that no matter how perfect we are, no matter how "good" we are, we will never be perfect or good enough to receive love from those who are closed off in their own hearts. In that recognition we release the longing for love that will never appear. We move beyond feeling wrong, or bad, or requiring ourselves to be inhumanly perfect; instead we recognize that those around us have failed us by not offering us the love that every human deserves. When we are willing to fully feel how we were wronged by not receiving unconditional love and positive regard, we can release the pain of our childhood.

It is rare for humans to move beyond our basic childhood programming. We carry this programming into the world as adults, rarely realizing that we have mistaken the world for our childhood homes. But we can heal the beliefs and understandings of reality that come from such a formative time. To do so brings us immense freedom; thus we gain initiation into spiritual adulthood. This is a state where we no longer react to the world as a child but instead we act from the perspective and reality of an adult. We no longer consider our parents as authority figures or reality makers; instead we see them simply as human beings who are imperfect. In this way we move on from childhood hurts.

Doing shadow work allows us to identify and heal the parts of ourselves that we have had to mask or cut off. It allows for us to reclaim a sense of power and purpose as we recognize and move beyond the restrictive roles that we had to take on to survive our childhood.

Greater clarity regarding the world and the self develops. With self-realization we gain emotional intelligence and the ability to feel and accept all our emotions. We recognize that our emotions do not need to rule our lives. They are simply messengers sending us signals and warnings. We learn to reconnect with the sensate aspects of ourselves and with an embodied experience of life.

Shadow work eventually leads us to simply be who we are, without any pretenses or masks. This includes a feeling of comfort and being "at home" in our bodies and our lives.

This also includes accepting things (and people) as they are, rather than expecting them to be a certain way. Out of this acceptance we develop greater peace and stillness within. We gain the ability to be in the present moment. An opening of the heart towards ourselves and others is the result of shadow work.

This work also enables conflict resolution. Relationships improve. Until we reclaim our shadows, we only see a small prism of what the world is and who people are. We see people as we need to see them in order to perpetuate our own stories about reality. It is by questioning how we see others that we can see where we are divided within ourselves. Self-realization can be referred to as the end of inner conflict, and shadow work is one of the most direct paths to get there.

Each one of us who is willing to do shadow work brings resolution to one small part of our societal, cultural, and world difficulties. This work creates waves of healing. This may be a small wave when it comes to the world shadow, but it can be a substantial wave in the shadow of our family or community. Taking back our shadows means that our pain is no longer creating world pain and conflict.

Being fully in our bodies brings us into full contact with our souls. A soul-level emptiness is pervasive in the modern world, and it propels us to keep searching for something to fill the soul-sized hole that we feel within. Out of emptiness of soul comes disconnection from ourselves, other people, the world, and the divine. A full, integrated soul allows us to replace this loneliness with connection. We recognize that we are made up of the same stuff as the person next to us. With this recognition we see that we are not the only person to suffer under the weight of what we carry. Others know this pain as well. When we realize this, our loneliness lessens and healing occurs.

When we do shadow work it is easy to get lost in rectifying past hurts or in seeing the hatred we cast out into the world. However, we have also cut ourselves off from our beauty and potential. These "lighter" qualities too get externalized into the world and projected onto the Other: we reject our own creativity, beauty, love, charisma, power, and light. Along the way we have learned to not be "too much," to not fully inhabit who we are.

As we lessen the conflict within ourselves, we more fully inhabit our light. In fact, our light rises the more we deeply accept our darkness, our emotions, and our humanity. Out of that darkness comes wholeness and the ability to accept every last bit of ourselves with love. When our personal conflicts lessen, we gain the ability to be of service to the world in our unique capacities. We can share our light with others, rather than being so wrapped up in conflict, competition, and the need for approval that once reigned over our existence.

The end result of shadow work is to embody the full continuum and potential of our humanness. In the Other we see another human, struggling just as we are. It is by embracing our humanity, our bodies, our emotions, our inner wildness, and everything dark within us that we can become fully and truly ourselves.

Chapter 5

Helpful Tools

*T*here are a variety of helpful tools that we can utilize when working with the shadow. Developing these tools can ensure that our shadow work is helpful and healthy for us. We can gain confidence in our shadow work by returning to these tools again and again.

Some of these tools are deceptively simple but in practice they offer us a depth of understanding that otherwise we would not achieve. Others may require a bit of practice to fully embody them.

An important tool while doing this work is seeking outer support. Work with a friend who is also doing shadow work or speak to a therapist or bodyworker about the shifts you are experiencing. Having someone in your life to help you navigate change is always helpful. Please know that the discomfort created by this work is temporary and usually a result of breaking through old patterns.

We get so accustomed to our habits and ways of being that positive change can be nerve-wracking. We get so used to being small that the idea of being larger, freer, or more in our power, more in our bodies, creates fear.

Having the mentality that change can be beneficial is also an incredibly helpful tool. We associate change with difficult things happening. We do not need to let fear rule our lives. It can instead be seen in its rightful place as a messenger, letting us know that change and uncertainty are occurring. We can learn to have fear and continue to do the work anyway.

The Open Door

Gautama Buddha is credited as saying to his disciples: "Believe nothing which is unreasonable and reject nothing as unreasonable without proper examination."

The open door is quite a simple tool but requires a bit of intuition. Each of us is open to different degrees regarding ideas, conversations, and considerations. We can consider this as a completely open door, a slightly open door (to varying degrees, such as a halfway open door or a slightly cracked door), or a completely shut door.

For example, a friend may have a completely shut door regarding politics, but an open door when discussing philosophy. Most of us have many doors that are open to varying degrees. It is rare to find someone with a completely open door, as that means that they are able and willing to consider any thought, idea, or conceptualization of reality that comes their way. This does not mean that they agree with everything, but that they are willing to interface with disparate ideas, consider them, and change their mind based off information that they consider reasonable.

It is an excellent practice to consider how open other people's doors are when speaking to them about a subject. There is no use in speaking with a closed door. It just becomes frustrating, and it is likely that the person will have an ego-based defense as a result. People change their minds or crack open their doors only when they are ready.

In noticing that another person's door is cracked open about a subject, you may wish to speak to them a bit. A door that is open wider would result in a more successful, substantial discussion. When you note how open someone's door is, you can meet them where they are. This means that you can tailor the discussion to how open they are.

Typical questions after hearing this include: "Why do I have to do this? Shouldn't other people meet me where I am?" Ideally people should meet you where you are, but in reality, people become conscious of others in their own time and in their own way. Learning to successfully communicate with others by seeing how open their door is, is worth the effort. It prevents you from feeling frustrated when you initiate a conversation that someone is not open to, and it keeps you from offering too much information for the person to process. You would offer a small child a much different lesson than you would to a university student. By approaching people where they are, you will find that they listen to you much more readily.

Questioning how open your own door is when you are presented with new information can be difficult. We tend to ignore things that we are not yet ready to accept and to dehumanize people whose ideologies contrast with our own.

The best way to open our door is to truly listen to people who have had vastly different life experiences. This includes considering differing political ideologies, ways of life, and ways of thinking. We tend to like people who consolidate our egos, as they say what we already believe. It is comforting to hear our beliefs come out of someone else's mouth.

To fully open our door, we can start where we have the least resistance. For example, you may be willing to hear the wisdom of someone several decades older than you. It may be harder for you to have an open door to a child or an adolescent.

It may be incredibly difficult to open your door to ideologies that express hate and division. However, if you see the humanity underneath the fear and anger you project onto them, you can take back a large part of your personal shadow. If you are willing to see the suffering behind someone's hateful rhetoric, you will take away some of their power. Those who express anger, fear, and divisiveness are showing their own self-hatred and ignorance. Behind the mask of any hate-filled rhetoric are feelings of powerlessness and low self-worth that come from fear of one's own shadow. Those feelings are magnified when you react to them. In the age of social media, when some people are attempting to provoke a reaction online, this is an important concept to understand. Our emotional responses and projections onto people give them a fleeting sense of energy and power. By reacting to them we are offering them the attention that they are seeking.

If we understand that deep at the core of our being we desire approval, love, and validation, we can see the suffering in those who express even the most hate-filled and ignorant viewpoints. With that awareness, compassion can develop for the person suffering, not the viewpoint.

When we are able to see at this level, we will no longer project onto them our own shadows, or offer them our power. By accepting the darkest of our own shadow within ourselves—our own hatred and ignorance—we will no longer find ourselves in need of an outer source to hate.

The Bottom of the Ocean

The ocean is a metaphorical representation of our subconscious mind. Most of what we think and feel is like the surface of this water, which represents the conscious mind. Mid-ocean level is where our thoughts and feelings reside that are beginning to arise into our conscious mind: we may be aware of them, but we cannot fully experience them with words or stories quite yet.

At the ocean floor, or the bottom of the ocean, we find our shadows—the parts of ourselves that have yet to surface or the information that we do not consciously know regarding ourselves. It has long been the role of shamans and artists to utilize symbols to help us access the deeper parts of ourselves. The information is there, but it simply has not been processed by the ego-mind yet.

When doing shadow work, assume that the answers arise at first are coming from the surface of the water. Ask internally what some mid-ocean answers to that same question might be. Then ask yourself what the ocean floor says, the real and true answer.

In time you can question which "layer" of the ocean the answers from within you are coming from. While working through the following chapters, you may realize that you have good access to your mid-ocean, but if you pause for a moment, you will sense a rising word or phrase that comes from someplace deeper and truer within yourself.

When reaching the bottom of the ocean, it is typical to feel a sense of resonance—a feeling of rightness or an emotional response. As we work with this tool what started as our ocean floor will become mid-ocean, or even surface waves. As we become more self-realized, what once was unconscious within ourselves becomes conscious. In time, we also learn to trust our intuition and things that are deeply felt, but perhaps not logically understood.

For those perfectionists out there, there is no "wrong" way of doing this exercise, or any of the other exercises. There is a gradual process of working with all of them in which the tool itself becomes more and more a part of your "toolkit" for life. Using the tool eventually becomes second-nature.

Magnification

When we react emotionally, it is unlikely that we are fully reacting from the circumstances of the present moment: our anger rises with rage from the past, our fear comes forward with memories of past panic. If we recognize this, we can begin to separate what is appropriate for us to feel in the moment from what is being magnified within us. Eventually we can fully feel what is helpful for us in the moment and validate it. Then we can process or release what emotions are arising from the past.

We are intended to feel all of our emotions. If someone crosses our boundaries, we should feel anger or irritation. If we are passed over for a job opportunity, we should feel disappointment and grief. All emotions are messengers, sharing with our conscious mind what the deepest aspects of our soul are speaking. Shadow work is not about removing "bad" emotions. Our emotions link us to our passions, and by fully allowing ourselves to feel, we become alive.

For example, a man cuts in front of a woman in the grocery store. She is rightfully angry. That is quite rude. But what also arises in her are past episodes when others got ahead to her detriment, including memories of the men who have spoken over her at work, and feelings of being overlooked in childhood.

She is not conscious of this. What she is quite conscious of is that she is incredibly angry over something that shouldn't make her that angry. Not only that, but she has been taught not to be angry at all, and not to show her anger, which magnifies it further. So she represses this anger like all of the rest of her angers. Or perhaps she is in a healthier place where she vents to a friend about the rude man at the market and releases the current anger.

If she had access to this tool, she could recognize that she has a right to be angry, but that her anger is magnified. She then could ask herself how much this anger is magnified. Working with simple numbers here is quite helpful. Is twenty percent of her anger justified? Is ninety percent? How much of her anger is from the present moment?

If we are able to ask ourselves these questions, we recognize that we are justified in our emotions, whatever they are. They may just be magnified. We can then validate the emotions we do feel and note what situations cause magnification.

You will find that some situations cause your anger to arise where ninety-nine percent of it is completely justified. Other situations will occur in which ninety-nine percent of your anger is an overreaction to the situation at hand. By noting the situations in which your anger— or any other emotion—is drastically magnified, you can start to see patterns in it.

Someone overlooking us may cause for us to feel intense grief and despair. Noting this once is helpful. Noting that it is a pattern, happening many times, will show us what is unhealed within us and what patterns (loops) are present in our lives that we can work on.

The simple practice of noticing when our feelings are magnified can increase our emotional intelligence and competence. By inwardly sensing what we are feeling and questioning it, we start to gain mastery of our emotions. In time we will be able to use this tool to process our anger and hurts as they are occurring so that we don't add to the backlog of unhealed emotions within. We can then work on the unhealed parts of ourselves that trigger these emotions. Over time we will notice ourselves reacting in the present moment without magnification.

What Age Am I?

We are each a constellation of many different consciousnesses. This means that there are parts of us still relating to the world as a child, or a teenager, or even who we were a few months ago. Then there is also a part of us that is operating in the present day, in our present bodies.

By asking "What age am I?" we can consider how we are reacting to any situation that we come across. This question gains more depth the more that we ask it. At first, we may be confused, or lack concise answers. As we ask this question more and more, we may hear that we are responding to a situation like a toddler or a teenager.

In time we will notice that specific situations trigger us to feel like a small child who was always teased, or like a teenager who wants to rebel against everything. We might find an infant who just wants its mommy, or a twenty-something who feels on top of the world and yet inwardly senses that she is not yet an adult.

Over time we will find patterns. If a reaction causes for you to feel like a two-year-old once, that might be something to note. If you react several times to situations like a two-year-old, that is a pattern to look at more deeply. That two-year-old part of you is frozen in time, stuck in its stage of development.

Through the awareness developed by asking "What age am I?" we can begin to separate our current, appropriate reactions from reactions that come from an earlier time.

This awareness in and of itself is quite healing. When we notice patterns, we naturally begin to change our behavior. If we notice that we are reacting like a teenager to everything, we are likely to change our reactions over time. This is to be celebrated, rather than something to be unkind to ourselves about. To notice that parts of ourselves are stuck is a sign of emotional intelligence.

Head versus Heart

Shadow work is a bit like playing detective. We question ourselves and outer situations until the need for that line of questioning ceases. We can simply allow ourselves to feel and to experience reality from an embodied state. We no longer project onto the outer world. The trick to this is that it does require healing work and frequent questioning for us to feel the full flow of reality pouring through us.

We tend to be quite stuck in our heads. In the modern world we experience a split between the head and the body, between thinking and feeling. Marion Woodman called shadow work and the work of individuation "putting the head back on the body." This is a process of allowing ourselves to deeply feel and then letting logic guide those feelings. If we consider the body as the polarity of feeling and intuition (classically "the feminine") and the head as the domain of logic and order (classically "the masculine") we can see how the world has long neglected the feminine polarity in favor of the masculine.

The objective of this practice is not to eradicate the masculine polarity. Intuition without logic is untethered from reality and disconnected from the body and the sensate world. Similarly, logic without intuition leads to a life without magic and the wonder of the unknown. If you have ever experienced the ecstasy of tasting the perfect bite of food, that was a result of being deeply connected to the sensate world and to the body.

In a healthy, fully realized system, the body and the head work together. We feel the flow of our emotions and deeply appreciate the passionate nature of our bodies, while that flow is given order and action by the head. Think of the head as being the banks of a river, creating sturdy boundaries and structure for that river to flow. Without that structure, our creative flows could not properly manifest in the world.

This tool is quite simple. When you feel or think something, ask if it is coming from your head or your heart. We are so used to being in our heads that it may take a bit of time to consider that something could be coming from below the neck.

Often what arise in our minds are thoughts of what we should do and who we should be. These can be helpful thoughts but they can also be incredibly nasty, untrue, or simply unhelpful thoughts. When our thoughts arise, we can feel into our hearts and ask for their response to those thoughts. We can eventually "hear" a response that comes from a deeper place.

Similarly, our hearts speak what our soul truly desires. It can take a bit of time to distinguish this from the voice of the ego. What arises from the heart is deeply felt and has resonance: it is the feeling of irrevocable truth that we cannot deny. This is how we can tell the difference.

When the heart speaks, we can then bring that information to the head. Our soul may be telling us to move to Hawaii. Our head may then tell us that we have a sick relative nearby who needs our care and that we have no way to financially support ourselves in Hawaii. If we return to our heart with this information, the heart may then reveal a deeper truth. For example, it may simply want to escape in some way. Negotiations between head and heart can occur. We may then decide that taking a day off work to go on a hike, or visit a new restaurant, is what our "escape" could be.

Initially we can begin to question whether information that arises in us is coming from the heart or the head. Both parts of us have wisdom, but the head may whisper lies and the heart may speak the truth without logic. The heart offers access to the soul-level feeling place within ourselves. It opens a gateway to the rest of the body and helps us feel and know ourselves on a deeper level. By questioning if something is coming from our heart or our head, we can gradually become embodied.

Superiority/Inferiority and Competition

Questioning if your actions or thoughts are causing you to feel superior or inferior to someone else can quickly reveal your shadows.

We may be better than someone else at certain things in our lives; we each are better and worse at different things. This creates a world in which (hopefully) those who have natural aptitude will feel called to careers or hobbies where they can utilize their gifts.

The ego likes to defend itself through the superiority/inferiority loop. While this will be further explained in the "Loops" chapter, suffice it to say that the superiority/inferiority loop engages us in continual competition with others in an attempt to justify our own existence. By fully integrating our shadows, we come out of this loop: we no longer need to feel superior or inferior to others as we are no longer projecting our inadequacies onto other people.

If you are willing to see situations in which you feel superior or inferior to others, you can clearly see a part of your shadow. By noticing this projection you can start to question more deeply what you have projected or defended against and eventually reclaim and reintegrate the shadow part. For now, simply notice when you feel superior or inferior to others and note common themes (for example, you may feel inferior or superior in specific situations, such as feeling inferior to people with more money, or superior to those with less education). Just doing this is a great start to integrating your shadow.

Practicing Boundaries with Yourself

We often talk about practicing boundaries with others. It is essential to learn how to say "no" to others and to consider how much of our time and energy we are willing to give to friends, family, and loved ones. Ideally, we would have naturally reciprocal relationships where we feel as if we give as much as we receive.

This may change throughout our lives as we experience crisis or need. Long-lasting friendships and relationships will cycle through different phases in which there is call for more one-sided support. This is quite different from being in a relationship in which we continually feel sucked dry, or stuck listening to their latest musings and never being heard.

We can also develop boundaries with ourselves. This is an essential yet overlooked aspect of developing boundaries. We are so used to "doing," to achieving, that we do not consider whether we are providing ourselves with adequate rest, relaxation, play, and fun. These are essential qualities in our lives. Simply put, they make the difference between a life worth living and a life in which we are on autopilot.

This becomes important with shadow work as well. Often, I meet individuals with the best of intentions, but they go overboard on inner work to their own detriment. This can result in anything from absent-mindedness to emotional overwhelm to complete disconnection from reality. Spiritual emergency can also occur, where material arising from the subconscious is too much to process consciously.

When doing shadow work, it is important to be aware of such possibilities. This work provides an excellent opportunity to develop boundaries with ourselves. There may be periods in life where this work can be done intensively, and other times where it may feel forced. Develop your intuition and the ability to say "no" within yourself. Recognize when there is too much going on in your outer life: work, family, and healthy fun, when your inner practices should take a back seat. Curiosity, willingness, or needing to take the next step in your life can be the clarion call to move forward.

This is profound and life-changing work, which can take some time to fully integrate.

I often get clients who come to me exhausted and don't recognize that they have every right to be exhausted. Their lives and what they are dealing with on top of work and attending to their household is exhausting. When we have the clarity to recognize that we are going through a lot, we tend to give ourselves a break. When we recognize that processing and integrating emotional and spiritual changes is just as taxing as physical labor, we can give ourselves time to rest, heal, and recalibrate.

If this work ever gets overwhelming, recognize that more work is not helpful. When overwhelmed, attending to the basics of our lives is in order. Physicality is often necessary to ground us back into reality. Long walks, spending time in nature or with (positive) friends and family, and taking part in pleasurable activities can bring us back to the present moment. This gives us the necessary space in which to process whatever is overwhelming us.

Sometimes we become obsessed with, or even addicted to, emotional and spiritual work, seeking catharsis. Catharsis can be an important tool, but we can also seek it out like an addict seeking their next high. An over-reliance on cathartic experiences can lead to ego inflation, an inability to adequately process what has come up, or a rejection of the work already done.

When we learn to practice boundaries with ourselves, we realize that life has flows to it. Think of this like tides coming in and going back out to sea. There are times where we can delve deeply into our inner work, and it feels like everything in our bodies and our lives is showing us where we are blocked, and what we should look at within.

There are other times where that tide is going back out to sea. During these times we can focus on integration and getting our external world in order, attending to our basic physical needs, rest, fun, chores, and relationships.

By recognizing these tides, we no longer have to force this work, or anything in our lives. We can take the opportunity when those tides come in to work with the heightened energies. When the tides are rolling back, we can allow ourselves to take breaks and not do as much. Offering ourselves grace and compassion will allow this work to go well.

While we all have aspects of our lives that we need to attend to, no matter how we are feeling, if we follow the tides like this, we will find that the culture of "doing" breaks down. We do not always need to be growing, doing, and achieving. We can be more productive and enthusiastic during times when tide is coming in, and less bullying of ourselves when it is going out—when it would be best for us to rest or attend to the necessities of our lives without adding anything extra to our plates.

Radical Acceptance

We often make the mistake of seeing people for who we want them to be, rather than who they are. It is wonderful to see the potential in others and to encourage that potential. However, asking someone to take responsibility for themselves before they are ready to is a foolish act.

The deepest form of love we can offer another human being is to accept them for being exactly who they are. Not who they used to be, or who they might be in the future. Not who we imagine them to be in our heads, or the roles that we have cast upon them.

Acceptance is radical because it means letting go of the desire to change others to fit our needs. Without realizing it we offer transactional love to those around us, and it does not feel good to them. Just as we desire unconditional love and positive regard, so do the people that we are in relationship with.

We often conflate acceptance with approval. We can accept that someone is a drug addict who will likely steal our television if we allow them to. We can accept that our boss or our friend can be a jerk. However, there is a danger in putting people into unidimensional roles as victim or villain. Your boss may be a jerk because she is stressed at work. On vacation or with her friends or dog she may be a lovely human being.

Seeing people clearly allows us to move beyond our own filters regarding who that person is. We see others through varying mental prisms which do not include the totality of who they are. When we see them clearly, we can transcend naivety and childhood narratives that blind us to the undesirable traits of others. If we do not fully acknowledge that a teacher gives us an uncomfortable, creepy feeling, our ability to protect ourselves from that teacher is lessened. There is a gift in fully acknowledging our intuitive fears, feelings, and first impressions. That gift is the ability to put up boundaries and to act and react with that knowledge in mind.

Radical acceptance is the ability to offer acceptance without any desire to change someone. When we radically accept someone, we meet them where they are. This is not done in any sort of condescending way, as if they are lesser. It is the unique ability to sense where someone is and to be able to speak to them exactly where they are. Those who have this rare quality will find themselves in better relationships, will be regarded more positively, and understood more regularly.

Radical acceptance leads to the clarity of truly seeing someone for who they are. With this clarity comes the ability to make decisions regarding your relationship with that person. If we are unwilling to admit that our friend is an addict, we might offer them money or an invitation into our homes to steal from us. If we are willing to accept that our partner is absent-minded, we will stop expecting her to remember where she put her keys. The small irritations we experience show a lack of acceptance of the other.

This form of acceptance accompanies the awareness that someone will change only if they desire to. We cannot change others. We can only change ourselves, and this may or may not affect or motivate others to do the same. Someone truly needs to be at a point of not only desiring change but being ready to make that change. Otherwise, we may dream of change but not be in a place of taking the action that is required to actually enact it.

We rarely recognize how much stress our desire for someone to change creates in a relationship. We can feel when someone disapproves of us, however small that disapproval may be. We can sense when another person does not accept us fully. When we accept someone for exactly who they are, space develops. They feel as if they can be who they are without judgment. There is less friction and adversarial, unspoken resentment in the relationship. Ironically, accepting someone for exactly who they are often creates the space for them to feel loved and appreciated enough to create change in their lives.

It is so rare that we feel the support that radical acceptance provides. It can heal hidden resentment and anger, and release our hopes that those around us become other than who they show us. When someone shows you who they are, take that as truth. Our behaviors, not our words, reveal the truth of who we are.

Radical acceptance brings peace and clarity. When you find yourself in friction with someone, take a mental step back and ask yourself if you are accepting that person for exactly who they are. Again, you do not have to approve of who they are. If you are not totally accepting them, ask yourself what would happen if you could accept them for exactly who they are with no desire to change them whatsoever.

The more that you question whether you approach others with radical acceptance, the more you will see how you desire to change others in small and large ways to suit your needs, likes, and dislikes. With this recognition you can become aware that others do not need to fit into a specific box. When we realize this, we can free the other person from the cage we have put them in and allow them to thrive as the person they are.

The more we radically accept others, the more we will radically accept ourselves.

Part 2

Working with the Shadow

*If any help was going to arise to lift me out of my misery,
it would come from the dark side of my personality.*

Robert Bly

*If you bring forth what is within you, what you bring forth
will save you. If you do not bring forth what is within you,
what you do not bring forth will destroy you.*

Gospel of Thomas

Chapter 6

Developing Emotional Intelligence

We are meant to have a full range of emotions. Emotional intelligence allows us to fully feel our emotions in a healthy, life-affirming way. By developing emotional intelligence, we learn to release the backlog of emotions within our bodies and to express ourselves genuinely and appropriately in any situation.

By learning how to work with our emotions, we come out of a helpless, victimized state into recognizing our power and capacity. Few of us move beyond childhood emotional reactivity into emotional skill and intelligence. In childhood, we learned self-soothing mechanisms, harmful behaviors, thoughts, and defense mechanisms to deal with emotions that were too stressful or overwhelming. Recognizing that we never learned how to work intelligently with our emotions can help us begin to shift the ways of relating that were ingrained in us at a very early age. We can learn skills now that we did not learn in childhood or adolescence.

When our emotions drive our behaviors, we respond reactively from our subconscious. To master our emotions we must become fully conscious of them. We can view our emotions as messengers offering important insights into the nature of our environment, the people in it, and how we interface with it. There is a reason to feel fear, shame, anger, sadness, joy, and pain. Each of these emotions is telling us something.

When we are so out of touch with our emotions that they have been cut off from our conscious control, we fear our emotions. They have been made shadow. As a result, our emotions lead us into reactions that we feel helpless to control.

When our emotions are embodied, we feel them fully, in the present moment. This means that we no longer backlog our emotions (by storing them in the body), or project them outwards. We recognize that emotions are simply energies and we can choose how to respond to them.

For example, if we are feeling anger, we can choose to remain silent, to leave the situation, to argue, to be diplomatic, or to punch someone in the face. We can also choose to walk off our anger, to dance, or to engage in other creative and personal pursuits with the anger as the fuel for what we are doing. These options should all be available to us with full embodiment of our shadow. This is true mastery—the ability to utilize our emotions as fuel and to make conscious decisions regarding what to do with their energy.

The purpose of shadow work is to integrate all aspects of ourselves and to become a full human being. In this integration we increasingly take back the projections and ideas that we have put out onto the world and we can see reality, and the people in it, with greater clarity. We can make conscious decisions regarding how to act and who to be.

One of the most important aspects of building emotional intelligence is validating our emotions. We are right to experience whatever emotions we feel in the present moment, and we were right to experience whatever emotions we felt in the past. We often seek to punish, shame, or bully our emotions when they arise: *I shouldn't be so depressed. That's stupid. I have a roof over my head and some people don't.* Or: *I shouldn't be angry because spiritual people don't get angry.* Another example of how we shame ourselves and one another is by saying or thinking: *You should be over your grief by now.*

When we shut down our emotions, and prevent ourselves from fully feeling, they don't go away. They reside within us, seeking to be fully felt. Much as we wouldn't belittle a small child for being sad (hopefully), we should not shame or harm ourselves into "getting over" whatever we feel or whatever we have experienced. We can move past whatever trauma or held emotions that lie unprocessed within ourselves only by offering grace to our emotions. They have a right to be seen, heard, and validated.

There is no such thing as transcending our emotions. Unless we fully feel our emotions, we are spiritually bypassing them. So many of us attempt to move to forgiveness and compassion without feeling the righteous anger and pain that another person or situation has caused. Until we fully feel, we cannot move into a state of acceptance regarding what we have experienced. Acceptance, not premature forgiveness, allows us to move forward in our lives.

Some emotions are simply too large for our bodies to process. These larger emotions need to heal in relationship—through relating with another person, council, or family system (which may or may not mean biological family). They need to be witnessed by another, and seen naked for what they truly are. Our ability to have our vulnerability seen in a safe way by another is the basis for authentic connection. As such, it is immensely healing. We have learned to shield ourselves from showing our vulnerability because, sadly, we have learned that our hearts can be used against us. In time we may learn that others can hold our deepest vulnerability as sacred. They just need to be the right people.

We can do plenty for ourselves on an individual level. Part of emotional intelligence is to recognize when we need another to help us out of a stuck place. We can forgive ourselves when we recognize that our emotional load is significant enough that we need to reach out for support. There is no need to suffer alone when others can help us.

E-motion

Our emotions are intended to have flow: they are e-motions. Much like the weather, our feelings are intended to pass. It may rain on our inner landscape for several days, but by fully allowing ourselves to feel, the storm will pass.

We often resist our emotions, especially the darkest of emotions: grief, despair, rage, panic, depression, loneliness. Through shadow work, we can learn to meet our emotions as friends. Even in the worst panic, or the depths of despair, we can sit with our emotions (experience them in the present moment) instead of ignoring, resisting, or projecting them onto others. This can only be done when we recognize that even the most difficult of emotions do pass through us, and that they do so much more readily when we allow ourselves to feel them.

To feel our emotions is often a step-by-step process. If you are just beginning to befriend your emotions, allowing yourself to feel small amounts of anxiety, jealousy, or sadness may be perfect for you. There is no need to stare into the abyss on your first day of doing this work. Doing shadow work means holding boundaries with ourselves and taking small steps that we feel are a bit outside of our comfort zone but will not overload us. If too much emotion arises, or if an emotion arises that we may need to process with others rather than by ourselves, we can let our bodies know that now is not the right time to feel this. Learning to practice boundaries with ourselves is an important step in self-regulation. Your mind and body can learn internal boundaries and how to self-regulate. It is just a skill that you may not have learned before.

With practice, our body and our emotions listen to what we have to say. We can also learn to titrate, to feel our emotions bit by bit. We can say "no," even to ourselves (this will be covered later in this chapter). We can also learn to say "yes," knowing that whatever we are feeling, no matter how terrible, will pass through us.

With emotional intelligence, we can start relating in a skillful and healthy way to our emotions. Our lives are filled with uncertainty and stress and we can develop the means to navigate whatever life brings our way. We can stop believing ourselves to be victims of life and instead become competent adults who recognize that we struggle because we are human. Struggle is inevitable and learning to navigate the pain that life brings, with resilience and skill, is the end goal of becoming emotionally intelligent.

Intuition, Instinct and Emotions

Each of our emotions has a reason for being, an innate intelligence, and a message to offer. They are like wave forms that move through us, offering us information about who we are and about everything that we intersect with. If we are willing to listen, we reconnect with intuition—the force within us that offers us instinctual information that we cannot yet process through intellect or logic.

Many of us have had our intuition overridden by a world that teaches us that feelings and intuitions are illogical or not worth listening to. This ignores the fact that humans developed instincts for good reason. As children our intuition is overridden by parents, schools, and friends who have different value systems that we must go along with to belong. This is a survival tactic, as on a deep, instinctual level we associate being an outlier with being cast from our tribe (family, social circle), ultimately leading to our death. We learn to listen to others, instead of ourselves.

A woman ignores the feeling of a man acting creepy on a bus for fear of being "impolite." She is then assaulted. A man has an odd feeling about the mother of his son's friend. He fails to stop his son from going over to her house. It later turns out the woman is violent and abusive. These are extreme examples, but they teach us the gravity of what happens when we do not listen to the instinctual and intuitive parts of ourselves.

As a result of unresolved trauma, we may be in a state of hypervigilance, in which our intuition incorrectly warns us that people or situations are dangerous. This may result from being victimized and not acting out our instincts. It remains stuck in our system like a giant flashing warning light, blinking each time we encounter a situation that reminds us of the original situation.

For example, a father is angry all the time at his son, but the boy is afraid to run and hide because he knows that he will be punished if he does so. This will lead to confused instinctual responses later in life. The adult man may now have difficulty leaving situations even though intuitively he knows that he should.

Even in less traumatic situations, when we learn from authority figures (parents, schools, and later peers and popular culture) that what we feel and know on an intuitive level is wrong, we learn to override our instincts and ignore what our body is speaking to us on an emotional level. In many ways, shadow work is about learning to listen to our feelings and instincts: "To thine own self be true," wrote Shakespeare. To develop the Self is to move beyond the sea of thoughts, opinions, and insights of others to discover what we truly feel, want, and need.

Embodied and Ensouled Emotions

Our vitality lies within the darkest of our emotions. Embodied rage gives rise to vitality and passion; without anger we are lifeless, we miss the spark of creativity that lets us live our days meaningfully. Within our sadness and the grief of all that we have lost lies the purity of love.

We cannot know happiness unless we have something to contrast it with, such as melancholy, numbness, or despair. Our despair reveals our cognitive dissonance: the way we are living conflicts with our true values. Who we believe ourselves to be and who we have become are at odds.

Anger shows us violated boundaries: irritation shows us mild boundary violation, anger shows us moderate violation, and rage points to severe violation of our boundaries. If we listen to the messages of anger, we understand our boundaries and create new ones that honor who we are.

Our hatred and ignorance defend us against seeing what is intolerable in ourselves. The starkest divisions within ourselves always show up in our hatred of the Other. If we see the humanity in others, the force of hatred is turned back to its source: self-hatred.

As we do shadow work, the pain of separation arises, as well as the grief, fear, and rage that we suppressed for so long.

Our emotions are a form of vital energy within us. All that we haven't yet allowed ourselves to feel or express stagnates within our bodies. All of our emotions are gateways to the shadow and lead to a deeper understanding of Self.

Our emotions are incredibly multifaceted. Grief is not simply grief: it is grief-rage, grief-despair, grief-longing. When we finally allow ourselves to sit with our emotions, we encounter a voice, something that wishes to be heard. It is only then that we can hear the true message that is speaking to us. Under the voice of anger we often find bitter disappointment and grief. Our melancholy reveals a lack of meaning and purpose. When we can hear those voices and listen to them, we encounter our soul.

The secret to regaining our passion, vitality, and creativity lies in our darkness. It is by embracing our dark side, by truly inhabiting our full range of emotions, that we are liberated. We can, through exploring our darkest emotions, regain our enthusiasm for living, our power, and our passion for life.

It is only through our emotions that we can feel and know what our soul is speaking to us. It is a quiet voice within, telling us not only what is wrong with our lives but also what is right. How we are cherished and valuable, and how we can contribute to the world. How we can find meaning and purpose and a desire to truly live. This voice is individualized—your calling is unlikely to be the same as your friend's. How you can create meaning in your life is not something that can be given to you by society, or your parents. It is something that is soul-guided and individualized. To access this voice—through the gateway of the emotions—is to fill the soul-sized hole that creates loneliness, isolation, and despair within each one of us.

While on its surface emotional intelligence is about processing past emotions and allowing present-day emotions to be felt, on a deeper level, it is so much more. To be in flow with our emotions, to allow them to move through us, is to have access to our vitality and innate creativity. We can think of our emotions as a misguided creative force. To work in concert with that force re-aligns it; we can now feel our full vitality and freely express our creativity to the world.

Our shadows represent large aspects of ourselves that are ruling our lives without our conscious recognition. When a part of ourselves is not integrated, it is outside of our conscious control. When our shadows are integrated, we can consciously understand and work with that part of ourselves.

For example, if we believe that to be angry is unladylike, we may have a large stockpile of unprocessed, unintegrated anger that has become shadow. Or we may want to prove to others that women are filled with rage, so we act out that rage. It erupts at times when it is triggered and spirals out of control. Even worse, it is likely that something small will eventually lead us to erupt in an entire volcano of repressed rage.

When we can feel that anger flow through our bodies—accepted and validated for its presence—we can direct that flow. Anger then becomes creativity, passion, or fuel to heal injustice. In its purest form, our emotions are the language of our soul. Fully feeling all of our emotions gives us direct access to flow—to creativity, passion, and aliveness.

The Nervous System

Picture your nervous system as a series of wires. These wires transmit information from below, from the digestive system/enteric nervous system, to the brain and from the brain to the body.

In the brain, the structures of the hypothalamus and the para-limbic system (including the amygdala) are particularly significant to emotional regulation. They are like the command post or regulator of our nervous system. They transmit messages in response to its environment, which we experience as heightened emotions like anger or fear. These messages are responses to perceived threats in the environment, activating the sympathetic nervous system. This results in physiological responses like increased heart rate, digestive issues, and other endocrine responses.

Put more simply, if we experience a threat in our environment, our brain will respond by creating the emotion of fear. This sends our body the message that we should fight, flee, or freeze in order to survive the situation. Our brains, if healthy and responsive, respond to threats appropriately. There is a reason why we may need to feel a rush of adrenaline and the fear and rapid heartbeat that accompany it: we may need to find our lost child or rush a loved one to the hospital. Our minds and bodies are wondrous things and when working well and in synchrony, they can respond to our environment and any situation in a way that is right for the situation.

When our brain is affected by trauma, these messages may be confused or out of sync. We may be in a continual state of overwhelm due to past trauma so that our "wires" are fried and cannot accurately transmit messages. We may learn to freeze in a situation in which running away would be the best response. We may have an ingrained response, like fawning (see below) that prevents us from recognizing threats, like people who may cause us harm.

During childhood a different part of our brain develops every four years. When trauma occurs, caused by emotional neglect, lack of safety, or lack of positive modeling, that part of our brain does not fully develop. The brain does not wait; it moves on to the next area to be developed. By looking towards our inner child (see Chapter Eight) we can find the parts of ourselves that never developed properly and learn to work with them.

Our bodies are a repository of emotions and they transmit messages up to the brain. If those messages are emotions that remain unintegrated, they could manifest as a continual message of fear, or feelings of immense grief sent again and again through these wires. Negative self-talk such as "I am not worthy" or "Everyone hates me" can also be transmitted.

When we can heal the emotions that lie latent in the body, messages like these will either stop or we will clearly see them for what they are. When we see that a message of "I am all alone" or a feeling of despair is being continually activated in our system, we can directly address that core suffering to resolve it.

The amygdala is the amplifier of the brain. It processes what is important in its environment, including stressors and fear. The hypothalamus and limbic system—the emotional regulator of our brain—as well as the amygdala can learn to re-regulate. This is done by healing past trauma and by becoming skilled in working with our present-day emotional responses.

Our brain consists of three "layers." The first layer, the oldest, is our reptilian brain. This contains our instinctual, animalistic responses. The limbic system is the second layer, which is largely responsible for emotion. The cerebral cortex is the third layer of our brain, responsible for higher thought and logic. When we are in a state of emotional overload, panic, or stress, the cerebral cortex (our "thinking brain") shuts down and we operate from the other two layers of our brain.

If we are living in a state of fear and hypervigilance, we will treat everything as a threat. This means that we will not be able to acknowledge and respond to actual threats in our environment. When we come more into our present-day emotional reality, our nervous system responds better and more accurately to the stimuli around us. It can clearly gauge threats and their severity. This is because it is not stuck in repetitive messages of the past; instead, those wires are transmitting clear present-day messages.

Our nervous system can move into several different states when it feels threatened. Some of these are lifesaving in certain situations. We may freeze if a dangerous predator is in our vicinity. Running away when someone is mugging us or shooting at us is the right choice. Or more moderately, we may wish to leave a situation (walk away or flee) when we recognize that an argument or a fight might break out.

We will each have a dominant tendency regarding how our nervous system reacts. This is something to notice, as it may not be the best response to every situation. Put more simply, shutting down (freezing) may be your automatic response to your angry partner. This may prevent arguments in the short term. In the long term, learning to be aggressive and fight (with words, ideally) would move you out of freeze and into healthy responsiveness to the situation.

We can learn to gain full access to our nervous system. The following sections provide some tools that can be used to respond to various situations.

Fight

Fight can be a very physical response, such as punching someone. It can also be an argument, or an internalized conflict. This conflict is a war between two parts of yourself; seeing this fight clearly can allow both sides to find their resolution and the conflict to end.

At its healthiest, fight is the correct response to threat. If we are unable to access this resource, we cannot punch someone who has punched us. Or we cannot argue with someone who needs someone to stand up to them. If we do not have enough *fight* in our system, we will be passive, and ineffectually hope for conflict to pass.

Darla wants others to think of her as a good and kind person. She does not share her opinions for fear of what others may think of her. Deep down, Darla desires to be authentic and to share her opinions and thoughts, yet she remains passive and frozen. Through shadow work, Darla recognizes that she no longer wishes to be passive and silent in her own life. She begins sharing her opinions and thoughts with others, knowing that some people may not like what she has to say. By becoming more assertive, Darla has learned to "fight" in a healthy way—to truly show up and connect with others. She now realizes that people may not like her if she is passive and yielding, and they may not like her if she is fully herself. So she may as well be fully herself.

Uma reacts to anyone saying anything negative to her by getting angry and responding maliciously. She believes that people will take advantage of her if she is not careful, and so she finds herself repeatedly in situations in which she feels others are taking advantage of her. In response, she argues, slanders, and cuts off contact with people who she feels have wronged her. If Uma were to examine the inner child that causes her to feel as if she needs to "fight," she would release her anger and recognize that conflicts do not need to lead to tantrums or other immature responses.

To engage in fight, it can be helpful to physically learn to fight. Training in practices such as boxing, weight lifting, or martial arts helps us to enact this biological instinct in ourselves. Working with the parts of ourselves that are hesitant or resistant to fight can allow for us to access this instinct when necessary.

Learning about conflict and conflict resolution can strengthen our verbal fighting instinct. Looking at parts of ourselves that have difficulty being assertive or argumentative when necessary is also helpful.

Flight

Fleeing from an attacker or a wild animal is often how we envision flight. This certainly is true, but it is not how flight shows up in our daily reality. We may leave situations, go for walks, spend time in our cars, scroll through our phones, linger after work or school, or hide in our rooms as a form of flight.

Naveed is incredibly stressed with work and home life. His wife Medina stays at home with their two young children, and she regrets the decision. She is frequently angry and belittling. Naveed spends an hour after work each day in his car smoking cigarettes and looking at his phone rather than going home.

Sara hates going home for the holidays. Her mother always criticizes her and her brother frequently remarks on her weight and food intake. When she goes home, she takes frequent walks or runs errands to escape the situation.

In its milder forms flight is a method of avoidance. It can be a healthy skill. Sara going for a walk is an entirely positive solution, even if a part of her wants to fight. Naveed would be better off seeking resolution and help for Medina and his family, but he would need to mount considerable internal resources to confront a reality in which he is miserable. Recognizing that he is running away would allow him to clearly see his misery and to eventually take steps to resolve it.

Freeze

We freeze when it is biologically advantageous. We seek to remain hidden for fear that a predator might find us. Our nervous system freezes when it is overwhelmed with too much information to process. Like trying to drink a too-thick milkshake that won't move up a straw, we need to sit and wait until things are calmer to be able to process the stimuli.

We also freeze when we are unable to make a decision. An essential conflict has arisen within us, and we are stuck between two states: should we stay, or should we go? Should we do this, or should we do that? We remain frozen when we are uncertain of what we should do next. We also remain frozen when we know on an instinctual level what direction we should go but we fear upending our life. For example, many people remain in relationships long after they are over. They have simply frozen out of fear.

Monique knows that her relationship is over with her partner, Wendy. They no longer talk, or even like each other. But they own a home together, and have a child, all reasons that Monique uses to stay in the relationship. She is miserable, and knows that her growing contempt for Wendy is not a good sign. She no longer wants to deal with Wendy's emotional baggage and has found herself watching excessive television and drinking in order to cope. When she recognizes that her relationship is already over (and has been for some time) she is able to successfully move out of freeze into taking action and making the decision to end her relationship.

When in freeze mode, it is helpful to move as much as possible. Take a walk, wiggle a finger, breathe slowly in and out. These small motions can help us to start to move out of the freeze state. Being frozen makes us small and hidden. The way out of freeze is to take our power back—to act, make decisions, and work on whatever part of us needs to remain small and powerless until it feels safe enough to be seen and heard.

Flaccidity

While fight, flight, and freeze are widely known nervous system responses, flaccidity and fawning are less well known but incredibly common nervous system responses.

When we are functioning at a basic level in our lives but don't have any resilience or zest for life, we are in a state of flaccidity. It is not a state of being frozen; in those states we cannot function much at all. In a flaccid state, we go through the motions of our lives but do little else. Hobbies, friends, and interests wane or disappear. We mark time until our inevitable death.

Mark describes himself as being in a continual state of melancholy. He goes to work, comes home, and watches TV or plays video games until he goes to bed. The next day he repeats the cycle. He derives no joy from work, feels numb while watching TV or playing video games, and only eats for sustenance. He has no meaning and purpose to his life and he feels like he is on autopilot during most of it.

Certainly there are plenty of things in life that we simply need to get through (the healthy state of flaccidity). But millions of people are stuck in this state without recognizing that they could discover meaning and purpose in their lives again. Learning to connect to others and to the world helps bring us out of this state. For Mark, having someone to bear witness to the weight of his shadow would help him discover some vitality in his life and body again.

Fawning

To fawn is to act from a learned pattern of putting others before the self. When we fawn, it is because we have learned at some point that we need to look after others in order to be safe.

Those who fawn learn that they are not important, that they need to make themselves as small as possible. They are often frustrated by louder individuals being seen and heard while they themselves are invisible. Little do they know that they have made themselves invisible as a safety mechanism. Fawning includes making large parts of the self, shadow.

People with fawning as a dominant feature tend to pursue helping careers. This allows them to put others first. Thus they avoid going through the trouble of establishing an individual personality, or discovering personal wants and needs and learning to express them.

Roberto is a therapist who loves his work being of service. He also finds himself frequently burned out and upset by his clients' needs. He is always there for his clients, and many of them offer gratitude for his willingness to text, email, or offer them time in between sessions. When Roberto goes into therapy himself, he finds that he always puts others first because this prevents him from having to live his own life. He has given his life away to his clients. By gradually establishing appropriate boundaries and by considering what he wants for his own life, he is able to move from continual burn-out into taking care of himself and considering his own needs and wants.

To be of service and to accommodate others is a beautiful addition to our lives. But to put others first, eclipsing any sense of individual self, is harmful. In addition, those who fawn will find themselves saddled with their opposite archetype—high conflict individuals and attention seekers. This fulfills the counterpart roles both individuals have taken on: the center of attention and the captive audience or caretaker.

To move out of a fawn state is to recognize the vital importance of putting ourselves first. In establishing a sense of self and discovering our own needs, wants, and boundaries, the fawning person may still be a wonderful caretaker for others. But they will no longer be a martyr and sacrifice themselves for the comfort of others.

Initiation Into Adulthood

It is incredibly rare for an individual to move beyond the conditioned responses of their childhood. By becoming initiated adults, we can recognize all that we have left behind, all that lingers in the shadows, and welcome it back into us. What we discover in those shadows is not just our pain, our fear, and our trauma, it is also our innocence, our play, our joy, and our enthusiasm for life.

There is a vast difference between the perspective of the adult self and the consciousness of the inner five-year-old. The adult may understand with clarity why the five-year-old is filled with rage, and dissect the circumstances with psychological insight. The adult can tell the story again and again about what that five-year-old experienced. But unless that five-year-old can express its rage through your body, the rage will continue. We heal by truly feeling.

We all have parts of ourselves that are fully initiated into adulthood. But we also have parts of ourselves that are stuck in infancy, childhood, or adolescence—or six months ago. The "inner child" of a sixty-year-old woman could be her inner thirty-five-year-old, grappling with her initiation into motherhood. We need space and time to recognize our former selves clearly and to see what needs have not been fulfilled.

Any moment of development is a type of initiation. We marry, give birth, relocate, graduate, divorce, and suffer job loss, death of loved ones, and disease. These are all situations in which a former self may become stuck in development. We can stagnate in a significant part of our identity that still feels incomplete or unsatisfactory. For example, a woman did not give birth vaginally as she had planned to; she had to have a cesarean. A man's first sexual encounter was disappointing. A child did not receive the birthday cake that she wanted because her sister—her mother's favorite—picked a different flavor. A runner twists her knee, prematurely ending her prospects of a path in collegiate track.

A man looks back and wonders how he, at fifty years old, ended up as a sales manager when his child self wanted to be a firefighter.

The largest initiations we undergo are bookends: birth and death. In between, we initiate into many different stages of development, including infancy, toddlerhood, adolescence, adulthood, and being an elder.

We probably recognize others who are stuck in some of these stages of development. For example, the friend who feels that they must on principle reject everything associated with pop culture is stuck as a teenager. The family member who continually melts down because she lacks the ability to emotionally regulate or recognize much beyond her own instant needs and gratifications is the eternal toddler. The neighbor who screams about politics remains stuck as the infant. The friend who has not developed any sense of self but who absorbs the emotions and moods of others is also stuck in infancy.

When we notice these stages of development in others, we can feel empathy. It must be hard to live in an adult body but be dominantly stuck in a toddler stage of development. It must be difficult to continually struggle like a teenager who feels everything so dramatically.

To notice these stages of development in ourselves shows us where we might be stuck. This is where healing is required. To have all parts of ourselves initiated into adulthood, we must meet the essential need that was not met at the earlier age—for example, to be heard, held, or loved. Something remains incomplete. By working with the inner child (see next chapter) and by asking "What age am I?" we can begin to recognize and integrate these parts of ourselves.

When working with the inner child, it is also important to understand the impact of initiating too early. For example, a teenager is emancipated from her parents at fifteen. She is thrust into adulthood, and as a result, it is likely that many years later she will still feel like that fifteen-year-old trying to act like an adult when she did not know how.

Other early initiations may be having a menstrual cycle at age eight, or a sexual encounter at age ten (or any time we are not ready for one). In childhood, we are purposefully meant to remain in a sort of cocoon of ignorance. Being introduced too early to the evils and darkness of the adult world creates issues in our emotional development.

For example, Moira was eight when her parents divorced. Her mother was very depressed. Moira began taking care of her mother and unwillingly acting her therapist. The impact of taking on such an adult responsibility at an early age has left Moira stuck as that eight-year-old, endlessly taking care of her mother (just with different faces and names) in the world.

Paul was the eldest son of eight. He was eighteen when his mother had her last child. He was initiated into adulthood too early— unable to have friends, participate in after-school activities, or even attend college—so that he could be an extra parent to all of the children. Paul now feels deep anger at the life that went unlived.

Significant impact also occurs when we do not go through the stages of initiation at all, or too late. Lauretta comes to her spiritual healer with a long list of doctors and practitioners she has visited. She has mysterious pain nobody can diagnose and while part of her deeply wants to heal, she regresses after each practitioner, medication, and practice to her former state. She admits a deep fear of becoming an adult with its accompanying responsibilities and pressures. A large part of her wants to remain a child, and as long as she is unwell enough, she does not need to initiate into adulthood.

Andrew gets coddled too much by his mother and does not know how to perform even simple tasks like laundry or cooking in adulthood. He expects his partner and his mother to continue taking care of these tasks for him rather than learning how to do them himself. He desires to remain a child, forever taken care of by his mother.

To be an initiated adult means living in the present moment, with emotional intelligence. A strong sense of Self is developed. We know who we are as an individual, and what our needs, wants, and likes are separate from the needs, wants, and likes of others.

This means assuming a certain degree of responsibility that we may understandably not care to undertake. There is something about remaining a child that allows us to hold on to a sense of hope and magic in the world, which we tend to lose as we move into adulthood.

With emotional intelligence, adulthood can still contain the magic and playful joy of youth.

As adults we have greater capacity to make decisions. In childhood, we were at the mercy of the whims of our parents and teachers. Working with our inner child is often quite fruitful when we help them to recognize the advantages of initiating into adulthood.

Chapter 7

Emotional Intelligence Tools

*M*any tools are available to develop emotional intelligence. By observing and working with our emotions, we take back large parts of our shadows and become initiated into adulthood.

Sitting with Emotions

A client once asked me what "sitting with emotions" meant. I realized that sometimes incredibly simple things need to be explained so that we can understand them fully.

To sit with our emotions means to offer ourselves a bit of space and quiet time to allow whatever emotions we are experiencing to rise into our awareness. This does not need to be ritualized in any way, or part of a spiritual practice.

You simply sit or lie down in a space that offers you safety. (As you progress, you will find that you can do this practice anywhere, but we typically feel more open and willing to be vulnerable in a place in our own home where we feel safe and comfortable.)

Take a few slow breaths in and out. Breathe in through the nose, filling up your abdomen with air, and exhale slowly through the nose. Some people like to count to four while breathing in, hold for four breaths, and breathe out using the four count.

Some emotions will likely arise, but this exercise is not about playing detective. If we start trying to figure it out, we go into our minds rather than feel with our bodies. The difficulty with this tool is that it puts us in receiving mode. We are so used to "doing" things that taking a step back, even for a few breaths, and seeing what arises from within, may be difficult at first.

When emotions arise, you can offer them the type of compassion you might offer a small child or a cherished friend. Your feelings are welcome guests, and you are offering them time and space to come forward and show themselves.

Memories may come up along with feelings. I will not say that these memories are not important, but for this exercise please reorient yourself from thinking about them. For now, stay in a space of feeling.

Another way to perform this exercise is to work with a specific emotion that is bothering you. For example, if you are overwhelmed, stressed, angry, anxious, or feeling any other difficult emotion, simply offer it space.

Sit down with intention: for example, "Okay grief, let us have five minutes together." Then allow yourself to feel. Keep good boundaries with yourself. It is not necessary to go overboard, which can sometimes be cathartic, but at other times be exhausting and unnecessary. Titration can help with this practice (see below).

When you start working with this practice, consider it to be like a muscle that you are building. Five to fifteen minutes of practice is all that is necessary.

In time, we can learn to process emotions from the past, as well as ensure that we are processing present-moment emotions in a healthy way.

Remember to meet whatever emotion arises in you with compassion. Whatever you are feeling is right—or was right when you first experienced it. Do not invalidate yourself or dismiss any of your emotions. We tend to treat ourselves and our emotions so terribly. We wish to bully them or erase them out of existence. If we treat them with the respect and grace that they deserve, they will share their messages with us.

If you ever feel overwhelmed, practice boundaries with yourself. Tell yourself that you are ending things for the day. Practice titration.

Reorient yourself to a practical activity. In time, you will learn that you can work with your emotions when it feels appropriate for you. When we discover this, we feel empowered rather than helpless and victimized by our emotions.

Color Breathing

In addition to your four-count breath, you can also add a color.

1 Picture the emotion as a color. There are no set colors for this. Your fear might one day be black and another day, purple. On another day your stress may be like a giant grey grease stain. Do not second-guess yourself, whatever color first comes to mind is wonderful.
2 While breathing (in four counts, hold four counts, out four counts) imagine that color leaving your body through your breath on the out-breath.
3 Do this breathing for however long feels right to you. If done correctly you should notice a palpable change in the emotion.

You can also do color breathing in high-stress situations, such as at a family dinner or during work. If a colleague or family member bothers you, first feel that you are annoyed by them. Then notice what color that annoyance is, and breathe it out of your body.

Titration

If we have an ocean of grief, it is not helpful to work with the whole ocean all at once. That is overwhelming and unnecessary. We may be ready to work with only a drop of grief or anger. We may be able to sit with a bucketful of rage, or a small pond of fear.

Evaluate where you are today and how much time you have. If you are completely stressed out but only have five minutes, that will naturally limit what you can sit with: "Okay I have five minutes to sit with this stress. Let us work with what we can." Sit and breathe in and out your four counts.

Or you may wish to practice boundaries with yourself by understanding that you have several oceans full of depression. That sort of darkness would be too much to handle all at once, but you may be ready to face a small glass of depression. Acknowledge the emotion within you, set the intention that you will work with one small glassful, and then breathe.

When setting boundaries with yourself, it is important to stick to your limits. That said, you may be ready for another glassful of grief to come forward and you may have time for it. But you might also be feeling uncomfortable, stressed, anxious, or unfocused. These feelings are all signs to end the work.

We tend to force ourselves to do things with the idea that catharsis or forcing is the right way to go about things. Introducing patience, boundaries, and respect for what is going on internally are some of the best tools to learn. Our bodies let us know when they are done with something; we merely need to learn to listen.

When you are done sitting with an emotion, you may wish to state to yourself: "Thank you for processing a pondful of anger with me." This clearly sets up a beginning, middle, and end to your sitting practice. Your body and mind will learn this over time, leading to a more successful sitting practice.

Titration allows us to successfully self-regulate. We feel empowered knowing that we can successfully work with our emotions and realize that feeling is healthy (rather than threatening). We can feel confident knowing that we are developing tools in emotional regulation and learning how to work with any emotion that arises.

Sphere of Possibility

Our most entrenched emotions are often the most resistant to change. We cannot imagine a life in which what we feel or how we view ourselves and the world is different. This voice may be entirely correct. Even after practicing the most helpful sitting practice for a length of time, your baseline emotion may tend towards anxiety. Put more simply, anxiety may be an ongoing emotion that is a part of you for the rest of your life.

This does not mean that anxiety, anger, or any of our emotions cannot change and shift. Or that we cannot learn tools to manage the anxiety that arises. Our emotions are deeply fearful of change, as they are defending us against further harm. If we understand them as protectors, trying to help us maintain what we already know and feel, we can understand why they may be resistant to change.

One of the things that occurs with a sitting practice is that the small voice within tells us that our panic, anger, fear, or depression cannot change. We are stuck. In your shadow work, arguing with this voice is beneficial.

Realistically, you may not be able to see yourself as a completely happy, shiny person filled with hope if you are deeply depressed. Yet you may be able to envision feeling calmer or in some way better for at least some days out of the month. Start wherever you are and with whatever you can imagine happening for you. This is called the "sphere of possibility." It is not helpful to imagine something for ourselves that we cannot ever truly believe will occur. But there is a sphere of possibility—an opening in which we can see a positive change in our lives that is not too threatening to our defenses.

When the voice arises telling you that nothing will change, sit with your personal sphere of possibility. You may feel like you will always be an angry person, but perhaps you can imagine yourself as someone who no longer punches walls or yells at the television. You may feel completely disconnected from other people, and in your alienation you may think that nobody will ever like you. If you truly sit with that, you may agree that you are not everyone's cup of tea, but that there are people from your past and present who get along with you. Your sphere of possibility now includes you developing more human connections.

Our sphere of possibility expands as we work with it. We can learn to manage our emotions and see the results of doing so; over time we can imagine more for ourselves. While doing this exercise, it is best to have a hopeful but realistic attitude. Nobody is ecstatically happy all of the time; we are meant to feel all of our emotions. Our lives have ups and downs, and we will feel the full range (the "motion") of emotions if we allow them. Every single emotion has a message and a reason for being.

How to Feel

1 Start by setting a time limit for your practice. Typically, ten
minutes is perfect for anyone, whether you are a beginner or more
experienced. Set an alarm to create this boundary for yourself. Set
an intention that you will simply feel for ten minutes.

2 Now, ask yourself how you are feeling. This may be "stressed,"
"angry," or any other emotion. It may be confusion, blankness,
apathy, or numbness. It may be an amalgamation of emotions
that is not so clear, such as "I kind of feel angry but also sad but
also hopeless but also like I kind of want to curl into a ball never
to be found." You may also be overwhelmed to the point that you
cannot recognize your emotions. This is perfectly fine: "I feel really
overwhelmed and disconnected and have no idea what I am feeling
other than super-stressed and freaked out." These are all emotions
that you can work with.

3 Choose an emotion you want to work with. If it needs to start out
more abstract, start there: "I feel like someone just punched me in
the gut" or "I feel a confusing whirl of sadness-despair-heavy like I
am in a dark cave and can't get out."

4 Now, do a body scan. Starting at the feet, up to the head, and down
the arms, ask for that emotion to show you where it is located in
your body.

5 You may notice a few places highlighted or that you feel drawn to.
Now ask what area you should focus on today. Pick an area.

6 Now, physically describe that area. Does it feel tight? Heavy?
Empty? Pulling? If your mind shares something else other than how
the area physically feels, bring it back to describing the physical
feeling. This "anchoring it in the body" allows you to feel, rather
than think about what you are feeling.

7 Now, describe how much space that physical sensation takes up. Is
it a large ball? Does it take up your entire chest? Is it a small knot?

8 Validate the emotion, no matter what it is: "Anger, I see you and
feel you and you have every right to exist. I deserve to feel upset
about this."

9 Just sit with whatever you are feeling for the duration of your ten minutes. If you notice yourself getting distracted, or thinking about other things, bring yourself back to the physical sensation in your body.

When you do this for ten minutes, you are setting healthy boundaries for yourself, which builds up your emotional toolkit. Creating boundaries like this also keeps you from being overwhelmed by your emotions. When you notice yourself getting angry, or feeling any other difficult emotion, you can let your body know that you will work with it—doing this exercise—later in the day. Over time you will begin to realize that you have the skill and capacity to handle any emotion.

Developing an Adult Self

Part of moving into adult initiation is to recognize our own likes and dislikes. For some of us, this may not be an issue. But many of us have been confused by what our parents or peers like, or hypnotized by advertisements. Or we simply may not have spent much time thinking about what we like or don't like.

Start quite simply. Do you like pickles? If so, what kind of pickles do you like? Your tastes may change. One week you may really like dill pickles and the next week you may love bread and butter pickles. This is perfectly natural. Discovering what you like, in non-threatening areas of your life, is quite fun and will consolidate your personal identity. Move on to art, music, books, movies. You likely know what is popular, or what your peers like, or what someone your age should like. What movies, music, and books do you like?

Sometimes we change our opinion based on what we read online. For example, we might really like a movie. We search online and see that it was rated poorly by movie sites. We then downgrade our own opinion of the movie. The reverse can happen as well. We did not like a movie or book but it has won awards, or all of our friends talk about how fantastic it is. We then upgrade our own opinion. Notice when this happens; it will help you separate your own opinion from that of others.

It is wonderful that you like a movie that others think is terrible. You now have a mind of your own.

This sounds simple, but by starting to question your likes and dislikes in this way, you lay the basis for an individual identity. You can then move on to more difficult terrain, like thinking about your boundaries and what your needs and wants are. You can then question your personal goals and contemplate what brings meaning and purpose to your life. Having a solid idea of what type of sandwich you truly enjoy, and knowing what your favorite toppings are for that sandwich, is where to start this process.

Noticing Nervous System Response

By noticing how our nervous system is responding, we can discover patterns within ourselves. We will naturally gravitate towards one or two responses. When we observe how frequently we respond this way, we will move towards questioning—and ultimately changing—our responses.

Simply notice what dominant response your nervous system has. Is it fight, flight, freeze, fawning, or flaccidity?

After you notice this, comment to yourself each time that you go into it. This is to be done without judgment. It is just basic noticing, such as, "Oh, I am freezing again."

When you have done that for a while, gently ask yourself if you could respond in another way. What would happen if you were to speak up instead of freezing and shutting down? It might not have been safe to speak up as a child, but the people around you now may want to hear what you want and need.

If you always flee, what would happen if you were to stay and work things through? What would happen if you were to argue or express how you feel?

If your response is always to fight, what would happen if you were to go for a walk instead?

If you always put others first (fawning) what would happen if you were to put yourself first? What would you do with your day?

If you could have meaning and purpose in your life, what would it be? Move out of flaccidity and decide that you can create your own meaning and purpose in life. Start by formulating some simple goals and acting on them. It may be brushing your teeth every morning or going to the gym. It may be affirming something positive about yourself and the world each day. If you engage with life, it will engage with you. Your passion for living can return.

Noticing Defense Mechanisms

Another useful tool is to notice what defense mechanisms you engage in. You can do so by looking at the list below. There will likely be one or two that are dominant for you. Notice yourself participating in them without judgment.

It is often easier to look outside of ourselves to see defense mechanisms. When you do this, do not point them out to people. Simply notice the defense mechanisms employed by the people around you. This will provide you with unique insight regarding who they are and what they may be struggling with. It may also deepen your empathy as it is likely that friends, family, and others around you enact the same defense mechanisms as you.

When you can see defense mechanisms clearly, you develop compassion as you see how we all sabotage ourselves and get in our own way. We struggle so much and feel the need to protect ourselves so valiantly.

When you are able to, consciously move to transmuting or integrating healthy defense mechanisms. Remember that there is a reason why we mask, deny reality, or shut down. Do not force anything. Treat the parts of yourself that desire to avoid or regress, with as much compassion as possible. They are doing the best that they can.

See whether any of these common defense mechanisms ring true for you:

- Denial
- Intellectualization or rationalization
- Disassociation
- Blankness
- Fantasy

- Avoidance
- Shutting down or numbing
- Masking
- Regression
- Repression
- Shielding or armoring
- Cognitive dissonance
- Manipulation and/or lying
- Gaslighting
- Distraction
- Deflection or displacement
- Projection
- Transmutation
- Integration

Chapter 8

The World as Mirror

*T*hink of the world as a mirror. What you see reflected is only a small fraction of reality. We notice things in other people and in the world around us for a reason.

We are the ultimate observers of reality. This offers us a certain degree of control. When we are being observed, we do not have that control. We are subject to the representations, projections, and roles that others place upon us.

When we are observing, we are continually projecting our shadows onto the Other—the observed. What we cannot or do not notice in ourselves, we react to in others. We so easily convince ourselves that the problem is outside of ourselves. Yet it is our own dissatisfaction, our own self-hatred, that is at the root of this. We see ourselves reflected in the outer world—and in other people—until our own inner nature changes. Then what we see reflected in the world changes.

We act out the divisions within ourselves in the outer world again and again. Both individually and collectively, we act out the pain that we haven't yet healed. The world, and the people in it, reflect back to us our own internal pain that we are not yet aware of.

We shove outwards what we are not ready or willing to deal with internally. We then lament that the same kinds of things keep happening in our lives, or that we keep encountering the same types of people again and again. These are called "loops" (Chapter Fourteen), and they show us exactly what we need to heal.

By noticing our projections, we can take back large parts of who we are that we have cast out. We have little awareness that our hatred or dislike of others stems from our own inner qualities that we have disowned. By observing others, we can begin to see the parts of ourselves that we have subconsciously separated from.

By noticing our projections, we can heal, resolve conflict, and develop empathy. Where we once perceived separation between ourselves and the Other—observer and observed—we can now see our shared humanity. This is the end goal of taking back our projections.

The beneficial part of thrusting disowned aspects of ourselves outwards is that it allows us to better observe them. We can recognize our own separated parts and our own internal conflicts by noticing what we react to in other people and what recurring conflicts arise in our lives.

This work, if done well, is life-long. At first, the world will be filled with our shadows, but as we continue with the work, we take back more of our shadows from others and notice them less in the outer world. This allows for us to be less reactive to others and develop a state of genuine connection and intimacy.

Noticing Projections, Part I

- For the next week, notice what advice people offer. Consider that they are giving themselves advice.
- The week after, notice what beliefs or ideas people repeatedly feel the need to share. Consider that they are attempting to convince themselves of these beliefs or ideas. When we know something to be true, we no longer feel the need to convince others of it.
- Now, notice what people warn other people about. Consider that this has to do with their own internalized fear. If someone is warning another person against doing something, consider that they might be stopping themselves from doing it.
- Notice what people claim about other people. If someone does this once or twice, it is something to note, but it does not necessarily show you their projections. What you are looking for are

repetitions—your boss who calls everyone *"idiots,"* for example, or your friend who calls everyone *"superficial."*

Observe people without judgment. You are noticing patterns, not commenting on them. Your power as observer shows you the shadows of others quite clearly. Observing this first allows you to then take a step back and notice your own shadows.

As you explore your own shadows, you do not need to do anything about them yet—awareness is always the first step.

- Notice what advice you offer and consider that it is for yourself.
- Notice what beliefs or ideas you feel the need to share repeatedly or convince others of.
- Notice what you warn others about and consider that to be a sign of your own fear.
- Notice what you claim about other people—not just comments you make once or twice, but repeatedly.

As we will discuss in the next chapter, there are very good reasons for you to believe that many people are jerks. They may fit that role perfectly. There is a reason why we project onto others, and often it is because they fit the part. But there are plenty of people with negative qualities around you. You notice and are bothered by jerks for a specific reason.

Even after practicing these initial noticing exercises for a short time, you may notice your reactions changing. When you keenly observe others, you see what limitations they struggle with and how they view reality. When you observe yourself, you have an opportunity to see your own shadows and how they populate your reality. Both help us recognize our own shadows and to begin to take them back.

Noticing Projections, Part II

Now that you have noticed some basic projections in yourself and others, you can begin to work with your own projections. To do this, we will build on tools that we have learned in Chapter Five, including Magnification and The Ocean Floor.

- Notice when another person bothers you for some reason— basically, when you are reactive to them in some way.
- Now, name three reasons why you are bothered by them. These can be single words like "selfish" or "narcissistic" or "rude" or it may be a phrase like "He makes me uncomfortable."
- These qualities probably occur in you between surface waves and mid-ocean level. They are unlikely to be the real reason you are bothered by them. Allow yourself to sink down to the ocean floor. Why are you truly bothered by them? Again, name two or three things.
- Of this list of qualities you have created, there is likely one reason that has resonance. It feels right to you—like the core reason this person truly bothers you—or it causes for you to experience an emotional reaction.

For now, simply create a list of some qualities that bother you about other people. When you observe other people and your reactions to them over time, you will notice a pattern emerge. You might be extremely reactive to selfishness, or people in the victim role, or machismo. Do not judge yourself for having these reactions; just being willing to notice them in the first place is not something that many people are willing to do.

Like any tool, this can take a bit of time to get used to. What helps many of my students is visualizing or sensing that ocean. Feel your initial impressions and answers as being surface waves or mid-ocean level and then sense yourself going deeper and deeper to the ocean floor, where the real reasons for your dislike or reaction to the person emerge.

It can be easiest to start with people that we interact with but do not have too much shared history with. Colleagues, acquaintances, and strangers are good people to start observing. We project much more onto friends, spouses, partners, and family. Due to the primary roles they play in our lives, it may take some time to learn to go into observer mode and be willing to see our projections onto them.

Noticing Projections, Part III

We will now consider whether the projection is simple, direct, or indirect.

- A "simple projection" occurs when we put all our pain and suffering onto another person. Consider this to be a "release valve": it is not specific to the other person, it is just an attempt to find a target for our internal suffering in the outer world. This is typically directed towards someone in a position of less power than us (for example, we cannot take our anger out on our boss without consequences).
- A "direct projection" occurs when we project disowned parts of ourselves onto another person. A woman is obsessed with other women's bodies because she is unhappy with her own. A man calls his son and many other people "losers" because that is how he feels about himself.
- An "indirect projection" occurs when we project qualities that we do not yet notice within ourselves. Perhaps we never had the ability to express that quality and make it a part of us. A man regularly watches food shows on television but doesn't know how to cook. Another woman frequently calls people "selfish" and when she gets to the bottom of her ocean, she recognizes that she has never had an opportunity to be selfish; she always had to think about others first.

These categories are helpful because they more readily reveal how our shadows populate the world. We not only cut ourselves off from our negative qualities but we also sever ourselves from our "shadows of light," the possibilities and joys of existence. If we notice our jealousy, hatred, and reactivity to others, we can notice all our shadows and the ways in which they play out in front of us.

In time, with shadow work we will likely see many indirect shadows and then move into being able to see them directly. For example, Marisa calls everyone around her angry. She at first sees this as an indirect shadow—she was never able to express her anger. In time she can see that she is quite angry, and that this is a direct projection. At first she was so cut off from her anger that she could not identify with it. After developing emotional intelligence and connecting with her anger and owning it, she no longer sees the world as populated with angry people.

Noticing Jealousy

Now notice people towards whom you feel jealousy or envy. Do the same bottom of the ocean exercise; name three qualities and then discover a resonant reason why you are jealous. It might be "because they have money," or "I am jealous they are on a beach, and I am in a snowstorm." These are simple and understandable reasons to feel jealousy.

It may also be a phrase like "why does he get everything while I get nothing?" Or perhaps even "she doesn't deserve him—why is her life so perfect while mine is garbage?" These are all common mentalities that arise when viewing someone who has a quality or life experience that we envy.

These are most often shadows of light—qualities of joy, wealth, peace, happiness, stability, or success that are an outer reflection of what we do not have (and wish for) in our own existence. They are also likely indirect shadows; for example, we may take an interest in a woman because she is so beautiful, when we have never felt beautiful. That quality is not a part of us; it is an aspect of our shadow that we have yet to meet or to fully own.

Noticing Television, Social Media, and Public Figures

We place the most rejected aspects of ourselves—the parts we identify with least—onto celebrities, social media personalities, politicians, and other public figures. Notice not only when hatred or dislike arise but also when you feel disgust and a desire to shame. We feel safe when we project our inner self-hatred onto targets that are more distant from us.

We can tell ourselves that extremists are worthy of our disgust without recognizing our own quieter forms of separating from others.

We so readily give our power away through projections. Without realizing it, we offer our inner beauty, spirituality, musicality, sexuality, fierceness, boldness, grace, and voice to those in the public eye. Whenever we project, we offer our power to another. With celebrities and public figures the projections of many people combine to create a specific type of glamor and power. These group projections can also contribute to the destruction or downfall of public figures. More regarding this will be discussed in the chapter on collective shadows.

Onto our televisions and social media sites we project our unlived lives. We may watch sporting events to live out our inner athlete or reality shows to live out our inner drama queen. We can start to see our shadows in what we choose to watch. This does not mean, however, that we watch shows on serial killers because we desire to become a serial killer.

Sometimes it is healthy to interact with a part of our shadow from a safe distance. We desire to understand the parts of ourselves that seek to harm, kill, or create havoc. Watching horror movies can help us come to terms with the darkest aspects of our nature. Refusing to watch horror movies may be due to a fear of encountering those aspects of ourselves, even from a safe distance. It may also mean that we are already aware of the darkness and horrors that reality can offer and we have no further need to explore them through the separation of observer-observed; we have lived and embodied that part of ourselves.

Many of us also indulge in "guilty pleasures" that show rejected aspects of ourselves. This may be cute animal videos because we desire the qualities of sweetness and connectivity that they offer. It may be projecting our inner light onto a specific singer. Through our screens, we can project and observe our unfulfilled needs. This may be as simple as watching reality television because we require a healthy escape from our lives. It may mean watching romance movies, as our relationship does not offer the perfection of love that is offered onscreen.

We may refuse to watch such shows—or deny watching them—because we want to believe that we are superior to those aspects of humanity. Yet it is in admitting to those guilty pleasures and seeing the humanity in them that we reclaim large parts of our shadow. We may never desire to watch reality television, or horror movies, but if we are vehemently opposed to them it is for a reason. By examining our own dislike, or the guilty pleasures we indulge in but would never admit to the world, we come out of shame and self-hatred. We can learn to accept every last part of ourselves.

Notice what your guilty pleasures are. What part of you that you cannot accept do you see on screen? What videos or movies do you gravitate towards and then feel ashamed about? Do the bottom of the ocean exercise. If you could name a quality that they bring into your life, what would it be? What would happen if you were to accept that you need this quality in your life? What would happen if you could see the humanity in every person that you watch?

What would happen if you could fully accept any part of yourself that you feel guilty about or ashamed of? This does not mean that this part of you is healthy; it may be outright destructive. But claiming that part of yourself brings clarity, which then opens you up to change.

When we completely accept a part of ourselves, we move away from bullying, shaming, or separating ourselves from it. If we neglect or shame any part of ourselves, that part thrives in darkness and will act separately from us. For example, when we do not accept our anger, we may act out in temper tantrums or by punching a wall. These actions are spontaneous and not led by our conscious choosing.

If we do not accept the darkest aspects of our nature—the erotic, destructive, and atavistic—we may find ourselves indulging in fantasies or watching movies where characters live that out for us. We may also find our creativity, dynamism, and power subsumed into listlessness and powerlessness. Embodiment of our emotions means that they are part of us and can flow through us. We can be in relationship with them, instead of being at their mercy.

Full acceptance of every part of ourselves lets us make conscious decisions regarding how we act. We become more authentic and whole if we embrace every part of ourselves.

Noticing Projections onto
Objects and Animals

We often project our emotions and desires onto objects. We kick a door in anger or buy a pair of shoes to feel trendy. If our desire for love and approval cannot be found in other humans, we project it onto material items, such as a car, house, or clothing. We can project our desire for perfection and health onto workshops or exercise classes.

There is safety in pouring out the love we have in our hearts onto an object or a pet. To love a car, or a dog, does not lead to the fear of abandonment or rejection. A couple may be afraid of loving one another, but they can pour out their love safely onto their cats, or into their jobs.

If we feel that we will be acceptable after our latest achievement—degree, job, or financial gain—we are projecting our need for love and approval onto these objects. If we believe that we will be healthy once we get an exercise bike, we are likely to find that our projections prove false; we still require the motivation to get on that bike and ride it.

When we take our projections back from the world, we may still really like owning our car or wearing a certain style of shoes. But we put the love and acceptance that we give to material items or to experiences in their right place. We can open our hearts to other people, rather than attempting to fulfill that connection in material ways.

Noticing Ourselves in Our Projections

We will now begin to work more directly with our projections. The simplest way to start is to notice whatever quality we are projecting outwards within ourselves. "Oh, that person is a jerk. I can also be a jerk sometimes."

This sounds so simple—and the most extraordinary tools often are—but it is effective because we are taking ownership of that quality within ourselves.

Let's look at how this works differently with a direct projection and an indirect projection.

Mark relentlessly complains to his colleagues about a new hire. He calls him pompous and arrogant. Mark follows that up by continually reminding his colleagues how he studied at a prestigious university with the preeminent teacher in his field.

If you were to ask any of his colleagues for honest feedback regarding the qualities they would ascribe to Mark, "pompous" and "arrogant" would certainly populate that list. In fact, none of them would describe their new colleague as arrogant or pompous at all. If Mark were willing to see this direct projection, he might recognize—with some embarrassment—his own arrogance and the feelings of insecurity that lie underneath. He might experience a spark of recognition: "I guess I can be arrogant or pompous sometimes too."

It is unlikely that someone like Mark would be willing to do shadow work, but this is a clear example of a direct projection. We all have met "Mark" in various ways in our lives.

Derek is really bothered by a woman in his support group. He does his initial shadow work and describes her as irritating and grating. He goes to the middle of the ocean. What bothers him is that she takes too much time at the meetings and pretends to know everything. He goes to the bottom of the ocean and the word "humility" arises. He reacts in disgust, recognizing that she has no humility. Derek always needed to be humble and tends to downplay his achievements. He notices this as a pattern now: a long line of people who he has disliked or even hated because they lacked humility.

Derek cannot think of a time where he has lacked humility. As he sits with this realization, he recognizes that he has never allowed himself to be fully proud of his achievements. He was always taught to be humble to the point of dismissing his achievements. With this recognition, the pattern breaks. He no longer feels disgusted by others who lack humility and he starts working on owning his accomplishments and feeling proud of them. He then starts to remember times in his life that he acted without humility, and he further reclaims his shadow.

When you notice a quality in someone that you dislike or envy, notice it within yourself. Recall times when you lived out this quality. Eventually, the people that you have cast into a unidimensional role to fit your unintegrated shadows will become more human. What you see in them will change because you have changed.

Inner Child Work

This work will build on the previous tools (from Chapter Five) of Magnification and "What Age Am I?" When you notice an emotion that is magnified, you will recognize it.

It is likely that there is an inner child within you that is reacting to people based on their pain. Your adult self may be totally fine with someone, but a part of you that is stuck at an earlier stage of development is seeing your pain mirrored in them. You will then ask "What age am I?" Your response may be "I am fifteen" or it may be more general, such as "I am a teenager."

Ask yourself what quality bothers you the most. If there are several qualities, don't worry—the world will always offer you the gift of showing you your shadows until you have taken ownership of them. You can simply pick one.

- Ask where in your body you store that quality—the reason why you are reactive. If there are many places, pick one.
- Utilize the skills of "How to Feel" to physically anchor: notice how the quality you picked feels physically and how much space in your body that physical sensation takes up.
- Now, ask your inner child to step forward. Picture them the best that you can. What haircut do they have? What are they wearing? Where are they?
- Get a sense of what is going on in the situation. Chances are that they are stressed, overwhelmed, traumatized, or suffering in some way. Ask them directly what is going on
- Ask them what they need to feel better, or to find healing. They will have some need that has gone unfulfilled. Often the need is to be seen, heard, loved, and/or accepted. But it may be anything.
- Once they express that to you, picture your adult self offering that to them.

As a child you were powerless over your circumstances. You could not leave home and get a job at age five. You could not change your parents or force them to love and accept you or create peace in a household of stress. Perhaps you could not show emotions because there was a culture of silence in your household, or you could not express who you were because your personality was quite different from that of your siblings or parents. As an adult, you can now offer those things to your inner child. You can also assure them that they have left their childhood circumstances and now have different options as an adult. You get to choose how to live your life.

If it feels like your inner child is stuck between stages of development, you can ask what they need to be willing to move from infancy to becoming a toddler or teenager, or from a teenager to adulthood. Chances are that fear of responsibility or change is preventing them from moving forward. By alleviating those fears, you can help them move through the doorway of initiation into a new phase of being. You may want to picture the inner child walking through an actual doorway into a new stage of their development.

Do not second-guess yourself in this work. Trust your intuition. If this work is done well, your life will shift in small or large ways. The same inner child may come up for healing many times. This does not signify failure—it just means that a specific age may require many layers of healing.

Paulina finds herself continually irritated by a woman at her job. She works with her observations and goes to the bottom of the ocean. She finds her loud laugh annoying (ocean waves), her presence irritating (mid-ocean), and the way she continually interrupts other people infuriating (bottom of the ocean . . . at least for now).

Paulina realizes that some inner child work may be helpful. She asks what age is the inner child who is bothered by this. It is a six-year-old. Paulina senses that this irritation at the woman at work is in her heart area. She feels that irritation for a moment in her chest. Her inner child is an ambivert (has both introverted and extroverted qualities), but she has an extremely loud and outgoing older sister. She was continually interrupted at the dinner table by her sister, and as this memory arises, she is extremely annoyed. Paulina asks her inner child what she needs, and it is to be heard. Paulina offers to hear whatever her inner child has to say.

After this, Paulina notices that she is still irritated by the woman at work, but it doesn't bother her at a deep level anymore. Her colleague is simply someone that she can interact with, if need be, but otherwise doesn't want to become friendly with.

Stefan notices a deep rage arise for no reason whatsoever. One day this rage comes up because another person at the gym questions if he was using the weights correctly. He observes that the slightest questioning of his ability causes him to feel rage. He feels at the bottom of his ocean a deep sense of rage and powerlessness.

In his current adult life, he is quite fit and does everything he can to exorcize his anger: boxing, weightlifting, running, and therapy. He has been in therapy for years and is still incredibly angry. He feels that an inner child is triggered and asks what age it is. The feeling of being a teenager, around age fifteen, comes up.

He feels this rage contracting around his neck like a vice. He sits with this feeling for a moment and asks the inner child to step forward. His inner teenager steps forward and tells him how angry and embarrassed he is that his family became homeless when his father lost his job. The inner child shares that he couldn't show his feelings at that age because he needed to be strong for his family. He felt like he needed to fix the situation but he could not. He felt powerless.

Stefan lets him know that he had every right to feel powerless and angry, but that it was too big a job for a teenager. It wasn't his job to fix. The inner teenager feels better, and Stefan asks him what he needs. He replies that he needs to feel worthwhile. His father always made him feel worthless. Stefan asks if he is willing to see his life now, as an adult, and witness how strong and capable he is. The inner teenager says "yes" and is amazed that Stefan can pay for food, clothing, and choose how to live his life.

Stefan finds that his anger is lessened. He notices feeling anger at other things, but he knows he can work with his inner child with these too.

The other way to work with your inner child is to notice a destructive pattern of relating to the world and asking where that pattern lives in the body. Anchor into that body part. Then ask the inner child who requires that coping mechanism to step forward. Be compassionate—as Maya Angelou so famously said: "Do the best you can until you know better. Then when you know better, do better." Your inner child was just trying to survive and to cope in the best way they knew how. Now as an adult, you have the chance to develop better coping strategies and to question the source of destructive behavior patterns.

For more in-depth instructions regarding how to dialogue with the body, emotions, and the inner child, see my book *The Body Deva*.

Saying Something Nice

This is another simple tool, but extremely effective. When you notice that you are truly bothered by someone, it is likely that they become a unidimensional character to you. They are no longer Jennifer who has a dog and loves her mother and is a fan of fishing, she is a mean gossip. This reduces Jennifer to the Other and takes away her humanity. We are not singularly good or evil, Batman or Joker, but a full human. This means that we are nuanced human beings that contain many qualities within ourselves.

When we notice ourselves projecting onto someone, we can not only observe and work with the shadow part, but we can bring some humanity back into our observations. We do this by finding in Jennifer three qualities that we like.

These may be quite shallow at first, especially if we have placed a thick shadow onto her or do not know her well. We may like her hair or her jacket. In time our list may also include her smile, her love for her dog, and the way she has a slight accent that comes out when she is excited.

When you find yourself disliking anyone, name three qualities about them that you like. Be genuine, and you will find that what you see reflected in the other person changes. On a deeper level, when we are more willing to notice the positive qualities in others, we are more open to seeing positive qualities within ourselves.

Spending Time with a Quality

When we notice an indirect shadow (a quality we have yet to own in ourselves), one of the best ways to become acquainted with it is to spend time with someone who embodies that quality. I first learned of this technique through W. Brugh Joy, who noted in his book *Avalanche* how our capacity to mirror the system of another provides us with a distinct advantage.

If we have never felt peace in our lives, we can find someone who truly embodies peace and spend time with them. On some level, our system will recognize that it is possible for us to experience peace. State with clear intention: "I love how Maria can get along with just about everyone." Move beyond jealousy (do your shadow work!) until you can truly appreciate that quality in Maria.

Sit in a quiet place. Bring your awareness to your heart area. Ask it if it recognizes Maria within itself. Work with your sphere of possibility. It may not be able to see getting along with everyone, but could it imagine having less conflict with others, or being a bit more peaceful? Ask if it is willing to embody that quality. Consider what you might need in order to embody that quality—therapy, a course in conflict resolution, stopping yourself from identifying as someone who cannot be peaceful in their interactions?

How this quality looks in you and how it looks in Maria may be quite different, and it should look different. If you do not have a Maria in your life, have you found anyone on screen or online who has this quality? It is best to start with someone you know, but we must all start somewhere, and starting with a character on television can open you up to the quality you are looking to embody.

When we have fully embodied our shadows, we reclaim all the qualities within us. Know that even the meekest of us has an adventurous and spontaneous side, even the most extroverted of us has an inner monk. How we have been identified in the world, and what we have experienced in our lives, contribute to who we consider ourselves to be. These labels are limitations, and we can meet new parts of ourselves if we are open and willing.

The world will be happy to show us where our shadows lie in one another. It is by seeing the world as a reflection of what is going on within ourselves that we take back the power and vitality we have lost through our projections.

When we are willing to see, what is reflected changes. This is because we are changing. While doing this work, take note not only of what you have left to work with, but also of how far you have come. Celebrate every step, every milestone, and every person who you meet who bothers you. They will become the greatest teachers and healers you will ever know.

Chapter 9

Understanding Our Play

All the world's a stage,
And all the men and women merely players;
They have their exits and their entrances,
And one man in his time plays many parts . . .

William Shakespeare

*C*onsider that what you believe to be reality is actually a play that
you have cast. Originally you were cast in the play of your parents
or guardians, but over time your own play unfolds. You develop a plot
and themes for the play, cast villains, heroes (yourself), victims (also
likely yourself), and main and supporting roles.

We are continually casting our plays; we grasp onto the themes,
beliefs, and narratives that comprise the central tenets of our plays in
our outer reality. Our plays and their themes and central cast of characters are set in our childhoods. When we go out in the world, we recast
our mother, father, siblings, and other figures from our childhood onto
the people around us.

We will cast our general family dynamics as well as individual roles.
We played a role in our family, and we are likely to keep performing
that role outside of our primary family structure. Whether it is being
a golden child, forgotten middle child, black sheep, scapegoat, or other
role, whatever we were cast as a child has a profound effect on us as an
adult. Just as we find our parents and siblings in the outer world, we can

also find our childhood role of being the black sheep continued in our adult workplace and relationships.

We project the roles of our childhood onto others until we can see what we are doing; then we can reclaim the power and energy that we gave to others by casting them in our play. Eventually we reach a point where we no longer need to have a play. We can see people as they are, instead of as roles. We can see reality as it is, rather than through the filter of our beliefs.

When we project roles onto others, we lose a bit of our power and vitality. It takes effort and energy to keep our play going. What underlies our plays are primary wounds that we developed in childhood. Who we cast most frequently in the outer world will be our mother or father. Until we heal our primary wounds, we will continue to feel powerless before the projected roles that we have cast onto others.

For example, Cody casts his mother again and again in his relationships. His mother was unavailable and unemotional, and he finds himself dating women who fit this type. He also finds that his boss, some of his female friends, and his idea of the archetypal "woman" all fit into the role of an unavailable woman who cannot fulfill his emotional needs.

Stephanie had a good relationship with her father and mother; she describes her childhood as idyllic and herself as a "daddy's girl." Later in life she becomes interested in spirituality and finds a spiritual mentor who fits the role of the doting father. In her relationships with men, initially they play the role of the doting father, but at some point, they see her imperfections and their adoration lessens. She then gets bored of the relationship and breaks it off, moving on to another teacher or partner who can once again provide the same type of devotion that her father did.

While historically, much has been said about interacting with an opposite sex parent in roles in the outer world, projection is not limited to an opposite sex parent or to "traditional" family systems. Whoever we lived with in early childhood and adolescence will be a part of our play: grandparents, guardians, foster parents, adoptive parents, birth parents, same-sex parents, and housemates in communal living situations.

Reclaiming Our Inherent Worth

Ideally, we would all be born into families that appreciate our unique qualities and foster them through praise and recognition. This creates self-esteem, self-worth, and an awareness that we are loved for who we are, rather than for what we can offer.

Unfortunately, too few of us are brought up in families like this. To claim our shadow means knowing our inherent worth. The concept of "inherent worth" was developed by Carl Rogers, who understood that all humans are inherently worthy of love and acceptance for being simply who we are. In an ideal childhood, we would experience this deep feeling of love and acceptance.

Far too often, we experience conditional worth. This is transactional love, rather than unconditional love. Instead of being loved for exactly who we are, we are taught that we are only lovable and acceptable if we fulfill certain conditions.

Transactional love is contingent on what we can provide for those around us. This may be by acting a specific way or liking specific things. It may be by taking on a specific role in the family, such as scapegoat, family therapist, babysitter (mini adult), golden child, or by pursuing interests or espousing beliefs that are in line with our parents' or guardians' interests and beliefs.

Transactional love feels very different from unconditional love. Transactional love leads to feelings of low self-worth, the need to achieve, and a desire for perfectionism and control.

As long as we are human, we are not going to be perfect. Shadow work is about accepting ourselves as we are. We can give up the quest for perfection, letting go of an arbitrary finish line when we will one day deem ourselves acceptable. Yet we can still have goals, desires, and things to work on within ourselves. Operating from a place of "okay-ness" where we practice radical acceptance and kindness to ourselves is much different from feeling broken or not good enough. We can accept ourselves as we are, as imperfectly human, rather than keep striving in the belief that one day we will be perfected enough to accept and love ourselves.

High achievers often have an underlying pattern of wanting approval or acceptance from parents, combined with a sense of low self-worth. They may feel like a fraud (imposter syndrome). High achievement is often followed by a sense of hollowness because what is achieved is only transactional love, in which we are approved of for our accomplishments rather than for our intrinsic self-worth.

With unconditional love and positive regard, you are loved no matter what you do, what you are interested in, or who you are. This does not mean that a parent does not punish for misdeeds, or approves of everything a child does. It does mean that there is an undercurrent of deep love and connection that fills those empty places in the soul, the child can go out into the world ready and confident in their capacities.

When we do not feel unconditional love, we learn to hide who we are. We learn to mask. Masking creates an essential conflict between who a person is and what they believe the outer world wants them to be. This conflict eventually creates massive separation between the individual and what they are truly feeling and experiencing. They learn to distrust their inner truth because they have been taught by their parents and the world that their intuition is "wrong" or "bad." This can be taught explicitly, with parents yelling at children or reprimanding them for acting in certain ways. This can also be taught in quieter ways. Often what we believe to be true or false, right or wrong, is what our parents thought was true or right. If we believe differently, we assume that we are incorrect. Part of individuation is considering what you believe to be true or morally correct, rather than unconsciously taking on your parents' beliefs.

As children we look towards our parents as role models: to show us how to act and who we should be. If we are different from our parents, our childhood brains do not understand that this difference is okay. We may then hide who we are through masking, even if our parents were not abusive in any fashion.

It is in early childhood that we receive the bulk of our "programming": we learn who to be and how to act in this world. When we are young, our universe is quite small, and we think in black and white terms. We often believe that the faults of the household are our own faults. We lack the consciousness or ability from an evolutionary stand-point to understand that our parents are not perfect. This is powerful biological programming, as we require our parents for considerable periods of time to nurture us physically and emotionally.

When basic caretaking is not offered, we are unable to see that the problem is with the parents rather than with ourselves. It is normal to carry this feeling of wrongness or guilt well into adulthood. The powerful drives within us that seek survival will not allow us to blame our parents, because we cannot fend for ourselves in childhood or adolescence.

When unconditional love and positive regard are present in a house-hold, we become confident enough to venture into the world without masks and without casting roles.

Our Role in Our Family

We are each cast into a role in our family. Long after childhood, we find ourselves still playing that role in our adult life. This role may fit who we are. For example, if someone is naturally nurturing and empa-thetic as a child, they will likely pursue a career that requires those traits. But that person may also get stuck in that role, that identity. They are more than just a "nurturer" or any unidimensional role; they are a complex human being composed of many traits and identities. The role of nurturer may also be destructive to the individual. For example, they may have learned early on to take care of others before taking care of themselves, leading to burn-out.

Someone may also be stuck in a role that does not suit them. For example, a father always desired a son who plays football and goes fishing with him. His son is not interested in these things, but he did them anyway, either because he was forced to, or because the unspoken narrative in the household was that if he did not do those things, he would not be loved by his father.

It is easy to point out outright abuse and a culture of fear in a house-hold, which cause a child to mask and take on roles. It can also happen in a household that is "normal" by societal standards or in which there is no outright abuse. We may have grown up in a household where technically everything was perfect but little emotional connection was developed; so we learned to wear a mask, much like our parents do, to prevent intimacy from occurring.

For example, a child grows up in a household in which nothing is spoken about beyond a superficial level. Large family topics are made secret, or simply not discussed with the children. His parents go to his rugby games and encourage his interest in music. However, there was no emotional connection with his parents on the deeper level that he needed in order to feel secure in himself.

Or an emotional child learns in her emotion-less household that emotions are not appropriate. So she bottles up her emotions and wears a mask so that no emotions are expressed or shown.

When we have not experienced unconditional love, we are continually stuck in a state of seeking approval and validation from the outer world. Any form of criticism, harshness, or dismissal is experienced as heart-wrenching. This is partially because rejection at any age is simply painful. But also it's because our inner child, that part of us continually waiting for unconditional love from its parents, never received it. We are left in a state of loneliness and emptiness, endlessly seeking from the world what we did not find in childhood.

Yet the world will never provide in adulthood what your inner child truly desires—to be seen and loved for exactly who you were at a much earlier age. Receiving accolades at age thirty will not appease the inner child, or only temporarily before the loneliness and emptiness sets in again.

Eric Berne, the founder of transactional analysis, described what we look for from the outer world as "strokes." This has popularly been understood as "ego stroking," in which we manipulate one another through compliments or accolades to get something in return. When we have not experienced true intimacy and unconditional love, we become transactional creatures, seeking approval from the outer world. We practice reciprocity, in which we offer some amount of goodness to someone in return for the same.

The "strokes" that we seek from others become a large part of our play, in which our interactions offer us assurances that we are good enough. This can be simple connection, in which we say "hello" to a neighbor and they say "hello" back to us. In this interaction we have received some small amount of approval, and a corresponding reciprocal stroke. If the neighbor ignored our "hello" we would feel bad, and likely project some rather nasty thoughts onto the neighbor.

Many of our interactions are transactional in this way. A husband and his partner count which chores they do and argue if one does more that week. A woman spends hours putting on makeup and taking hundreds of photos to get the perfect shot in order to receive compliments on social media. A teacher pores over his students' reviews of him at the end of each semester, on the one hand lamenting how much energy he gives and how obnoxious and oblivious his students can be, while on the other hand savoring each compliment as if it is gold. An employee is devastated to be ignored at work but she lights up each time her boss even looks her way.

When we feel inherently worthy within ourselves exactly as we are, we take back considerable energy from the outer world. No longer does the world, or the people in it, have the power to deem us acceptable or lovable enough. We determine internally whether our actions and creations are worthy, decide what we value about ourselves, and choose what we need to work on.

When we drop the "game" of receiving strokes from the outer world, we stop comparing ourselves to others. We no longer feel superior or inferior to those around us. We can then truly move into a state of "okayness" where we feel basically good about ourselves. It is then, and only then, that we can recognize how tiring it was to continually achieve and attempt to prove ourselves to an outer world that is mercurial at best in its decisions as to whether we have a right to exist and take up space.

At that point we can move beyond any childhood roles, loops (repeated patterns of wounding), and plays into simply being who we are. Closing the chapter on our childhood, we can step into adult wholeness.

Moving into Adulthood

As an adult we can learn to accept any abandonment, rejection, or abuse that occurred in our childhood home. Once we come out of denial, we can fully feel the anger, grief, depression, and other emotions that originated from not being fully accepted and loved by our parents.

Becoming a spiritual adult means addressing these wounds head-on and clearly recognizing the hopelessness of the situation. The most healing thing that can happen for our inner child is to recognize that our parents did not have the capacity or willingness to offer us unconditional love, and to let go of the hope that they will someday be able to do so. Then we can move on with our life, grieve our childhood, and find love in relationships with people who can actually offer it—including our adult self.

We can see our parents as human beings, ones with their own flaws and wounds. This does not mean forgiving them for wrongdoing; it means moving away from a childlike relationship with them. This balances the power in the situation. As children, our parents had all the power. We were powerless over the bigger decisions in our lives and couldn't exert control in our environment. Reclaiming that power as an adult allows us to see our family members as people. This creates acceptance as well as the ability to move on from any detrimental patterns, roles, and needs for masking or approval. Until we go through this process, we subconsciously experience "repetition compulsion"—our inner child experiences denial, represses emotions, and repeats the childhood pattern of hoping our parents will offer the love and approval that we still crave as an adult.

By letting go of this hope, the child can move on, and the adult no longer needs to cast the role of parents in the outer world. We can then offer ourselves the love, approval, acceptance, and positive regard that we were never offered in childhood.

Often the first step in healing the inner child is to understand the ways in which we have been harmed or victimized. Even in cases of outright abuse, this may be difficult to see. It is even more challenging in cases where the adult claims that they had an idyllic childhood or that they have nothing to work on regarding their childhood. Perhaps for the rare individual this is true. Those holding on to the bonds of childhood the tightest are often those who have been harmed the most. However, those whose wounds of childhood were shrouded in silence, who grew up in homes where "technically" nothing was wrong, but where unconditional love and acceptance were not present, require healing as much as anyone else. We tend to so readily dismiss our pain because we can point to others who have it worse. However, we all need to feel inherently worthwhile and be accepted for who we are. If we are not there yet, we have some work to do.

The next step is for the inner child to feel the full weight of our victimhood. We cannot move beyond identifying with the role of "victim" until we have fully validated the emotional pain of our experiences. When we fully feel and accept that we were wronged, then, and only then, can we move beyond being a victim into a place of feeling more hope and power in our lives.

The end result of working with the inner child is understanding that our parents are simply people. They may have their flaws and faults; they may have done things that are simply unforgivable. But in most cases our parents are a mixture of bad and good, struggling with their own childhood conditioning just as we do. To move our parents out of static roles of hero or villain is to take our power back from them. Just as they have cast us into roles, we have cast them into roles. Releasing all the roles allows us to move beyond the bonds of childhood and to relate to the world as an adult.

Casting Other Roles

Most of the roles that we cast come from our childhood. While the role of mother and father require careful examination, we project other roles as well. Any authority figure that we care about during our developmental years can become a character that we can cast later in life.

For example, Antonio found in his gym teacher a father figure. Mr. Vallo was tough but fair, and truly cared about Antonio. Mr. Vallo died while Antonio was in high school, and Antonio deeply grieved this wonderful man. He found as he went out into the world that bosses, friends, and others could not live up to his gym teacher. He was often outraged by the behavior of others, without realizing that he was attempting to cast others in the role of his gym teacher.

When we cast someone into a role, we usually find that our projections onto that person do not quite fit. It is likely we have cast someone into a role because they meet the bare minimum to fulfill that role—for example, they are a woman, or an authority figure, or similar in temperament to the person we are casting.

When the role does not fit, we feel threatened and disturbed by the person. They are not acting as we wish them to; our projections onto them, the role we have cast, don't fully mesh with who they are and how they behave. We then unconsciously act in ways that attempt to get them to play the role that we desire.

Dakota idolizes her new art teacher, Olivia. She tells her about all her prior art teachers and how they damaged her; she says how much she loves and appreciates Olivia. Very quickly Dakota starts behaving inappropriately to both Olivia and her classmates. Dakota has projected her relationship with her mother and the painful environment of her childhood home onto Olivia and her classmates. She alienates her classmates by acting superior to them and she sends Olivia emails disparaging her work. The roles that she has cast require Olivia and her classmates to reject her and treat her poorly. Dakota of course does not recognize this. She believes that she is a victim of a world full of rejecting and abusive people. When Olivia dismisses Dakota from her course due to her behavior, this fulfills Dakota's need to be abandoned and rejected yet again.

Paul frequently posts negative thoughts online, tirades about everything from climate change to sexism to cultural appropriation. He talks over others who are more informed on the subjects of discussion. He grew up with a father who was a pillar of his community. His father was successful in marriage and career; he was loved by many friends and relatives. Paul was a bit shy and awkward and felt like he could never measure up to his father. His father never abused him and was kind to him, but Paul has cast the role of his successful father onto others; he is deeply bitter that others are succeeding in a world where he feels like he cannot get ahead. While online, Paul expects to receive hatred, threats, and negative reactions because that is how he feels about himself in comparison to his father.

These attempts to cast ourselves and others into roles in our play often work. We feel comforted when others move into the roles we have cast, while our own role is dependent on our cast of characters acting in specific ways. If someone fails to fulfill their role, the whole play is at risk. For example, if someone treated Paul with kindness, or even with pity, he would need to question his self-hatred. In some cases, Paul may do exactly that, and take back a part of his shadow. To keep the play going, Paul will focus on those who are expressing hatred towards him, calling on moral outrage. He may post something particularly hateful to generate the response that he subconsciously desires.

If the person does not fit the role that we have cast them in, or they don't follow the narrative for how our relationship will play out, we may call upon our sense of moral outrage to defend ourselves.

To call upon moral outrage is to believe ourselves to be simultaneously the victim and the hero of our reality. The other person plays the role of villain. We feel disgust, hatred, or disbelief regarding the behavior of the person who does not fit the role we have cast. By doing this, we separate from them by denying their humanity and their right to be a fully fledged human, separate from our projections.

In doing basic shadow work, we begin to understand that those individuals that we feel morally outraged by can be viewed as a part of ourselves with which we have not reconciled. Our need to feel morally superior comes at a steep cost: a part of our shadow. When we cannot see the humanity in another, we have separated from the parts of ourselves that we dislike or hate.

If we question our moral outrage, we can take back our shadows. We can take back our vitality from our projected plays and from the people we have cast in roles. When we can see ourselves mirrored in another, we take back the energy that we formerly cast outward. When we recognize the roles that we have cast, we can gradually let go of our need to cast others as actors in our play.

Identification

There is a folk legend about a pot roast. A woman cooks a roast each Sunday, just like her mother did. She cuts off the ends of the roast before putting it into the pan. She asks her mother why she should cut off the end of the roast. Her mother says, "I don't know, it's just what my mother did." Her mother then asks her own mother why she cut off the ends of the roast. The grandmother says, "It was the only way that it fit into the pan." This story perfectly describes how identification works.

We learn to inhabit the role of "adult" through a process of identifying with our parents. Without our being aware of it, we take on the ways that they inhabit the world. This can include simple things like how they pay bills or how they exercise, but it can extend to everything from cooking, holiday traditions, hairstyles and clothing, parenting practices. It can determine what our family and home should be like in adulthood.

Often we insist on doing things the way that we learned how they should be done in childhood, simply because our parents did it that way. This has both good and bad qualities—our mother may have been a fantastic cook, or your family's holidays may have created a lot of joy that you wish to continue.

It may also mean that rigidity develops. We do things simply because we believe as adults that we should act out the role of "adult" the same way as our parents did. We easily inhabit the same role already played by one, or both, of our parents, without questioning if that role suits us.

Abe insists that the Christmas tree be set up a specific way and that his children open presents on Christmas Eve, leaving only one present for Christmas Day. On Christmas Day a specific potato dish must be served, and the family must eat at midday. He must be served while seated at the head of the table. This is the way that his childhood family celebrated Christmas, and so he insists on following this tradition as well.

Julia insists on both cleaning her home and providing the majority of childcare even though she has a full-time job and is exhausted. Her mother was a stay-at-home mother, and their house was always very clean and tidy. Her mother would get quite upset at loud noises, clutter, and dirt; Julia grew up feeling like she could not get dirty or basically act like a child in the home. Julia is more forgiving of childhood noise, but she still feels the need for her house to resemble her mother's, and to take on the majority of childcare and household chores even though she has money to hire babysitters or house cleaners.

Ahmed insists that his wife not work, even though she would like to and they could use the extra income in their household. His father oversaw all the finances for his household and was quite stingy with spending. Ahmed becomes the same way, even though a part of him desires to take vacations and recognizes that if his wife worked it could significantly help the household.

Identification most commonly arises as we take on the role of our same-sex parent in adulthood. How we lead our lives, who we are, and what we consider to be an "adult" or "adult female or male" largely entail us moving into the same role that our mother, father, or guardian inhabited.

This will happen even in children who vow to never be like their parents. Many children in early childhood make a secret pact not to be like one of their parents. They end up with a split identification: they act out the role of their mother, father, or guardian without awareness and they simultaneously act out the vow of not being like them. Yet in this vow they are still identifying with the role of their parents; they are simply acting out against that role.

Radha grew up with a young mother who was a neglectful alcoholic. Her mother was quite poor and got divorced and re-married several times to a series of violent men. Radha vowed at an early age to be nothing like her mother. She chose to remain childless as an adult and strove to ensure her own financial success. However, she found herself dating men who were addicts. They were not violent but they neglected her. Radha felt like she had to do everything on her own, just like her mother did. This part of her mother's role remained.

For Radha to break free she would need to release all identification with her mother, including the vow to be nothing like her mother. Even though this vow has its benefits, it is also confining. If we are in opposition to someone, they are still controlling us—we must act and believe in opposition to them. Radha should be able to choose on her own whether she wants to raise children and whether she wants to focus so much on financial success.

Trauma Bonding

We often relate to others because they have experienced similar pain as we have. In them we find a mirror that directly reflects our own experiences and understandings of life. There is a sense of safety and certainty that develops when we surround ourselves with our own reflected beliefs and understandings of reality.

This means that you likely relate to someone because they have gone through a similar form of suffering as you. They reflect the same pain that you carry. This can create empathy, friendship, and states of interbeing in which you can support and connect to one another.

This can also mean that you dislike someone, or do not get along with them, because they remind you of some shadow part, some pain, that you do not wish to admit to. This pain has been repressed and denied for a reason.

Although she does not know him, Opal truly hates Franco. They are in the same consulting field, and she frequently sees his online posts and responses. When she questions her hatred of him, she recognizes in him something of herself: the same sort of insecurity and inadequacy combined with a desperation to be acknowledged.

Heather truly loves James and calls him her "twin flame." They have a deep friendship that feels like they have known one another forever, even though they only met a few years ago. James starts going to therapy and doing significant work on himself. Heather finds that James feels more distant and that they are no longer as compatible as they once were. This is because James has healed considerable inner child material and they no longer share the same abandonment wound and loneliness that once tied them together so closely.

When we project our shadow parts onto others, in the short term it can be quite positive. Eventually, however, we notice how we mirror one another and how we use our shared experiences as a way to connect. Sometimes with personal work, we find ourselves moving on from a role, a friendship, or a relationship because we no longer need to project and cast roles the way that we used to. We have changed, we have healed, and our play and its roles and narrative will reflect that.

In some cases, when a person changes, the friend or partner adjusts over time to the new reality. Growing pains in relationship are very real, as we acclimate anew to the roles that we inhabit and the roles we have been cast in. Once the other person gets used to the change, for many relationships and friendships, releasing roles or changing them can allow for growth and healing in both individuals.

But in some cases, this growth can cause difficulties in the relationship. The other person needs you to inhabit a role with a specific script and you no longer fit the bill. This will cause them to feel uncomfortable and confused. They may act in specific ways in an effort to put you back in the old role. The crucial question is whether a partner or friend is in your life simply to reflect your pain or cast a specific role, or if there is true intimacy between you.

Casting Other Roles in Our Play

Although the roles of mother and father (or any authority figure from our childhood) are considerable characters in our plays, we also cast other people in roles.

If we are traumatized in adulthood, we may respond to that threat by casting others as perpetrator. Marla experienced a home invasion and she was severely shaken. She now is hypervigilant in her house at night and fearful of anyone who resembles her home invader. Thomas was bullied in his first job and is now highly reactive to anyone who jokes with him or makes fun of him.

We also end up casting roles as a result of popular culture and our relationship with online spaces. Everything we do online is tracked, then bought and sold by corporations and advertisers. What is then brought into our awareness—videos, music, advertisements—is based on who we are, what we say, and what we search for on the internet.

When we have children, our own identification with them and projections onto them can create complex roles. For example, Ida was ecstatic to have a son and loves him immensely. When he started dating, no woman was ever good enough for him. She could not release her grip on her son because she wanted to be the only woman in his life. She still thought of him as a child. She attempted to sabotage his relationships and projected her hatred onto her son's wife, continually disparaging her to anyone who would listen. She cast her daughter-in-law in the role of "villain" because she could not accept that her son has grown up and has individuated. She cannot see that her role has changed.

Reyansh loved all of his children but he did not understand his youngest son, Advik, who had always been interested in computers and who spent long hours playing video games. Reyansh wanted his son to be extroverted, to get married and have a child so that he could be a grandfather. Advik's wife was pleasant enough, but Reyansh lamented that she and his son could not have children. Reyansh blamed his daughter-in-law for not having grandchildren and he loudly proclaimed his disappointment, shaming her and Advik at every family function in the form of "jokes" about how they could not continue his bloodline.

It is typical for parents to project roles onto their children's significant others. These roles are often extensions of their projections onto their children. We consider children to be a part of ourselves, and so when they become individuals, living their own lives, there are times when a parent feels grief, disappointment, and disapproval. In a healthy relationship, the parent is excited for their child to individuate, even if they do not agree with all of their adult child's life choices. They can celebrate their child's career, spouse, or life path, even if it is not what they would choose for themselves.

In unhealthy relationships, the parent still sees the child as an extension of themselves. They exert control to keep the child acting the role of "child" no matter what their age. In considering their child to be a part of themselves, they subject them to their own immense shadow—their hopes, unlived dreams, unacknowledged emotions and traumas. They may express their disappointment regarding their child's independent decisions in developing their own identity.

While we project a "mother" or "father" role onto our spouse or partner, we also project the largest parts of our disowned shadow. This will be covered more fully in later chapters.

As we age, we are likely to transition from thinking of every boss we have as a surrogate parent to developing our own idea of what "boss" should be. We also discover large divisions between ourselves and others in politics, ideology, philosophy, religion, spirituality, and way of life. These divides are subject to the projections of the darkest aspects of our own being.

As we discover the roles we have cast, we can clearly see the play that we have projected onto the world and the people in it. Our narrative about reality, how we interact with others, what we see in them, and what we know about ourselves can change. We confine ourselves to a play that was largely set up for us in childhood. As adults we can take conscious steps to release this play and move into the open space beyond it.

Chapter 10

Casting Roles

When we cast our play, we look for others who will fulfill specific roles beyond those of mother and father. These roles serve a specific function and have personality traits, ways of being in the world, and even physical characteristics set by us subconsciously. We find others who have the wounding patterns that fit the roles required to carry out our play. In the previous chapter we saw examples of this, like a man looking for an emotionally unavailable woman who is small and plump like his mother to play out the role of "mother" so that he can act out the role of "child."

When he casts a woman in this role, he requires that she be emotionally closed off and that she physically resemble his mother. If she were to significantly change—for example, to become a warmer, more open person, or to change her hairstyle or weight—she would no longer fit her proscribed role and he would become upset.

When we cast someone in a role, we need them to remain static. They must always be a "mother," a "narcissist," a "villain," or a "witch." If the other person steps out of this role, we unconsciously try to move the other person back into their cast role. For example, if this man's wife were to desire intimacy, he might subconsciously act out by going out drinking to move her back into her static role of emotionally unavailable "mother."

If his acting out succeeds, she will move back into her assigned role. If his acting out is unsuccessful, problems will erupt in their marriage.

It will then be up to both of them to determine whether they desire to work through those issues and grow beyond these roles, or decide that the relationship is at an end. If the issues are not resolved, the man will move on, seeking another woman to fulfill the "mother" role for him.

When we cast a role, it is to fulfill specific emotional and physical needs. For example, a boss looks to cast an individual in the role of "employee." To this particular boss, the employee role needs to be filled by someone who is hard working, able to perform specific computer-related tasks, and also willing to bend to her sometimes unreasonable requests. If the employee is hired and is unwilling to work extra hours, or if he pushes back against watching the boss's child when she brings him into the workplace, the boss will be upset as the employee is not fulfilling the static role that she had envisioned of "employee."

"Archetype" is a Greek word meaning "original pattern" or "model." Archetypes provide a broader understanding of a role and represent fundamental characteristics of a prototypical image or thought. We collectively and personally form images and stories around our deepest understandings of the human experience, and we utilize these images and stories to make sense of the world. As humans we like to see patterns, and archetypes offer us the opportunity to see the broadest of roles enacted on the world stage. For example, George Lucas famously utilized Joseph Campbell's work on the archetypal hero and the hero's journey to inspire *Star Wars*.

Archetypes are stories around our most basic impulses. Our instincts arise in popular consciousness as symbol, myth, sound (and music), math, and story. From time immemorial, fairy tales, folk legends, and myths have illustrated the struggles and motivations of human nature.

For example, many of us might feel at times like Sisyphus rolling a boulder up a hill only to have it roll back down from the top each time. The belief that "no matter what I do, I end up at the same place" is hard-wired into our psyches and on some small or large level we all live out this myth. This myth also shows our basic human instinct to continue following the same habitual patterns even if they offer us nothing in return. When we feel like we're struggling against the collective, or we think we are being punished by outer forces, it's like pushing that boulder up the hill again and again despite knowing that it will roll back down. How different that story might be if our friends or community helped push that boulder, or if we decided to stop pushing that boulder altogether.

Our myths and legends, along with their impulses, are shown today through movies, television, and social media. Social media influencers, reality television stars, actors, politicians, musicians, and others in our public sphere show us our collective archetypal figures.

In collective archetypal figures, we observe static roles and patterns on a larger stage. Similar to the roles we set in our individual lives, these collective roles lack any sort of nuance. The hero, victim, villain, lover, creator, and many other roles reflect our own individual impulses and struggles.

On an individual level, a role and an archetype can have significant overlap. However, what one boss decides to cast as "employee" and what another boss casts as "employee" can be quite different. What you decide to cast as "boyfriend" will be different than your image of the archetypal "boyfriend." For example, you may subconsciously cast someone as "boyfriend" who is tall and intelligent and also helps you repeat the pattern from your childhood where your parents struggled to communicate with one another. Archetypally, "boyfriend" may mean an unavailable movie star, impossibly good looking and perhaps rakish in character—and, of course, adoringly devoted only to you.

Or perhaps you are someone who has had a poor relationship with men and so the archetypal male and possible "boyfriend" is selfish and boorish and doesn't help out with chores. This kind of relationship satisfies the role of "boyfriend" as well as "male."

An archetype is our conceptual model of someone based on our experiences of them. This may be as simple as picturing the archetypal dog as a golden retriever due to a movie seen in childhood or having a golden retriever as a family dog when growing up. Archetypes often consist of our romanticized notions, or perfected ideals, regarding that role. One popular example is the archetypal boyfriend being a "bad boy gone good."

Our archetypes can be skewed by our perceptions and personal experiences. For example, difficult experiences with men or women will cause the projected archetypal man or woman to be an object of hatred or wounding, rather than a source of desire or perfection. On an even more complicated level, we can have both a skewed and a perfected archetypal image of the same thing, resulting in confusion and conflict within ourselves. For example, a man hates women but he also idealizes specific women that he considers "perfect," while subjecting all other women to scorn and dehumanization. He is split between archetypal women—the perfected beauty and all others.

We carry all archetypal figures and roles within ourselves; some are just dormant or simply less active. We all contain masculine, feminine, and asexual/ambiguous aspects within ourselves. We each contain witch, explorer, romantic, stoic, hedonist, tyrant, addict, and all other archetypal roles. It is by embracing all archetypes and roles within that we become a whole human being enjoying a fuller and freer life. This dissolves inner conflict as we claim the shadow parts that we have projected into the outer world.

For example, Edra was afraid of planes but she loved watching documentaries, especially ones about travel to distant places. She could not claim her archetypal explorer, and so she passively watched others embody the "explorer" archetype on screen. If she could embody "explorer" in her own way—perhaps by taking trips that do not require flying—she would find her own inner explorer.

To reclaim archetypal figures, we often need to reconcile seeming paradoxes within ourselves, in order to claim our multidimensionality. For example, a man loves his strength and frequently mocks those who do not exercise or work out, or whom he perceives as weak. If he were to embrace the "weak" shadow aspect of himself, he would no longer see a world divided (and he would also stop spending so much time and energy on disliking the weak Other). He also would be able to more wholly embrace his strength. It would become something that he is, rather than something that he feels the need to outwardly prove to others.

All of the roles and characteristics that we carry within also contain their opposite. The strong man needs to point out the weak man outwardly to displace his inner shadow of weakness. Those with true strength utilize it to help others who are weak, knowing that one day they too will be weak—through illness or old age. Those who fully embody their strength can clearly see areas of themselves that are weak, with acceptance and mercy. We all have areas in our life where we cannot carry on individually and where we require support. We all have parts of ourselves that are not fully formed or that are "weak" by nature. It is by embracing seemingly opposing roles that we break free from the cages that we have put ourselves in.

This work is not about changing archetypes, it is about allowing them to become their purest expression. Some facets of our personality are fixed, even if we fully reclaim our shadow. We may always be stubborn or somewhat melancholy. We can develop a good relationship with these parts of ourselves, rather than separate from them. By fully inhabiting who we are—without bullying or shaming ourselves into being something else—we can become wholly ourselves.

We define ourselves across such a narrow spectrum, and in such specific roles and archetypal figures, that we rightfully feel confined. Being imprisoned in a specific role and its expectations means that we cannot express ourselves or live the way that we wish to. Everything that we desire outside of that role is projected onto others, either onto those close to us or onto public figures. Our deepest desires play out through our religious and spiritual principles or across our screens.

In considering roles and archetypes, the problem is not that they exist within us. The problem is that our perceptions of them have become skewed by personal experience, and we cannot break free from their static requirements. When we see ourselves living out these roles, we can see how they limit us. We are not just "mother" or "son" or "employee."

We can look into the stories that we live out and move on from defining ourselves through such narrow paradigms. Additionally, we can claim archetypes that feel distant or non-existent in our lives. When we recognize that all archetypal figures and roles play out within us, we widen our perception of who we are, what we can do, and who we can become in this world.

The Victim

The most common role that we play is that of victim. We have every right to cast ourselves in this role. We have been wronged—morally, physically, sexually, and emotionally. The harm and suffering in the world and in our lives is never okay, and never right. Only by fully embracing the extent of our victimhood can we move beyond the confines of this role.

Our victimhood requires us to be fully seen and heard in our pain. At some point in our lives, we were rendered powerless. We have been traumatized, damaged, and we have created defense mechanisms so that we will not be hurt in that same way again. We believe differently, we navigate the world differently, and we *are* different without the power that has been taken from us.

If we have been abused, our abusers rely on breaking us just enough so that we are still functional enough to play a role for them. We are still needed to care for children, to work, to do chores, and to look okay enough for the world to think that we are living normal, quiet lives. But our abuse is contingent on us being silent, passive, and broken. In such relationships, the pile of unprocessed rage and resentment will one day boil over, leading to an eruption of emotion. Or we will step out of passivity and powerlessness and move beyond the cycle of love and abuse to take charge of our own life. To step into our power again, taking it back from those who stole it from us, means to become the hero.

This process is much more complex in the case of systemic and cultural abuse; we can only free ourselves so much from these cycles. In those cases, clear recognition helps, as well as moving beyond ideologies that project laziness, inadequacy, craziness, or immorality onto those who are suffering due to systemic oppression. Those in healthcare and teaching and factories and fast-food production do some of the hardest, most soul-crushing jobs on the planet and gain little from the experience.

Shadow work requires us to see that we are all victims in one way or another. As part of the human experience we all suffer under the weight of collective trauma. We all have had experiences in which we have been rendered powerless, or subjected to the authority of another. By recognizing our commonality in this archetype—*we have all been victims*—we can move beyond feeling isolated in our pain. We can stop comparing our victimhood to another's. Every individual or group has known suffering. When we are willing to accept the role of victim wholly within ourselves by clearly seeing how we were wronged or rendered powerless, empathy develops for the suffering that is the human condition.

To fully integrate this archetype, we need to admit to ourselves the full extent of our victimhood. We tend to readily dismiss the pain we have experienced; we can always point to someone who has experienced worse. And we cannot see our parents, or our friends, as villains because to do so would mean to come out of denial and fully contend with the pain that they have caused us. When we fully feel and validate the full extent of what we have experienced, we can move past being stuck in a victimized role.

When we are willing to clearly see ourselves as victims of systemic financial, cultural, and spiritual oppression, we take back the collective projections and ideologies that are offered to keep us complacent. Collective patterns require collective healing.

The belief that one cannot be a victim means that others can victimize us and we will be blind to it. Spiritual teachers and other authority figures utilize this mentality because it allows them to victimize their followers without question. If we do not claim our victimhood, it means that we are not willing to see the full extent of harm that has befallen us throughout our lives.

We will play victim as a dominant role until we truly close the door to our past. What we have been through leaves marks: emotional, spiritual, and physical. If we do not tend to our victimhood, we will pass it along to another. We harm others in the same way that we have been harmed. Seeing this brings home the idea that "hurt people hurt people" because they truly do. But this leaves out the understanding that "ignorant people hurt people" or that "evil people hurt people." We hurt others far more out of ignorance than from any other factor. When we know more, when we become more, we can look back and reconcile within ourselves any hurt or pain that we have caused in the world. When given the chance, we can reconcile it outwardly as well, without requiring the victim to absolve us of any guilt or to offer forgiveness.

When we are stuck in the role of victim, we will filter reality so that we always remain the victim. We do not notice the light aspects of life, nor the good things that come our way. We are so immersed in the darkness that any light is suffocated. The world is awful, people are terrible, and everyone is out to get us.

Subconsciously we act in a way to make this true. So much obnoxious or ill-intentioned behavior is acted out by those who are simply so stuck in a childhood victim role that they continually cast others in the role of victimizer. For example, Willow believes that nobody notices her. Her parents only noticed her when they needed to—particularly when someone else made a comment that reflected poorly on the family. She makes awkward comments and dresses in a punk style. When she gets the negative feedback she secretly desires, it reinforces her belief that she is a neglected, victimized child. If Willow were to heal this childhood dynamic, her dress and awkwardness may remain the same, but her childhood loop of "poor me" and its accompanying inner narrative would change. Others would more easily relate to her because she is no longer subconsciously casting herself in a victimized role, in which she needs to act inappropriately to receive attention.

Shauna grew up as one of the only black children in a predominantly white school system. She was bullied and victimized but she always needed to remain calm and quiet so she could avoid being punished as well. She rightfully grew up to be angry, as well as wary of friendships. While it was not an easy task, she learned to understand the difference between her feelings from her childhood and adolescent experiences, which required healing, and her righteous anger at the state of the world and at people who viewed her only as a person of color. Once she saw herself more clearly, she could react appropriately to present-day circumstances, from an adult perspective rather than from the vantage point of a harmed child.

When we accept our past as being fully in our past, we can move beyond moral outrage and shut the door on what happened long ago. It was unfortunate, but it does not need to define who we are today. We can move beyond living out the wounds of our childhood.

The Villain

The moral outrage that we feel against others fades as we come into contact with our own inner villain. We can move on to fully claiming our inner perpetrator, understanding that we have the capacity to harm, to abuse, and even to kill. What differentiates us from those who do such things is the conscious choices we make regarding how we act. We can harm, but we choose not to. By reclaiming both our inner victim and our inner perpetrator, we can let the victim role fade into the background.

There must be a perpetrator for there to be a victim. If there were no "bad guy" there would be no "good guy"—no divide between good/evil, moral/immoral, or just/unjust. We must work through many layers of victimhood to reach a point of seeing that we carry the villain within ourselves. We have—typically without awareness—created pain, taken power, or participated in injustice for our own benefit.

The role of the villain is the ultimate Other. We cast our darkest shadows onto it, and it is typically the last part of ourselves that we claim. It is much easier to cast our villains onto comic book characters, politicians, prisoners, and serial killers. Daily we are exposed to extreme examples of polarizing behavior in video clips and news stories. Onto them we place our darkest shadows.

To see the villain as more than a strictly evil presence in the world is to render the villain human and capable of complexity. We are all heroes and villains. We are all perpetrators and victims. When we can see this, our desire to paint the Other into a unidimensional corner ceases. Our villains are no longer strictly evil, they are nuanced, with both good and bad as well as plenty of qualities in between.

Recognizing the grey areas within us is a significant step on our path of greater self-realization and healing. Real life includes villains who may also be lover, creator, healer, explorer, provider. When we see this, the façade of the comic book supervillain releases, and we are left with humans—deeply ambiguous, unaware, mostly trying their best—and the hypocrisies they leave behind. To witness both the villain and the victim within ourselves is to fully embody both our darkness and our light.

Hero

There is much written about the "hero's journey," an archetypal adventure to overcome some type of darkness. It is a quest in which our hero goes out into the world, meets the foe, and returns home changed. On a deeper level, the hero's journey represents coming into consciousness. The shadows of the unknown, repressed and denied, come to the forefront to be reclaimed.

We can see ourselves as the protagonist of our stories: the hero on a journey who emerges triumphant after a battle or trial. To believe ourselves to be on a hero's journey means that we embody the light, continually battling the forces of darkness. To be the hero means always having a foe, a conflict, acting with meaning and purpose. We are able to defeat the monster and return a changed man. We can take back the stolen treasure, and come back as a more enlightened woman.

The problem with being the hero is that we always need to engage in a quest. A hero doesn't rest, they are always looking for the next monster to slay. They are never present with themselves, or their bodies, because they are off at war, journeying to find a Golden Fleece, or defending their community.

While we like to think that the hero has a definitive end to their journey, those of us who live out the archetypal hero know that this is not true. There is no satisfaction because a new monster, a new destination, or a new endeavor always arises. Achieving a goal simply moves the goalposts. There is no enlightenment, there is only one perilous journey after the last.

When we can recognize that there is no quest, simply our idea of a quest, we can release the hero. We can call on our heroism as needed, but to define ourselves by this role means that we must continually sacrifice our lives for a greater good that never fully appears.

There is a tension between creating meaning for ourselves, knowing our purpose in the world, and freeing ourselves from the archetypal hero. The idea of a quest is conferred to us by the outer world—we must achieve certain things in this world to be successful—and we stagnate in nihilism and anguish when we realize how illusory this quest is.

To create meaning and purpose for ourselves is necessary, otherwise we cannot live our lives. Yet to believe that everything is a lesson denies the fact that there are some things in life that we simply need to grit our teeth and bear. Not all experiences are lessons, and we do not emerge victorious from every quest. Sometimes an experience creates nothing but pain that we must learn to endure.

Perhaps this is the real role of the hero—to endure despite all odds. When we embody the hero within, we know that if we get knocked down by life, we can get back up and continue moving forward. One benefit of age is that we recognize that death, birth, disease, and hardships simply occur, and we somehow manage to carry on.

Whatever quest we are on can be relinquished with a recognition of the futility of it. Our finish lines are arbitrary; they disappear and fade into the background once we cross them. When we release our need to complete the quest, and realize that the quest itself is illusory, we can feel the immense fatigue of our inner hero. He can let go, stop fighting, and learn to rest and simply be.

The Drama Triangle

Roles create specific patterns of interrelating. All the roles that we inhabit require an Other to fully live them out. We do not live in a one-person production of our play; we must enlist supporting characters to act out all the other roles.

We can understand the ego as an organizing structure of our reality. However, this reality does not remain static. Each time we take on a different role, that organization changes. For example, one day we may wake up as the eternal optimist, ready and able to take on the world. We notice the birds singing and smile at each person we pass. The day unfolds pleasantly, and we feel that all is right with the world.

The next day we wake up as the depressive. There are horrible people doing unpleasant things in the world and we focus on any bad news that comes our way. We participate in *Schadenfreude,* the particular brand of shameful joy we feel when we see the suffering of others.

In both of these instances, our ego is organizing, and thus filtering, our reality in a specific way so as to match the role that we inhabit that day. We may change our role much more quickly due to specific happenings of our day as well. For example, Hawthorn spilling hot coffee on her shirt may quickly shift her out of an adult mediator role (calm and pleasant to everyone) into the role of a child who wants to throw a tantrum. Jackson is in a terrible controller/dictator role at work where nothing meets his specifications, but in a doting father role once he arrives home from work.

The roles that we place on one another, the ways that our plays intersect, cause us to inhabit roles that have specific ego structures, patterns of relating, and narratives. The "drama triangle" is a model developed by psychiatrist Stephen Karpman that shows how the roles of persecutor, rescuer, and victim destructively relate to each other.

While one individual can inhabit one of these roles in a static way— for example, by always being the victim—it is much more common in our relationships for the roles to be more fluid. We switch between these roles to fulfill the requirements of our play. We may feel some satisfaction in letting the characters in our play run through their expected lines with one another, but on a deeper level we realize that what happened was destructive, rather than helpful.

This model points out that we require others to inhabit certain roles in order for a type of transactional relationship to occur. We cannot be a persecutor without a victim, or a rescuer without someone to rescue. In time we see how we fulfill each of these roles, moving from one to the other, depending on the relationship we are in.

In our workplace we may be king and leader, while at home we are victim and rescuer. To have the fluidity to bring out roles consciously and purposefully, in a healthy, life-affirming way, is the goal of considering how we interact with others and the roles that we play.

Child, Adult, and Parent

In the book *Games People Play*, Eric Berne develops a model of relating that includes a constellation of roles including child, adult, and parent.

Our inner child can be understood as an aspect of our wounding that is stuck at a specific stage of development. They relate to the world as a child, which can frustrate those around them. A refusal to complete basic tasks of adulthood combined with the emotional immaturity of a child creates issues in relationships, friendships, and other interpersonal spaces.

However, Berne was careful to show how the child role is not simply a negative and wounded inner child, but also a source of qualities such as joy, play, and wonder. To recover childhood innocence, creativity, wonder, and open-mindedness while remaining in an adult role integrates the positive aspects of the child role into our lives.

In relating, the child often plays opposite a parent role. If one friend is the stable therapist of the group, that means that the others can remain in the child role, getting drunk, creating conflicts, or having meltdowns. The parent role assumes responsibility over the child role. This dynamic creates quite a bit of friction in relationships and friendships. The parent tires of taking care of the child, and for always needing to be the adult in the relationship. This can happen at quite a young age as well.

For example, Erica's parents divorced when she was ten years old. Her father was devastated, and when she visited him, he would loudly complain about her mother and place Erica into the parental "female" role: cooking dinner, cleaning up, and ensuring that he went to bed and woke up for work on time. He would act like a child and get upset at her when she didn't perform these tasks. Erica was given an adult role from age ten with her father, while he inhabited the child role. In her adult life, Erica still finds herself in an adult role with her father, frequently listening to his hateful diatribes about her mother and stopping at his house in her spare time to perform basic tasks for him. She also finds herself in relationships where she needs to do all of the household chores, childcare, and caretaking for her partners.

Sometimes the role of parent can feel quite good on some level. To treat another as a child is to deem ourselves in some way as superior or more capable than them. Maria is a spiritual teacher. At a young age she cared for her ailing mother. As a teacher, she treats all of her students as children, and it makes her feel good that her "children" need her as their "mother." In reality, while a teacher expects some of their students to be stagnated in development, it is their job to help the student to grow up, insofar as the student is willing. Maria doesn't want her students to mature because she loves that they see her as a mother figure. She tends to attract students who desire someone to play the role of mother so they can act like children. She has terrible boundaries with her students and is frequently tired and ill from "mothering" so many students. She is unwilling to look at the reasons for her need to parent others, and how it stemmed from caretaking for her mother in childhood.

To step out of the role of parent is to stop taking responsibility for the child. When we do this the child will either flounder or grow up. If we look at our inner desire to parent others, we can see that it creates a type of resentment within ourselves at needing to act in this role while the child gets to act freely and irresponsibly. The parent is often a martyr role, believing that they have the weight of the world on their shoulders. To step outside of this role allows an individual to rediscover their own inner child, and to move away from needing to parent other adults.

The adult is the neutral and whole individual in this constellation. It is our present-day self, free from the role of parent or child. To act as an adult is to see others as humans on the same level and composed of the same stuff as we are. We neither take too much responsibility for others nor do we neglect our own responsibilities out of childish selfishness. There is balance.

The Golden Child

The golden child in a family is the favorite who in the eyes of the parents can do no wrong. Each achievement and every special occasion in this child's life is given full attention by the parents or guardians. If this child becomes difficult, or creates a problem, this is quickly deflected onto the "scapegoat" (see below) or denied altogether.

While this may be a favored position within a family structure, the golden child is bound by the hopes and desires of their parents. Typically, the golden child is required to achieve what the parents want for them, and the child is not seen as their own independent self. They are an extension of the parents who identify with them so strongly that the child's accomplishments become their own. Any unfulfilled desires of a parent become lived through the child, and any accomplishments that a parent wishes to relive from their youth becomes a necessity for the child to achieve.

The golden child often feels pressure to meet impossibly high standards set by the parents and suffers from never feeling good enough. There is a deep-seated anxiety about continually needing to achieve, as well as a desire to please people, particularly authority figures and institutions. Golden children often grow into positions where they are expected to work hard and excel with little complaint or pushback.

For the golden child, it is often necessary to work on developing boundaries and a separate sense of self. Being so enmeshed with a parental figure understandably creates confusion about individual wants, needs, and goals. One advantage of clearly seeing how they were the favorite in the family structure is to connect with siblings regarding their family experience and commiserate with them regarding their own particular suffering.

The Forgotten Child

There is not much to write about the forgotten child because they are, quite simply, not noticed. Whatever they do or say is not met with attention, care, or regard in any way. Even acting out in negative ways is ignored by parents or caregivers.

There is a tendency for the forgotten child to be either the middle child or the youngest child in a long line of children. If it is a large family, the older children are expected to be quasi-parents to the youngster. While this may forge a strong bond, a child taking care of another child, even if a decade or so separates them, is not the same as a parent providing love, care, and attention. The eldest in the parental role is likely to feel resentment at caring for the child; even when unspoken, it becomes part of their relationship dynamic. This also happens in households where another child is sick or has a disability. The healthy child then becomes the forgotten child, frequently inhabiting the role of "mini-adult" to assist the ill or disabled sibling.

The forgotten child feels invisible, and in adult relationships they struggle to stand out. They play their invisible role convincingly, creating a physical appearance that ensures that nobody notices them. Until this child is able to find a voice and a stable sense of self, they will remain forgotten and invisible. Abandoning the childhood role and letting go of any wounding is necessary so that this child can step into the limelight.

As children, many of us became invisible so that we wouldn't cause issues for our parents. We figured that if we were not a burden, if we became so small that our parents forgot that we existed, we would be loved. We might be praised or we would at least avoid being punished or shamed for having basic wants and needs. To recognize as an adult how terrible that is, and to see that every child deserves to be cherished, can allow the forgotten child to become a remembered adult.

The Scapegoat

In ancient Greece, a goat was sacrificed ritually for the good of the collective. The people believed that heaping the energetic and emotional "sins" of a community onto an animal would absolve them. Such ritualistic scapegoating continues today within family structures.

In families the scapegoat is often referred to as the "black sheep" of the family. It is the problematic child or the child who is different from the other members of the family. While the golden child can do no wrong—their every accomplishment is seen with pride—every mistake the scapegoat makes is magnified and seen as a terrible offense.

This creates significant confusion and distortion in the scapegoated child, who is likely to grow up feeling "bad" or "wrong" about themselves because they were shamed or punished for perfectly normal misbehaviors.

The scapegoat is conditioned to accept the barest scraps of "love" in return for hiding who she is in an attempt to win love and approval. Because her work is not recognized, she must accomplish more, and sacrifice more of herself, in order to achieve any sort of recognition.

The scapegoat often grows up with a deep fear of their otherness or "wrongness" stemming from their childhood family dynamics.

When a child exhibits problematic behavior, the healthy parental reaction is to find the required help for their child, not to shame and blame them for their issues. A child is a reflection of their parents and of the family home, and the scapegoat becomes the lightning rod in the household for all blame. Issues within the family, including with siblings and the parents, will be deflected onto the scapegoat.

In this way, scapegoats often grow up feeling as if everything is their fault and they take over-responsibility for interpersonal situations. The scapegoat often meets others who wish to deny their issues or who want to utilize him as a therapist. As he so readily learned to absorb the issues of his household, others will learn to use him in this capacity as well. The scapegoat requires boundaries and clarity to lay fault correctly in any situation. While empathy is certainly a gift, the scapegoat needs to be careful that they are not taking on blame, drama, or the pain of others in their quest to garner approval and acceptance. Additionally, the scapegoat will often need to look at their tendency to overwork for little benefit. Only by resolving resentment about this pattern can they move forward in their lives with an ability to say "no" and to set better boundaries overall. Most significantly, the scapegoat needs to understand that there is nothing wrong with them. They were just made to feel that way as a child.

We inhabit many roles, both in our childhood home and in our daily lives. Becoming aware of the roles that we took on in childhood allows us to examine the other roles we take on in our lives. We see clearly how they may limit us and how they play out in our current lives. By doing so, we break free from them, or we can decide to inhabit a role to the degree that it serves us.

Chapter 11

Recrafting Our Narrative

*I*n our personal play, we all have central themes and a narrative structure. The script and themes of our play and its cast of characters repeat in loops. If we notice these loops, we can break them. We can heal the pain underlying our script, change or expand roles, and even release that play entirely.

For example, if the central theme of our play is "I am all alone," our reality will prove to us again and again that we are all alone and that we cannot count on anyone other than ourselves. We will subconsciously place others into roles that are rejecting, punishing, or unreliable. We then prove ourselves right, never recognizing how our main character continually pushes others away and places them into rigid roles.

Our minds will repeat to us the beliefs that hold together the play: "I am all alone. Nobody likes me. Nobody wants to help me." We repeat the conversations with others that allow us to feel rejected and alienated. Without recognizing it, we project thoughts, ideologies, and emotions onto others. For example, Sheila believes that she is all alone, so she apologizes profusely anytime she asks for anything. She may not ask for anything at all, so as to avoid rejection. When interacting with others, she assumes that they do not like her, and she subconsciously acts in ways that garner disapproval from those around her. Sheila may also believe that she is strong for not needing anyone else.

Part of us deeply desires a change in our narrative, and so we have a rift between different parts of ourselves: one part that is deeply invested in the play that is already set, and another part that wants the play to be quite different. This conflict repeats over and over in our outer reality until we acknowledge it and release our need for it.

For example, Hudson has a central narrative that "nobody likes me." He was five years younger than his sister Valerie; starting from when he was born, she made it clear that she hated him. His parents dismissed it as normal sibling rivalry. Valerie made it clear throughout Hudson's childhood that she disliked him and that he wasn't wanted. Hudson took on the rejection of his sister and the ambivalence of his parents. Understandably, he created a central narrative that nobody liked him. As an adult he now has difficulty making friends.

Taoko was her parents' only child and they told her from an early age that she needed to become financially successful so that she could provide for them in their old age. They insisted that she become a doctor or lawyer—nothing else would do. She developed anxiety in school because no matter how well she performed, her parents always questioned why she didn't do better. She developed a belief that nothing she did was ever good enough. She carries this belief into her work as a physician as well as into her relationships, including her relationship with herself. She continually bullies and berates herself for not achieving her goals, though she fails to notice that the goalposts change once she achieves something. She could run five miles at the gym—her original goal—but that wouldn't be good enough because she didn't run ten miles.

The Inner Critic

We all have an inner voice that is critical. Being critical of ourselves can be healthy; to appraise what we have done and see where we could do better next time is helpful and inspires growth.

But our inner critic is rarely healthy or life-affirming: it is most often a bully. It seeks to demean and punish us; it tells us that no matter what we are doing, it is not enough. Theodore Roosevelt once said, "Comparison is the thief of joy." Our inner critic constantly compares our life to the lives of those around us. We may intellectually know that we can never truly experience the inner reality of another person, and we may understand that social media posts rarely reflect reality, but that does not stop our inner critic from using this material as fuel for envy or self-hatred.

Our inner critic is often formed through "introjection." We internalize the voices of our parents (or the most dominant or critical parent or guardian), which creates the basis of our inner critic. We then add onto it: bullies, teachers, friends, celebrities, and advertisers all contribute to its formation.

Our life experiences, our successes and failures, and our perceptions of the world and our place in it are then added into the mix. As adults, our inner critic becomes its own animal, whispering to us words and phrases of self-hatred and worthlessness.

Our inner critic is often like a tape recording, repeating messages in the mind. However, we would not feel compelled to repeat something to ourselves if we knew it was true. We would already believe it. The simple fact that this loop repeats itself shows conflict within the self. This conflict is good, because a part of us understands that our inner critic is not speaking the truth.

No matter how sick our mind may be, or we believe our mind to be, we still have healthy parts of ourselves. We each have an inner encourager, an inner sense of positivity and goodness. This part of ourselves is often drowned out by the negativity. There is a valid reason for this: we prioritize messages of fear and negativity out of basic biological programming because we need to react appropriately to threats in our environment. However, the mind often ends up damaging our health and well-being rather than properly assessing present-day danger.

With this knowledge, it can be extremely helpful to externalize the inner critic. Either draw or visualize what your inner critic looks like. It may shift from day to day, but it will generally look somewhat similar (until significant healing has occurred). Now, give that image a funny hat, odd glasses, a clown outfit, or something else ludicrous to carry or wear.

When your inner critic begins to bully you, imagine that voice coming from the figure that you created. It sounds simple, and perhaps a bit odd, but engaging with this exercise breaks through the stranglehold that the inner critic has on your life. It allows you to contextualize the words the critic is saying so that you can reexamine them. For example, let's say that your inner critic is a fierce-looking grandmother who glares sternly at you while berating you for being horrible and worthless. If she is wearing a large fuzzy top-hat and clown shoes while she says it, this voice will have much less power over you.

Developing Empathy for Suffering

Some people are so hurt that they cannot help but react to the world like a wounded animal—defended, guarded, and rightfully so. The world has hurt this person, injured their soul in such a way that, broken-hearted, they have lost faith in the world. An essential trust, a bond, has been broken.

It can take a long time for trust and faith to re-emerge after such a betrayal.

This betrayal can be healed. It can be seen for what it is, and in that, the person can see that they have a reason to feel hurt. Something unjust has occurred, and the emotions surrounding that injustice should be validated, not pushed aside.

If someone hurts us, we should feel anger. We should be disappointed or grief-stricken, and experience the deep unsettling loneliness and fear that accompanies feeling unwanted or unloved.

When our true selves are told enough times that we are wrong, we go into hiding. We no longer show the world our uniqueness or our brilliance. How could we, in a world full of people looking to place their fear and self-loathing on anyone and anything rather than feel it within?

When we look at others, we often see their defense mechanisms, as well as our own projections onto them. When we take back our projections, we see their suffering clearly. We know that we have arrived at this point when, instead of judging or criticizing the person for being who they are, we see them as a person in pain. This is empathy. If we walk away from an encounter with them feeling harmed, we can recognize that they always carry that pain within themselves. We get to choose whether to remain in the presence of their suffering—they do not.

When we see people in this way, empathy and even love can develop. It must be difficult to suffer so much. They are expecting to be judged as harshly as they judge themselves. In fact, they may be acting in a particular way in order to receive the expected harsh judgment. This would affirm their every defense mechanism, every destructive and self-hating thought. There is no need for you to play a part in upholding their negative thoughts about themselves and reality.

Radical acceptance frees us from being cast in their play and projecting our own inner pain onto them. We can stop being "hooked" into situations that create chaos.

When we work with our own projections long enough, we begin to recognize that others are projecting onto us. You cannot do shadow work for anybody else. Each of us is responsible for the difficult work of self-growth. As you begin to see the projections that others are placing onto you, the roles that they are attempting to cast you in, you can choose not to participate in their play. They want you to act a certain way and to treat them a specific way so that you mirror back to them their beliefs about themselves and reality.

When you treat someone with empathy instead, or even neutrally, they may be frustrated because you are not treating them the way they want you to treat them. When you notice other people projecting onto you, you can set internal boundaries. Do not act the way they expect you to or engage in the conversations they expect you to have with them. Do not fulfill their desire for you to mirror back their negative qualities to them. Treat them differently than they expect; they might even appreciate it.

Releasing the Mother and Father Roles

If you think that you are enlightened,
go and spend a week with your family.

Ram Dass

It is very common for us to live into adulthood while projecting our relationship with our parents onto friends, loved ones, partners, and others. There are several ways to investigate this.

The first is to see if you are still relating to your parents as if you were a child. If they are still alive, question what age you feel while you are at home and notice what role you are cast in. Chances are, both you and your parents are relating as if you were still a teenager, or even a young child. Holidays are a good time to notice our regression to a much earlier age.

The second way is to notice patterns, or loops, in the outer world. Do you notice that you are always attracted to the same type of woman or man? This could be a preference for certain physical characteristics, or it could be a specific emotional pattern of relating. We will have these patterns even if we didn't have a parental figure in our childhood. For example, Kyra's father left when she was five. He was an alcoholic who always promised to visit but never could be counted on to show up. Later in life she notices that she engages in relationships with her "absent father": men who not only resemble her father physically, but who also are addicts who promise her the world but do not deliver.

Another example is Ramona, whose father worked at a very important job and was never home. When he was home, he did not interact with her much. She found in her adult relationships that she dated high achieving women who prioritized work before her.

Notice your relationship with authority. This will also show you quite a bit about your relationship with your parents. Do you distrust authority? Do you rebel against it? Do you want someone to provide all of the answers for you? Do you continually place others ahead of you as if they are more adult or worthy than you? Or as if they somehow have it all together and you do not? How do you interact with female or male individuals that you perceive as having authority? Do you feel as if you do everything wrong? If so, there is something worth exploring regarding your "play" and how it was cast in childhood.

You can also become aware of resistance. Perhaps the idea that we project our relationships with our parents onto others sounds too simplistic to you. The logical mind will seek to obscure and over-complicate things. We may not want to see how our spouse resembles our mother.

Noticing the projection of our parents and guardians onto others is a major step in releasing the play we have cast and taking back the power we have given to others. This will automatically allow us to act differently and to recognize possibilities beyond spending a lifetime stuck in patterns of childhood relating.

When we fully recognize how tiring it is to project a role onto others, and release the emotional need for that role, we can break free.

Questioning Roles

Beyond mother and father, we cast others in many other roles. These roles may be cast onto our own children; discovering that we have created a golden child or scapegoat dynamic in our own family allows us to take ownership of our projections and heal the family as a whole.

When identifying roles, it is easier at first to see them outside of ourselves. What roles do you see in the people around you? They may be clearly defined roles, such as employee, or they may be descriptors: sad sack, jock, overly-enthusiastic, drunk, suck-up, witch, addict, tyrant, hero, clown, artist.

First consider the actual roles they play in their lives. Are they a mother, sibling, or employee? What is their career? What hobbies define them? What do they discuss most frequently? What culture or religious group do they belong to?

Note if you feel any judgment. Are you looking down at *coffee girl* because she is female, young, and serving you coffee? If so, that is something for you to do shadow work on. It shows that you are seeing her as separate, rather than appreciating your shared humanity.

Consider the roles a person may inhabit that are less concrete. If you were to describe three characteristics regarding them, which would you choose? For example, *he is scientific, obese, and quiet.*

These three characteristics define his overall role. For example, if he were to lose weight, acquire an interest in healing crystals, or become more gregarious, his role would change. We can often figure out defined roles fairly easily, but we need to notice how people interact with one another to identify the role they inhabit emotionally.

It is much more difficult to define our own roles. This is why developing an understanding the roles that others play can be crucial to seeing our own.

Consider the roles that you inhabit. Start with concrete roles: are you a mother, father, son, granddaughter? What is your profession and how do you spend your spare time? For example, upon honest examination, Matthias replies: *son, stoner, gamer.* Julia replies: *mother, website developer, runner.*

Now consider your characteristics. How would your best friend describe you in three words? How would a stranger describe you in three words? These considerations can allow us to move past self-judgment (and the inner critic) to develop a more honest self-evaluation.

If the roles and characteristics you come up with are entirely negative, try to think of at least one positive characteristic that describes you.

Now consider what characteristics you have determined that make up your "character" or role. If you were a part of a play, what would your character bring to that play? If the play were centered around your character, what would be the central narrative? What would she be trying to overcome or achieve? What would she be struggling with?

When we clearly see our own roles, and those of the people around us, we realize that what we see is but a sliver of reality. We are much more than three characteristics or a unidimensional role. What people see of us at work or school is not who we are—we all have hidden depths and many characteristics. The qualities that have defined our role can change. By consciously noticing them, we begin to question our part in the play—what works for us and what does not.

We can then decide what parts of ourselves we desire to change, and what parts we *can* change. For example, Alexis defines herself as *disabled, creative,* and *kind.* She cannot change the nature of her disability, although she may change her relationship with that role if she feels negatively about it or if she has not fully accepted it. She does not wish to change her creativity, but she notices that she often expresses her kindness by acting like a doormat. She wants her role to change by developing boundaries. In this awareness, she clearly sees how she wants to shift her role, and what she can work on to improve her overall play.

Our Central Narrative

When you consider your play, ask yourself what type of play it is. Is it a comedy? A tragedy? Is one part of your life a light-hearted farce and another part a dark night of the soul?

To understand our play, we can consider how we see the world and our place in it. This will teach us what our central role is, or basically what our play is about. Some of us view ourselves as being on the hero's quest, a journey to overcome and conquer, despite all odds. Others may feel like our play centers around cycles of renewal and growth, where we are continually being reborn. Some of us may feel trapped in a play of ennui, in which existential despair and meaninglessness are the central tenets. Others may feel like we are in a video game, continually striving to surpass our previous level of existence. Some may feel like they are in Plato's cave, slowly awakening to being in chains, seeing their shadow upon the wall, and climbing out into the sunshine.

If we consider what we believe about the nature of the world and the people in it, we can tell a lot about our play. Do we believe that people are predominantly good? Do we believe that we get what we deserve? That the world is fair and just and orderly? Do we believe that no matter how hard we try, we will never get ahead? Do we believe that the world is full of cruel and vindictive people who are just waiting to harm us?

What we believe to be true about the world and about human nature provides insights regarding our current play and the roles that we cast in it. If in our play we believe people are generally good with a light of the divine in their heart (which they may or may not notice) we are more likely to cast others in that role. Similarly, if we believe that everything is meaningless and that people are stupid, the world will be filled with meaninglessness and populated with stupid people to justify our worldview.

If our play changes, the nature of the world itself does not change, but what we focus on and surround ourselves with does change. However, there is one caveat. If we believe that the world is on one end of the pendulum or another, that severity will come at a price. If we singularly focus on goodness and light and ignore all evil and darkness, sooner or later the dark will come crashing into our play. If we believe that we singularly control our reality and everyone in it, something will eventually happen in our play to prove us wrong. If we believe that the world is nothing but darkness, the light will come in eventually, whether we acknowledge that light or not.

Our central narrative is created by what we believe to be true about ourselves and about the nature of reality. It expresses the meaning and purpose we give ourselves as an individual human being. A seeker on a quest will have a much different narrative from someone with a narrative of continual evolution. Someone who believes that their narrative is about fighting evil may have a similar narrative to someone on a quest, but it will diverge in some ways as well. The person fighting evil has the subject of evil, or a monster, as their purpose, while a person on a quest expects to encounter difficulty but eventually achieve a specific goal and triumphantly return home.

One of the ways to deconstruct this narrative is to consider what we believe regarding people or the world, while understanding that we also are people and we are a part of the world. I am not a separate observer. Basically, if our worldview is based on the idea that "people are stupid" or "people are awful," then at some point we need to recognize that we are also talking about ourselves.

Our script follows our central narrative and the roles that we cast in our play. Within our script we hold beliefs and "truths" around which we organize our identity and our place in the world. The single easiest way to notice your play is to hear when your script repeats. Our scripts are quite static, and so the same language and roles will recur in our play. Our role, and the roles of others, require a specific narrative. Notice repeated conversations and phrases—what you say or think to yourself, what you say to others, or what others say to you. There is a reason for this repetition; it is a necessary part of your play and the roles that have been cast.

When you notice the script, you understand that it is based on cast roles that have specific expectations. You are expected to respond a particular way based on the role that you have been cast in (or that you have cast yourself in). If you respond differently, you change the script.

You change the narrative. The other person must adjust, or you must adjust your own notions regarding who you are.

Daria is known for being high energy and volatile. She initiates arguments with her boyfriend in which she accuses him of cheating, and then throws things. She notices that this is her script, and that this narrative exhausts her and never ends well. The other person either grows smaller to accommodate her or leaves her. During the next argument, Daria takes a walk instead and keeps her jealousy to herself. Her boyfriend is confused by this, but eventually a new script forms in which Daria goes to the gym, or takes a walk, instead of arguing or breaking anything.

It is when we move beyond having a script that we begin to experience genuine intimacy. When we are no longer guided by a central narrative, we can choose our own meaning and purpose in life. We do not have to continually be questing, fighting, or growing. We do not need to follow a central narrative. We can simply be ourselves. We can decide what brings us meaning, set our own goals, and choose what to do with our lives. This is true freedom.

When working with a script, we may not be ready to change our behaviors. But we can change the script. We can learn to use language consciously. Our scripts "loop": they repeat the same circumstances, arguments, and conversations. Even if we keep the same script, if we modify a few words, the script will slightly change.

Alexandra always thought "I can't believe he is doing this again" when dealing with her brother, Thaddeus. He was immature and always asking her for money. Their script included him calling her only when he needed help. He would quickly ask how she was doing and then launch into a recital of the terrible fates that had befallen him. He would then invariably ask for a quick loan that he would "totally pay back." She would relent and offer him money.

She noticed this script, including her internal script. Next time he called, she changed her internal script to one of dark humor: "Who wants to bet what he is calling me for?" When she answered the phone and he asked how she was doing, instead of answering with the usual "Fine," she listed every single bad thing that was happening in her life.

Thaddeus was not accustomed to her requiring him to listen. He kept trying to interject with his own problems, but Alexandra continued bringing the conversation back to herself. Thaddeus became frustrated; he interrupted, asking if he could borrow some money. Alexandra agreed, then added that she would send him a contract for him to sign, agreeing to repay her the full amount within three months, otherwise she would take him to the small claims court. Thaddeus complained to their parents, who called to yell at her for not sending him the money. Alexandra then suggested that her parents offer him money, and they stopped yelling. Thaddeus, miraculously, no longer needed the money. The next time he called, he had a slightly different script. Alexandra recognized more who Thaddeus was and the role that he wanted to inhabit. She felt acceptance toward him rather than resentment, no longer playing the role of responsible sibling who picked up all the pieces for him anymore.

One of the ways that we can determine growth in relationships is if our script changes. In time, our overall narrative may change as well. We may be a rescuer to our innocent ingenue of a girlfriend, or an over-worked mom to an equally busy husband, but those narratives and scripts can change with recognition and effort.

Releasing Causality

In our narratives, we often have beliefs about reality that require examination. They may be entirely false or they may be conferred to us by others without our conscious consideration. For example, the beliefs we develop about cause and effect are often based on logical fallacies, making sense to us emotionally but not rationally.

Howard was laid off on a Saturday. His wife and sister both passed away on a Saturday. Howard now believes that Saturdays bring bad news, and he is anxious and upset every Saturday. Keisha believes that if she does not stop at the café and get coffee before work, the day will go badly. She experienced a truly awful day a few years ago when she had desperately wanted coffee; since then, she has linked that experience to not having coffee.

These are often small things in our lives, but they lead to some amount of personal imprisonment based in fear. We may think that if we do not listen to a particular song, or if we do not follow our usual routine, something bad will happen. We may also experience false equivalency in which something good will happen if we go somewhere or do something in a particular way.

Richard eats at the same restaurant every day. The food is simply "okay," but he believes that this is his "lucky" restaurant; he meets clients and friends there because he feels things will go well. He may be correct, but the "luck" he ascribes to the restaurant can be taken back, and the link can be broken between cause and effect. His client may prefer a different restaurant, and things might go even better there. His friends may appreciate a break in the routine of meeting at this specific restaurant or want to try a new place.

If we question the causal links between things, we can deliberately take both mental and physical action (by acting differently) to test out the smaller strands of our narrative. Noticing and freeing ourselves from causal thinking can change our narrative in substantial ways and bring more spontaneity, freedom, and fun into our lives.

Projection onto the Past

A northwestern medicine study (see Further Reading for link to resource) has shown that every time we remember an event from our past, we remember it differently. Our memory is not concrete, it is mutable and subject to the stories, recollections, and filters that we have created.

Our mother may love retelling a story about our childhood that she thinks is cute, but we do not. We may have experienced bullying that overshadows our present-day reality but the person who bullied us never gives it a second thought. We may have very different memories of our childhood than our sibling does.

Each time we remember something from our past, we are not recalling the original event but the narrative that we have created around it. Our memory becomes subject to our recollection, and over time it becomes skewed. The memory changes each time we remember it in small or large ways: large traumatic events can be dismissed, and smaller events can dominate our childhood narrative.

When we hold so tightly to the narratives that we have created about our past, they become omnipresent and overshadow our present-day reality. Many of us have experienced negative or troubling occurrences in our childhood and early adulthood; shadow work does not suggest that we can undo what has happened in our past. Our past has created and shaped us, and we have known the darkness of the world from our encounters with abuse, stress, violence, and struggle.

However, our past can be placed firmly in the past. We no longer need to hold on to an extensive narrative, we simply understand that something unfortunate has happened to us. When we fully voice our victimhood and allow our inner child to be seen and heard, they integrate in our adult selves. They no longer cry out for love, acceptance, or healing. Our stories can change from tales of feeling stuck, forever repeating the harms that have befallen us, to stories in which we have survived an unfortunate past but emerged alive and whole.

We can never fully release the stories of what we have endured, nor should we. But we can, with healing, find our book of pain condensed to a chapter or a sentence. This allows our past pain to be a footnote in our lives, rather than the central narrative.

Playing the Tape Forward

This is a simple skill but it allows us to work through our fear-based narratives. Our projections onto the future are often ambiguous, which creates panic because they are so open-ended. We so desire control, and part of that desire is to have a clear knowing of what will happen to us and our loved ones in the future.

Shadow work ultimately teaches us to sit with uncertainty. It allows us to accept "not knowing," especially regarding matters like sickness, death, relationships, and career. To be able to flow with things and accept that we are impermanent beings is a difficult task. We can know intellectually that change is the one constant in our lives, and that we are changing each minute, day, and year. But this is rarely embodied by us welcoming the continual changes in our existence.

One way that we can move towards this place of accepting uncertainty is to question: *And then what will happen?* This grounds our abstract fears into a concrete reality.

Maurice is afraid of a big presentation at work. He starts by visualizing himself giving the presentation. He then asks: *And then what will happen?*

- He pictures himself blanking out and forgetting what to say.
- *And then what will happen?*
- He sees himself reaching for his notes or asking his colleague for information and then regrouping and continuing.

Or let's say that Maurice is quite the negative thinker. He assumes the worst-case scenario for himself in this presentation:

- He visualizes himself giving the presentation.
- *And then what happens?*
- He stutters and drinks too much water.
- *And then what happens?*
- He needs to go to the bathroom but cannot since he is presenting.
- *And then what happens?*
- He gets more and more nervous, and everyone gathered starts talking about how terrible he is.
- *And then what happens?*
- He totally fails at his presentation and his boss needs to finish it. She looks at him admonishingly and tells him that they need to talk later.
- *And then what happens?*
- He is called into his boss's office and fired.
- *And then what happens?*
- His boyfriend leaves him and he can't pay his rent.
- *And then what happens?*
- He must move back in with his parents and give up his dog because his father is allergic.

This is obviously a giant pile of horrible consequences. Intellectually, Maurice knows that the likelihood of this scenario happening is incredibly slim. However, playing this out in his mind—even the worst-case scenario—offers a type of concreteness that calms his mind and body. It sounds odd, as most of us want to visualize ourselves excelling at a presentation and receiving accolades. But visualizing or thinking through our worst fears actually allows them to be fully seen and heard. Our fears have not often had the opportunity to be witnessed, as we are too focused on denying them or living in continual, abstract fear.

"Playing the tape forward" allows us to ground our fear in reality. By doing this, Maurice realized the unlikelihood of his worst fears coming to pass, but he also felt prepared for any scenario. His fear had spoken, and once it was able to be heard, it abated.

This tool works for anyone, even those with panic and anxiety disorders. (In fact, panic attacks often occur because of abstract fear, and grounding the fear this way helps considerably.) If you are particularly prone to panic or anxiety, this may be a tool you wish to work on with others first. That way you can talk through your fears with another person listening, which brings even more light to the situation.

By playing out potential scenarios, we can accept all of the eventualities and uncertain circumstances that are a natural part of our lives. We can come more into the present, realizing that we are grasping towards the future in a way that is not helpful. We have no control over the future. However, we do have control over the present, in which we make decisions that pave the way to our future. By taking back our fear-based projections into the future, we can live fuller and more present lives.

Part 3
Collective Shadows

Give a man a mask and he will tell you the truth.

Oscar Wilde

We have all the layers within us, figures which are not as modern as consciousness; parts of us are in the Middle Ages, parts in antiquity, and parts naked on the trees.

Marie-Louise von Franz

Chapter 12

Archetypal Figures

*W*hile by no means a comprehensive list, this section is intended to help us identity the archetypal figures that we are playing out in our lives. Seeing the broader roles that we identify with can help us understand the stories and impulses behind them. We can then also consider how to choose which roles to play, as our tendency is to continue living out our stories, even when they no longer benefit us.

This section is composed of both "classical" and more modern conceptualizations of archetypal figures. While utilizing this section, first note which archetypes you identify with. Then, note what their narrative is and how their script plays out in your life. For example, the archetype of "martyr" is accompanied by a specific belief pattern, behavior tendencies, and script.

Bring your attention to the archetypes you notice in the people around you. The "office gossip" may not be listed below, but she is a common archetypal figure in many of our work environments. She lives out that role and she also expects you to receive her role in a specific way. She may place you in the role of "listener" or "active participant" or even "target." When we notice our interrelating roles and how our archetypal figures play out in the world, we can gain deeper understanding of our play—as well as the plays that we have been cast in.

It is also interesting to note which archetypal figures that you cannot identify with at all. We carry all archetypes within ourselves. Some may be more dominant than others, even when we have wholly reclaimed our shadow. However, the absence of an archetype within us suggests an area of potential growth. Find someone who embodies that archetype and spend time with them. Or consider how that archetype could be "activated" within you; ask yourself what activities, beliefs, and patterns of thought might be preventing this archetype from expressing itself.

By retrieving all archetypes within ourselves, we not only reclaim our shadow but we also become more able to freely express to the world who we are as a unique individual. When we reclaim an opposing archetype—such as the strong man accepting his weakness, or the individualist accepting connection—the archetypes we identify with most strongly can become even healthier.

What you will notice about archetypal figures is that they all have strengths and weaknesses. No archetype is singularly negative or positive. We can embody an archetype fully and become aware of its tendencies. That creates balance: our inner explorer can find peace at home and our inner physician can welcome outside advice.

The Explorer

Interested and curious, the Explorer seeks to find new terrain, both in the outer and inner worlds. Always striving and continually finding new frontiers, the Explorer may present as a world traveler, eager to visit the next country on their list. The inner Explorer may be passionate about discovering new frontiers within themselves. Other Explorers achieve breakthroughs or find new terrain in science, art, technology, and other fields. The Explorer's enthusiasm and excitement might also come with a type of restlessness in familiar territory.

To temper the Explorer, embrace the joy of simple things, being rather than doing, and settling into steady routines. This can be the final frontier that they need to explore.

The Warrior

Representing strength and leadership, the Warrior is on the frontline of the battle. Their excitement comes from beating their enemies, the thrill of conflict, and standing up for causes. The soldier, doctor, protester, and social worker commonly embody this archetype. Other Warriors are those who have fought valiantly against trauma and health issues within themselves.

When fighting for larger causes, daily life can become mundane. Peace after wartime can leave the Warrior unsettled and unsure of themselves. To rest after battle, and to release the hypervigilance that is required during war, is the ultimate battle of the Warrior.

The Observer

With a knack for seeing situations clearly, the Observer's keen insights into people and how the world works make them excellent writers, creatives, therapists, and philosophers.

The Observer is never a part of the story, and so they may feel separate, on the sidelines of their own life as well as of life in general. Releasing their beliefs and the trauma of feeling separate and Other makes the Observer into an active participant in their own lives, while retaining their valuable skills.

The Romantic

The Romantic sees life as an adventure, filled with love, joy, and passion. They paint the world with broad strokes and are enthusiastic about the next possibility on the horizon. They see the beauty of the world in a way that makes people naturally gravitate towards them and feel special in their presence. The Romantic excels at torrid love affairs and memorable outings, and they are full of an enthusiasm that is contagious.

For the Romantic, the real world can quickly become a disappointment. The trip or gathering they created isn't the picture they envisioned, and the person they fell in love with reveals themselves to be human (and more than just an object of their passion). The Romantic's excitement and devotion can be tempered by pragmatism, planning, and paying attention to details. The Romantic can retain their inner passion while also grounding their enthusiasm in reality.

The Martyr

Classically, the Martyr sacrificed himself for a much greater cause: the divine or humanity. How the Martyr plays out in our daily lives is often an individual sacrifice to a smaller cause, such as a workplace or a family. The mother and the employee are classic Martyrs, who sacrifice their own health, well-being, and identity to care for others. Many people in "helping" careers, such as nurses, massage therapists, farmers, and customer service representatives also fit this role by sacrificing their bodies to take care of others.

Resentment quickly piles up for the Martyr, who is rightfully exhausted by the demands that others place onto them. With their gas tank running on empty, they are asked to give more. By listening to this resentment, the Martyr can recognize that it stems from offering too much of themselves and receiving too little in return.

To care for themselves so that they can be of service to others is a necessary undertaking for the Martyr. To have boundaries and to step out of the role of Martyr requires evaluating what the Martyr gets out of this role in the first place. Someone dominantly playing the role of Martyr has difficulty giving it up, especially if it means changing their world view to one in which they can receive and others can be of service to them. To let go of sacrificing oneself takes practice, as does the ability to ask for personal needs and wants to be fulfilled.

The Physician

The Physician occupies a role of authority, and they often step into this role either out of a sincere desire to help others or to attain the societal acclaim and status it provides. While the Physician can readily be embodied by medical doctors, we all have friends, family members, and others in "helping" professions who play out this archetype. Even those we look up to, such as celebrities and gurus, can take on this role of authority.

We project our inner wisdom and body consciousness onto the Physician. They tell us what to eat, how to be healthy, and how to thrive as individuals in body, mind, and spirit. The Physician separates themselves from the "common person" by taking on this role: they know more and therefore are a "superior" human being in their expertise.

When we accept the limits of our knowledge, we can bring the inner Physician into balance. We do not have all the answers, no matter how much we have studied or practiced.

For many actual Physicians, such as surgeons, there is a certain degree of dehumanization that needs to occur for them to function. However, the Physician can permanently remain cold and removed from their own humanity and the humanity of others. Connecting empathetically with others allows the Physician to step down from their pedestal and recognize that the world is filled with people who all offer different types of knowledge and authority.

The Mediator (Peacekeeper or Diplomat)

To keep our own true thoughts and emotions at bay in order to calmly and neutrally mitigate a situation is the superpower of the Mediator. Our inner diplomat knows the right words to create peace, soothe animosity, heal discord, and facilitate agreement between two or more parties.

This role is assumed by lawyers, directors, and counselors. However, in a family or a social circle there is often one person who takes on this role. This is the person that all others come to for a sane and measured assessment of a situation.

While mediation is an essential skill, the peacekeeper or diplomat can sacrifice their own feelings to serve this role. They fear being too much: too loud, emotional, dramatic, or irrational. The Mediator needs spontaneity and an outlet to express their true thoughts to balance this role. By learning to show emotion rather than remaining neutral, the diplomat can use their essential skill but not let it be the only feature of their personality.

The Fundamentalist

We all have an inner Fundamentalist, a part of ourselves that holds on to a specific belief or understanding of reality that is so fixed that it overshadows our entire world view. This can include political, religious, and spiritual views, but it also can pertain to diet and lifestyle. There is no greater Fundamentalist than a vegetarian who looks down on anyone who eats meat (or who will not hear any viewpoint originating from someone whose diet differs from their own). Similarly, there is no greater Fundamentalist than a person who insists that they need to eat meat with every meal.

We can see our inner Fundamentalist through who and what we hate or separate ourselves from. If we view the world in terms of this versus that, or ourselves versus another person or group, our inner Fundamentalist is creating false divisions and a skewed version of reality.

The inner Fundamentalist can recognize their passion for specific ideologies and realize that their lifestyle choices may be perfect for themselves, but they do not need to create hatred or moral outrage toward those who do not ascribe to their specific dogmas. This archetype creates massive shadows, with the Fundamentalist hating the Other.

By focusing instead on what brings happiness, purpose, and meaning into their own lives, the Fundamentalist can stop creating such strict divides in reality and within themselves. It is exhausting to continually hate others who do not believe, behave, or look like ourselves. The Fundamentalist can examine this hatred and address their own massive shadow of self-hatred and ignorance, if they are willing to look.

The Tyrant

Our inner Tyrant is typically our inner toddler. He wants things now, and in a specific way, or otherwise there will be hell to pay. There is a desire within each of us for instant gratification, for others to satisfy our primary wants and needs.

The Tyrant rules over others as a form of control. No one else can express their thoughts or ideas unless they are in line with the Tyrant. In other situations, the Tyrant will take on thoughts and ideas of others as if they are their own. They lack the capacity to acknowledge others, and must be the center of attention.

This role is often taken on by bosses, but it is also seen quite regularly in relationships. The Tyrant will likely find a partner with a passive, agreeable personality (who likely grew up in a home with a similar Tyrant figure) who will step on eggshells to avoid incurring their wrath. The partner's life will revolve around the Tyrant and their needs and desires.

We all have an inner Tyrant, and in most of us, it comes out when we have an unfulfilled need or want. Those who express the Tyrant role often need to look at their inner toddler, or their desire for control and safety. Too often, the Tyrant does not want to see this role, because underneath it lies fear, trauma, and feelings of powerlessness.

For one to step out of this dominant role, these difficult aspects need to be confronted. One must explore the basic selfishness and unhappiness that underlies this archetypal figure. The Tyrant eventually realizes that they would be happier in their life without controlling others; they would feel better if they were in some way of service to others instead.

The Addict

The Addict is trapped in a cycle of misery and non-being. Addiction is the worst form of self-sabotage; each time the drug or habit is used it is a kind of self-murder. In addiction, time stops; reality is set aside while the Addict enters a liminal space—a cocoon of non-being in which the person no longer worries about the world or its stressors.

At its most basic impulse, the Addict is embodying the pleasure principle in a misguided way. Following their instinctive drive to seek pleasure and avoid pain they have found a shortcut to bliss, but it comes at a high cost: money, time, and life force.

It is typical for our inner Addict to recognize itself and to lament its addictions. They recognize the cycle of addiction and contemplate how to get out of it. Far too often, the contemplation phase fails to lead to action. Each time they act out the addiction, they question how to leave the cycle; yet every time they abstain, they wonder when they can get their next fix.

While it is common to think of heroin, alcohol, or other drugs when talking about addiction, we can become addicted to so many things: gaming, shopping, sex, sugar, social media, work.

We may dismiss "lesser" addictions because we think of an Addict as an alcoholic or heavy drug user who requires hospitalization or rehabilitation to recover. Thus we ignore our addiction, though it creates the same cycle of avoiding life by seeking a shortcut to pleasure. We all have an inner Addict for whom "one is too many, and a thousand is never enough."

The opposite of addiction is stepping back into time (the present moment) and actively engaging with our lives. When the Addict becomes free from addiction being the primary focus of their life, the backlogged emotions and the life gone unlived come front and center. By building emotional intelligence and healthy coping mechanisms over time, the Addict can learn to step out of the cocoon they have created for themselves and live their lives again. The Addict can build hobbies, friendships, and relationships outside of addiction, and find more fulfillment in the basic responsibilities of adulthood. By fully initiating into an adulthood that they were previously not willing to step into, the Addict can realize that life can be fulfilling. Over time, the Addict can realize to what extent their addictions have held them back, and reconnect to the world and to their own potential.

Connecting to ourselves and to others can allow the Addict to primarily exist in the physical body and to engage in healthy escapism, rather than addiction. Healthy escapism is consciously chosen, moderate by nature, and creates expansive feelings like wonder, curiosity, and a feeling of freedom. Going on a hike or out into nature, exercise, concerts and theatre, social events, reading, trying new foods, and volunteering can all foster healthy escapism as well as connection.

The Depressive

The Depressive is stuck in a dark void from which they cannot escape. Life itself becomes a struggle, and the chores and demands of life become Herculean tasks, rather than simple pursuits. For the Depressive, life is seen through the lens of melancholy and wrongness. The light of goodness and hope becomes dim or absent entirely.

The Depressive can be an insightful and conscious realist who perceives reality in a way that most people block out. The chaos and decay of the world is depressing, and to see the world clearly is understandably troubling. We so often block out the nature of people by assigning a sort of moral goodness to them without recognizing that people so rarely achieve that goodness. The Depressive becomes immersed in recognizing the ambiguity and negativity of the human condition, and the false concept of the superior, moral human.

For the Depressive, life has lost meaning. Julia Kristeva wrote, "When meaning shatters, nothing else in life matters." This eloquently describes the Depressive's attitude towards life.

Healing begins when they recognize the absurdity of existence, and see how we are conferred meaning and purpose in ways that do not benefit us as individuals. To purchase material items or work more for the gain of our employer does not ultimately provide the type of meaning the individual soul is looking for. The Depressive—seeing the meaninglessness of what society and advertisements offer them as meaning—has the opportunity to move towards an existence in which meaning and purpose come from within. When we seek individual purpose, the darkest aspects of the self can turn into the blinding light of radiance.

The inner Depressive does not need to be cajoled into this light or bullied into being something other than what they are. They require understanding and validation in their quest for meaning, and assistance in finding it. Many Depressives rightfully feel as if their lives are terrible or soulless—because they are. We all have times in our lives when we have every right to feel depressed.

Grounding our Depressive into the present moment, rather than the abstract, allows the Depressive to greet life as it is, and to move through the grief of life not being what we were promised it would be.

The Depressive seeks to remain in the realms of idealism, spirituality, and philosophical intellectualism, rather than face a more concrete daily reality. It is, however, in the quiet, simple moments of life that we find purpose and meaning. Ernest Hemingway referred to these as "irrevocable moments"—moments in time similar to a single photo, in which we feel a sense of perfection and finality. These moments stay with us; they are what life is composed of. A quick laugh with a friend, a perfect Christmas opening of a present, a cat jumping on our lap and purring, a feeling of love that permeates a family dinner. The love we receive through connection offers us a sense of perfection; this can't happen if we are removed from our bodies and our lives.

Hemingway also wrote: "Every man's life ends the same way. It is only the details of how he lived and how he died that distinguish one man from another."

Washing the dishes, doing laundry, the seemingly trivial interactions that compose our days—these are the stuff of life. When we live our lives fully, we can move out of existential misery and into finding meaning and purpose right where we are. Even the changes that come with life—chaos, uncertainty, life and death—are what provide us with the stories of survival, hope, and meaning that remain with us as we get older and look back at our lives.

When we were younger we were promised many lovely myths that do not pan out in our adult reality. Sometimes we work hard and that just means more work. If we are kind to the world it is not necessarily kind back to us. We hold on to our childhood naivety because it is incredibly nice to think of the world being a place of compassion and comfort. To come into maturity is to recognize that the promises we were offered as children were false. This understanding comes with immense grief.

We can move through the grief, the injustice, and the moral myths into a clear, adult perspective on reality. We can learn to stand in reality just as it is. Beyond the despair we learn to choose our actions and our motivations, without the falseness of morality and without the naivety that we once had. For example, we can choose to be a kind person, not because we are afraid of being immoral, or because of our desire to be seen a certain way by others, but because we know that the world is filled with suffering. We have a choice whether to create more suffering or not in this world. The journey of the Depressive takes us to a vantage point where we can accept the suffering we were once so immersed in. We simply view it as the human condition, part of the natural cycles of human life.

The Fool (Jester, Comedian or Clown)

The Fool uses sarcasm or humor to deflect their inner pain. Their smile masks an inner despair and belief that if they were not the clown, they would not receive approval. Nobody would like them if they were simply themselves.

The Jester can learn to remove their mask and set aside their shielding humor and start to authentically express themselves. The Comedian inhabits a unique role in this world in that they can test boundaries, point out truths, and be unique in their way of being. This may include using humor or sarcasm, but these are no longer ways of hiding their inner pain, they will be a genuine expression of the self.

The Individualist

The Individualist is frequently someone who carries the weight of Western philosophy on their shoulders, like Atlas condemned to holding up the sky. Western culture is based on rugged individualism, and our inner Individualist desires to be seen for their uniqueness and their inherent specialness. We are frequently taught to assume the responsibilities of adulthood at too early an age, and so the hyper-individualist is someone who was taught by parents that they could not rely on others. In learning this, they decided to take care of everything themselves, since they could no longer count on their parents—and by association the world—to take care of them.

We all have a rugged Individualist within us, as we live in a culture in which we are expected to work, and to perform beyond our physical and mental capacities. Beliefs like "I could have it all if I only tried hard enough" are imprinted into us at an early age, and so we view our successes and our failures as the measure of our goodness. If we were to see that we fail or thrive based on larger forces than our individual selves, we could move out of this false equivalency.

In healing, it is important to recognize that feelings of abandonment, rejection, loneliness, and overwhelming emotion are too much for an individual to contend with alone. Our aloneness and the rejected parts of ourselves require another individual, or community, that offers space and acceptance. We can do tremendous work on our own, but there are times to reach out for support. There is no need to work through years of suffering alone when another individual can help us lift that heaviness.

Whether we see it or not, we are a member of many communities: the human race, the place where we live or grew up, our culture, and other groups. We can recognize that in addition to individual happiness, family and social connectivity offer great meaning and purpose to our lives.

The Collectivist

The Collectivist recognizes the need for community and how we thrive in our interconnectivity. Work, healing, and social change can be achieved much more readily in groups rather than through an individual. The Collectivist is often a romantic, believing that bygone eras and tribal cultures are preferable to the modern age. Yet they might ignore the individualistic nature of the modern world and be hypocritical in their denouncement of individual notions of self. In collectivist cultures, there is a yearning for individuality, and a desire to achieve for the self, rather than the collective.

In individualistic cultures, there is a yearning for the collective. If we recognize that we require both individual and collective, the pendulum can stop swinging between individualism and collectivism. Then we can take the best of both worlds, and recognize that our individual self and its wants, desires, and needs are also important. Our work on an individual level, if done well, is of service to the collective.

The Common Person

The Common Person is a neutral archetype. They are a bit of a trope, an "every person" who is a bit of a blank slate. They are appealing but slightly bland, with intellect, talent, or aptitude neither above nor below average.

This type of person tends to fade into the background and often plays a supporting character in their own story. To develop themselves and their story to the extent that they become an individual would mean stepping into the limelight.

In archetypal work, the Common Person offers us an understanding that we all carry neutral parts within us. We do not always need to have a goal, a story, or a purpose, nor do we need to be the center of the universe. In recognizing this, we can attend to the simple things of life, and realize the joy and purpose in simply being human.

Chapter 13

Animus and Anima

*W*e each contain both masculine and feminine polarities within ourselves. Instead of considering these to be strictly "male" or "female," we can view them as archetypal understandings of the Self on a masculine to feminine continuum. To come into contact with all aspects of our continuum—masculine to feminine and everything in between—is the objective of shadow work.

To complete this task we do not need to change our tendencies or self-expressions. We can be fully strong and dominant in our masculine tendencies while enjoying knitting as a hobby. We can be fully dominant in our feminine tendencies and know how to barbecue ribs or repair a toilet. We can even be fluid, or androgynous, and decide based on the day, or the occasion, which parts of the continuum we want to express.

Integrating our masculine and feminine polarities allows us to consciously choose who we are and what we enjoy, rather than resisting or hating any aspect of ourselves. Once we become comfortable with our full continuum, from masculine to feminine, we no longer judge or despise others for their choices. When we hate either the masculine or feminine archetype, we hate half of ourselves.

The archetype that expresses the universal feminine characteristics is called the *anima;* the archetype that expresses the universal masculine characteristics is called the *animus.* Every male has an inner anima, and every female has an inner animus. Intersex or more androgynous individuals may have access to both their inner animus and anima. On the other hand, they may also have difficulty exploring or expressing the continuum of masculine to feminine due to fear or past trauma.

We all have a *persona*, or a public face that we present to the world. We can actually have many personas, such as a "work" persona and a "home" persona. It is also common for people to have an "online" or "social media" persona. This persona may closely resemble the authentic self, or it may create a significant divide between our authentic self and that persona.

Masks are a protective mechanism. They help us feel safe and secure because we do not need to show our "real face" to the world. Showing our authentic self to others creates vulnerability. Some individuals must wear a mask in order to be gainfully employed or to fit in at school or in social circles. We all wear a mask in some small or large way to hide our true feelings. This can be entirely appropriate; for example, we may be in a cycle of grief and want to avoid sobbing in a crowded restaurant. Yet we may wear a mask to hide ourselves so completely that we lose access to any part of who we truly are. To find ourselves, and to remove the mask, is the greatest work we can do.

We can consciously learn how to put on and take off masks. The term "persona" derives from the Latin term for masks worn by ancient Roman actors. Learning to work with physical masks lets us consciously choose a persona; we can fully embody an emotion or a part of ourselves that we would not otherwise be able to. With a physical mask, we can fully inhabit a role that is quite different than who we consider ourselves to be. This can break taboos and allow us to fully access the darker aspects of our shadow.

Learning to consciously play with masks—through working with physical masks, makeup, or dress—helps us take control of how we present ourselves to the world. We can also energetically decide how we will act for a specific occasion, putting on a "mask" of personality or confidence. This places us in a seat of power. We most often use masks unconsciously as a defense mechanism, and it is a much different reality when we decide what mask we will wear.

Animus and Anima

Generally, masculine consciousness is binary—this versus that—while the feminine expresses itself in liminal spaces—what is in between.

The feminine represents the body, emotions, intuition, chaos, and also the essential simplicity of being. Though it seems paradoxical, the feminine contains both rage and stillness, non-doing and frenzy. The mind will never be able to fully categorize the feminine polarity because it is continually creating and recreating itself. It contains the very power of creation, and in such a way, represents the primordial movement from death to rebirth, from one polarity to the next.

In modern culture we tend to revere the "light" feminine, but the dark is still often dismissed and hated. Marion Woodman referred to self-realization as "putting the head on the body" and by this she meant pairing the feminine (the body) with all of its emotionality, feeling, instincts, and intuitions, with the head (the thinking, order-creating polarity).

We often separate our animus and anima, as they are the most basic divisions of our shadow. They represent darkness and light, yin and yang. When we understand that these two polarities can work together, our basic divides can be healed. The full power of intuition, feeling, and creative flow can arise through the body and be sorted by the head so that it can decide on appropriate action.

The anima represents the entirety of the unconscious. We deeply fear it because it is the unknown: uncertainty, death, and the Earth. If we contact our anima, we move beyond the head and delve into the body. We have cut off our bodies and have learned to shame, disregard, and repress our physical selves. If we learn to "feel," we begin to gain access to our anima.

It is only by exploring our darkness that we can gain full access to our light. Without connection to our body, our head thinks itself into a tailspin. The body is the present moment, and without it we are disassociated, nothing but abstract thoughts and logic without anything to ground into.

If we consider the primal force of the anima arising within us to be a vast ocean, then the animus is the shore of that ocean. It contains the ocean and gives it direction, action, and order. If the entirety of our subconscious were to arise in us without such a boundary, we would be lost in an ocean of feeling. We require tools, a map, and an understanding of what is going on within to find ourselves again.

The animus is the military-like precision and discipline that offers us routine. It also represents achievement, protection, and strength. Our anima certainly has strength, but masculine strength is the bamboo that can weather a significant storm—even in the worst of storms, bamboo bends, rather than breaks.

Placing the Head on the Body

To place the head on the body is to embody and connect with both polarities and the continuum in between. Consider which parts of yourself are uncomfortable with the feminine, masculine, or androgynous parts of this continuum and find ways of exploring them.

If you are fully stable in your masculinity, then trying on a dress, being nurturing, or allowing yourself to feel will not create insecurity. Similarly, if you are fully stable in your femininity, then doing home improvements, wearing a suit, creating a schedule, or converting ideas into action will not create insecurity. While these are incredibly simplistic ideas, the point is to consider your personal barriers and to explore them.

One of the most taboo-breaking ways to become embodied, to access the feminine, is to learn about sexuality. Learn what the genitals look like and how they work for both men and women. Explore the different ways that you can experience pleasure or offer pleasure to another. The shame we feel in Western culture around sexuality is for a reason—we are uneducated purposefully. Our sexuality is the home of our body, a way to access our individual power and pleasure. By learning about our bodies and the bodies of others, we can move away from shame and hatred into seeing and experiencing the magnificence of human physiology.

In both men and women, the anima is largely unexplored, containing the largest aspect of our shadow. To learn how to be, rather than do, is quite the task for the modern individual. Being okay with silence and stillness, without looking at phones or getting caught in the millions of distractions of modern life, can bring us into contact with our anima.

Our bodies love to sing, dance, play, and feel. We have become afraid of feeling because we have learned that emotionality is wrong, or because we experience the emotions that we do feel as overwhelming or stressful. We confuse past trauma for feeling, and so we do not understand that our emotions, when expressed healthfully through us, can feel really good. If we recognize that we never received an education in emotion (in the way we were taught mathematics, for example) we can release our shame and learn to become emotionally intelligent creatures. We can begin to sit with our emotions and hear their messages.

When we come more into our bodies, we listen to our intuition and instincts. There is a reason why the hair stands up on the back of our neck, or why we have a concern (without logical reason) about our new neighbor. When we learn to listen to our emotions, they provide a gateway to our instincts. We can move beyond the childhood traumas of being told that we were wrong, and the cultural traumas of being told that we should rely on logic alone. When our instincts and feelings arise, we listen to them, and then we logically decide what to do next. This is how we pair the head with the body.

The Unrevered Masculine

Societally and personally, we inhabit the masculine much more than we do the feminine. Historically, when women entered the workplace, they understood that they needed to express their masculinity to fit in. The parameters for "normality" in workplace and society had already been set by a select few, and so the feminine aspects of women retreated into the background.

All Others (including women and people of color) wore a mask of masculinity until we collectively began changing. This is because historically anyone other than the white male was seen as Other, and thus, as part of the energetic feminine polarity. While we are still living out the shadows of this, we also are significantly shifting our expressions of the masculine and feminine polarities in our world and our workplaces.

Individually and collectively we recognize when something is not working long before we act on it. Basically, we have a period of contemplation before we take any type of action. The actions we often first take collectively are stumbling steps, rather than solid ones. We also often swing to the other side of the pendulum; we overcorrect and must then seek balance.

What this means in the modern world is that we have a genuine need to revere the masculine. We are currently suffering from the child or adolescent male within each of us being uninitiated into healthy adult masculinity. The adolescent male is unsure in his sexuality as well as his place in society; he has not learned to express any emotions other than anger and frustration. The masculine left unexpressed turns to violence and hatred of the feminine. It is an oppressive force, rather than a protective force. By revering the adult masculine, we can develop resiliency, stability, and healthy expressions of sexuality.

However, this should be accompanied by the understanding that the masculine expresses in each and every one of us. We so often project the masculine onto another and do not claim it within ourselves. It is incredibly common for women who come to my practice to complain about having to take on both feminine and masculine roles in their heterosexual relationships, while the man gets to remain a child. If we were to view this situation as unfortunate and recognize that it may not be healthy or ideal for the inner masculine to be stuck in perennial childhood, then we can see the wounded masculine for what it is.

It is surprising that, when offered the opportunity, many of us have an inner masculine that desires to step up, to act boldly, and to protect. The wounded masculine within each of us can recognize itself and come out of the cocoon of childhood. It may need to be coaxed, as the child parts of ourselves feel comfortable with little responsibility. However, understanding how little meaning and purpose this childlike existence offers to the inner masculine can allow it to grow up.

We can honor the healthy masculine by seeing it and appreciating it in our daily lives. There are several archetypal figures of the masculine, among them the Magician and the Wild Man.

The Magician represents our cognitive faculties and can equally be viewed as the archetypal sage. He is a powerful figure, one who is wise not only in the material realms (and logic) but also in philosophical, artistic, and more magical worlds. How we wield our power shows our character. Power is the ability to make conscious choices, and our inner Magician can choose how to behave and what decisions to make.

Our inner Wild Man is passionate, strong, and aligned with his most basic instincts. He is at home in nature. This is frequently our inner shadow male, the masculine part that we seek to dismiss—it would not be civilized to pillage a neighboring town. Our inner Wild Man does not need to rape or create harm, nor conversely to be tamed or obedient. There is a real need for all of us to seek out nature, to learn how to live off the land, and to allow the aggressive parts of our personality to arise safely (and in a way that will not harm others). Learning basic nature or survival skills, hiking or camping in the wilderness, or engaging in healthy competition will bring out our inner Wild Man.

The Absent Masculine

The absent masculine is an archetype that expresses with our collective inability to see the masculine as nurturing and concerned with domestic matters, including childcare. We assume that the masculine will be "absent" from the lives of our children, only offering financial contributions. When some people see the masculine participating in the household or in the lives of children, they respond with fear and confusion.

Peter describes an experience he had at the park with his daughter. He understands from the looks of others parents, and from past experiences, that he should not interact with any of the other children. He feels the projections of fear and a feeling of shame, as if he were a predator, in their glances.

His daughter is enjoying herself in the park and when she comes up to him, a woman he doesn't know walks up. She looks at his daughter and asks her, "Is this your father? Do you feel safe?" She then looks at him disapprovingly. She is about to pick up her phone to record or photograph him when he tells his daughter it is time to leave. They go home, and he now feels hesitant about visiting that park again.

Each of us needs to understand this fear so that we can consider our projections onto the masculine. It impacts our personal lives, but collectively it is creating a generation of men who are in liminal space: they desire emotional intimacy and feeling, they want to access their inner anima. But they are subjected to so many unhealthy projections by others that they cannot express themselves.

We still expect stoicism and childlike behavior from our inner masculine, and we project the dark shadows of violence, abuse, and sexuality onto it. To move beyond this is to recognize that we are all capable of such darkness, but to also take enough of our shadows back so that seeing a father taking his child to a park or doing something nurturing is normalized. That would be revolutionary. Our animus could fully grow up and take his rightful place in this modern world.

The Witch

There is a reason why so many women identify with the archetypal figure of the Witch. She is wholly herself, full of rage and magic, gifted with healing capacities and power. We cannot help but desire for her to arise within us.

She is totally unapologetic for what she wants, and she gets what she desires. She no longer represses her emotions, resents her place in life, or suffers quietly at the hands of the masculine. Instead, she is angry, whipped into a frenzy, freely getting back at those who have wronged her and freely emoting.

In most of our ancestral lines, the female has a legacy of abuse and lack of freedom. Without education, independence, and financial capacity we may be trapped, with our children, in unfortunate circumstances.

To be fully herself, despite the shadow of the abusive parts of the masculine, is the power of the Witch. Our inner witch has every reason to feel rage. The feminine has had its power stolen, and is continually dismissed, rejected, called "crazy," objectified, and hated. She is Other, and so can never fully find her footing in a world that is designed to oppress her.

By fully giving ourselves right to feel both our thwarted power and our rage, we can move beyond the "light" feminine archetype that requires us to be nice and continually obligated to others before attending to our own needs. We can learn what we want, what we need, and to fully validate the rage of our oppression and dismissal. All of us would benefit from embodying this dark feminine power and freeing ourselves from the thoughts and minds of others. It is not our role to fit in, but to stand out.

Cassandra

In Greek mythology, Cassandra was a priestess who uttered truth but was never believed. She was dismissed or ignored entirely. There is a part in all of us that identifies with this role, especially when we know on a visceral (or logical) level that what we are saying is completely true. To learn to speak our truth, despite the responses of others, without doubting or changing what we think, allows us to move out of righteous indignation into a state of calmly and clearly recognizing when those around us are simply idiots.

The Devouring Mother

It is typical for women to give up a sense of their own identity when raising children. They become the archetypal mother, and that can be their only role for quite some time. As her children grow up, the mother may regain her sense of individual identity and fulfill other roles.

For some women, this does not happen. This mother permanently infantilizes her children so that they will never have to encounter or deal with the "real world." She finishes their homework, picks out their clothes, and fiercely opposes or interferes with any burgeoning independence or individuality in the child. The Devouring Mother will hate any reminder of their children growing up or no longer needing them, including finding romantic partners.

This mother "devours" her children—mind, body, and spirit. They grow up feeling guilty for individuating; they fear moving out from under the mother's control. Many times, they do not grow up. They remain instead as stagnated children, their mother taking care of their every need.

Many children with Devouring Mothers need to take care of their mother emotionally. They are a mini therapist who fulfills their mother's needs and whims. This is a form of control, and the child wishing to drop this role is often met with contempt, abuse, shaming, or even threats of violence. By consciously recognizing this pattern and being willing to let go of these roles, both the Devouring Mother and the child can individuate. Through discovering who they are as individuals, healthy connection to one another can now happen, rather than an enmeshed relationship that does not allow either individual to thrive.

The Death Mother

The idealized picture of the mother is one of a woman who selflessly provides infinite love and compassion. We rarely consider the shadow side of the mother, in which the sheer difficulty of child-rearing, the energy and time required to fulfill this role, breeds resentment and hostility.

The Death Mother views her role as a mother with contempt, hatred, or disinterest. She feels the same way towards her child, who grows up knowing on some level that their mother wishes that they were never born. This creates immense fear as well as people-pleasing (or mother-pleasing) tendencies in the child, who feels helpless to change the household environment, no matter how "good" they are.

Another variation of the Death Mother is a woman who enacts her own fantasies through her child. If the mother could not play soccer while growing up, her child will now play soccer. The child becomes an extension of the mother, rather than their own person, living out the "dead" mother's unlived childhood dreams.

With this archetype, it is important to understand that both mother and children lose energy and power in this dynamic. Many women feel forced to have children, or they fail to receive adequate sexual education. This results in cycles of animosity, repressed anger, energetic depletion, and loss of bodily autonomy.

The mother "dies" because a part of her can barely repress the rage at having to fulfill this role. The child then "dies" under the icy stare of the mother, losing vitality and eventually becoming depressed by the knowledge that their mother would on some level prefer that they did not exist.

We present motherhood as a time of infinite joy. While most women understand that pregnancy and child-rearing will be difficult, the actual physical and emotional toll still surprises many of us. By allowing our true feelings to arise regarding women and the role of "mother," this role can come out of the shadows and into the light. All parents, no matter how healthy and loving, experience moments of unhappiness, despair, and even regret in terms of their children. Accepting those feelings as normal, or seeking help for extreme emotions, can make all the difference, both individually and collectively.

Seeing Projections onto Our Spouse

We often struggle to see our projections onto those who are closest to us. This is why we start shadow work by looking at those who we are not so intertwined with or emotionally attached to. However, we place the most divisive parts of our shadow onto our spouse or partner. If we are willing to look, we can see our disowned animus or anima in the other; these are the parts of ourselves that we have the hardest time reclaiming.

Until we fully integrate our inner masculine and feminine, we split ourselves in two. Our animus or anima lives within our partner, unrecognized until we become conscious of the split. If we are brave enough to withdraw our projections from our spouse, we face the darkest aspects of our shadow. We see our unrealized masculinity, femininity, or androgyny. We see the skills and talents and potential that we have neglected.

At the same time, we peer into a mirror of our own self-hatred. What couples fight about, the things we mutter under our breath, what most bothers us in the other, all reveal inner divisions within the self. These divisions are primary and substantive; they are the very things that prevent us from becoming more self-realized.

When we see our shadow in our spouse, and thereby reclaim it, we heal on a personal level. This also engenders dynamic shifts in the relationship. Arguments can cease, as both partners take back the roles that they have placed on each other. When we withdraw the projections, true intimacy can occur. We can see and love our spouse or partner for who they are, rather than through the roles we have projected onto them.

Chapter 14

Loops

*H*ave you ever noticed yourself engaging in the same conversation again and again? Or perhaps the same conflict, just with an endless rotation of names and faces? Sometimes it may be the same conflict and conversation with the same person, like grocery shopping with a spouse or going to your parents' house for a holiday dinner.

Maybe you are even aware of how you feel fifteen years old again when you visit your parents. Or you may feel exhausted by the repetitive patterns that dominate your life. There is a reason for all of this. We often repeat our scripts without recognizing that there can be resolution. By changing the script and changing our role we can find a pathway beyond the play.

The first step in shifting our role is to notice how we repeat certain actions, behaviors, and words. We may start to notice how many times we have met someone who is acting out the same role. For example, we may encounter the same woman again and again—just with another face and name—who has angered us, stolen from us, or engaged in slander, gossip, and animosity.

We cannot control such a woman. She has her own reasons, her own pain, for being who she is.

But there is a reason for the loop. There is a reason for your reactivity, perhaps a reason for you to be proven right about how women act. Or perhaps how women who vaguely remind you of your mother behave. Once the loop is broken, this woman or this type of woman, will still exist in your world. However, your reactivity, role, and script with her will have changed. She will no longer be a central role that you have cast . . . and that makes all the difference.

Loops are the actions, scenarios, thoughts, and belief systems that we experience repeatedly. They constitute our "programming" and how we filter reality. By understanding loops, by noticing them, and by breaking them apart, we can move beyond them. We then experience reality more as it is, rather than through our programming.

A common type of loop is a repetitive behavior that arises out of trauma. Something within us seeks closure, and so we recreate the original trauma again and again, casting the same roles (often just with different faces and names) hoping to find resolution and healing. Ultimately, healing comes from the traumatized aspects of ourselves being properly seen, heard, and nurtured.

We also have behavioral loops that follow a specific routine that creates harm, exhaustion, or rigidity within us. These are loops in which steps occur in the same order established over time —A happens before B and then on to C and D.

Looping can also occur through language and speech. Speech loops involve us repeating the same phrases and opinions to ourselves and others. A common way that people do this is by offering advice to other people that is actually more applicable to themselves. Another way to notice these loops is to observe how people tear others down; they typically fixate on a particular subject in order to induce shame, to gossip, or to express hate, always using the same language.

We also employ repetitive speech loops when we do not fully understand the meanings of the words or phrases we are using. Inwardly this may be because there is a desire to understand them. Put more simply, we have found a new word or phrase that feels important, and that has perhaps impacted us on a deep level, but we don't truly understand it yet, so we repeat it until we do.

Repetitive words and phrases are also very much used to program us. By paying attention to the current phrases of the day and how often they are repeated in advertising, news and media, we see what is being "sold" to us. By recognizing these repeating phrases and words, we can question what type of reality is being woven into our collective and personal webs. We can then understand deeper layers of reality, how large corporations and groups may seek to manipulate our reality, and how they create their own language for their own purposes.

We also have biologically based loops, or survival loops. Our ancestral DNA contains memories of being cast out, chased, harmed, or threatened. We needed to enact certain behaviors to survive. In the modern world, these behavioral loops and thoughts rarely make sense. For example, in present-day reality, being cast out of our friend group may be a difficult experience for us. In the not-too-distant past, however, being cast out of our tribe meant death. We respond in the modern day with the fear of death being a possibility after being kicked out of a group, even though it no longer makes sense for our response to such a situation to be so severe.

Understanding Loops

The first thing to understand about loops is that they are comfortable and even pleasurable. We have a vested interest in keeping our loops. They express who we consider ourselves to be and what we view as the basic "stuff" of reality. What we consider to be our personality is often just a set of tightly held wounds. Our preferences and ways of being arise due to trauma. Our stories keep us as we are, and cause us to see others through a distorted lens or role.

Our past trauma creates barriers to experiencing reality. The beliefs that arise out of trauma, the choices we make at the time of trauma, and the survival mechanisms that we enact as a result of trauma, are all a part of the loop.

The neurons that fire together, wire together.

Donald Hebb

Our brains develop tracts, many of which originate in early childhood or even *in utero*. Our minds filter the information that they receive. The mind rejects anything that does not fit into what it believes to be reality. As we move through our lives, we stop using anything beyond the pathways that have already been set up. To put it simply, why should our brain use a county road when a super-highway is already in place?

Except that super-highway filters reality for us in a very specific way. That super-highway may repeat the message that we are worthless, for example. The more that we require specific beliefs to be true, and the more ingrained our tracts are, the more we will ignore anything outside of them. We will filter it out.

We filter many things out without conscious awareness—our natural filters cause us to engage with information that only fits with our loops. If we have tightly ingrained loops with a vested interest in being a certain way, we will more viciously defend our loops. We will deny anything that opposes or contradicts our loops.

We most commonly deny lived experiences because they are not our own. We do this out of ignorance, rather than malice, although someone denying the reality of another person's experiences is a form of intolerance and hatred.

The more rigid our loops are, the more defenses they need. We vilify and project onto the opposing messenger. We will tear them down, silence them, shame them, or even violate them emotionally or physically if we can. We will find some part of them that is human, and thus imperfect, to tear down, or we will lose ourselves in self-righteousness to create a battle with them, with ourselves emerging as victorious. We will do anything to prove the belief systems that have emerged out of pain and trauma correct. We will defend our "truth" and become emotionally reactive towards anything that opposes it.

We rarely have an authentic experience of someone or see them in their totality—we see only a fraction of who they are. Rather, we see what we project onto them, our need for them to be a specific way or to play a specific role. We may even have ingrained loops that we defend so fiercely that our relationship has no basis or grounding in any sort of connection with the person. This commonly happens with celebrities, teachers, and other public figures.

We should have a healthy laying of tracts that tell us that it is safe to connect, that we are human, that enable a healthy blueprint with a clear mind that creates safety, self-worth, curiosity, openness, and discernment. We can only pay attention to so much of reality (there is a lot of it!) and so we should naturally have filters, things that we pay attention to more than others. Even in healthy, non-traumatized states, we are still denying large parts of reality and creating filters to focus on our specific experiences of this world, simply because other frames of reference are not a part of our "world." While our baseline filters typically remain reasonably static, they also shift based on what we are concerned with or focusing on that day.

Have you ever read a book and realized that you didn't process any of the last few paragraphs? You may be tired or distracted, but it could also be due to your mind "blanking" to protect you from "digesting" information because your filters are not set up for you to do so. You are either not ready for that information yet or your defense mechanisms are preventing you from seeing that information and absorbing it.

For another example, have you ever had an experience in which you were discussing something important with someone, let's say a doctor, and suddenly you find that information everywhere? Your doctor was talking about thyroid conditions, and out of nowhere your friend starts talking about their thyroid, a news segment is featuring the thyroid, and you see a book at the library about thyroid issues.

All of a sudden, the word THYROID is everywhere. Your filters have reset to focus on this topic in your reality.

Our loops emerge out of survival mechanisms and remain ingrained as impulses that have emerged from our biological imperative—to keep us safe.

We do not create reality; we create restrictions to experiencing reality. Our mind determines our loops and then believes that they are defending us against "intruders" when it encounters anything that does not fit in with that programming.

On a cellular level, we believe that by reinforcing our loops, we are defending ourselves against death. Through human evolution over eons, we have learned that our organism needs to preserve and protect itself, and we define anything that is beyond "I" or "us" as invaders, foreigners, and enemies.

We feel that we must defend ourselves due to our fear of anything beyond our conceptions of reality.

These biological imperatives and survival mechanisms are wired into us. They are activated by situations in which our survival is threatened; they get further activated by trauma, with neurons continually sending the message of survival and how to achieve it.

The difficulty is that we create most of our loops in early childhood or *in utero*, and we react to them and live them out for the rest of our lives. These loops and their accompanying messages are still being replayed; we will continue living them out until they can be noticed and healed.

The Laying of Tracts

When we are young, our universe is quite small. We form the baseline of our reality at a young age, so our beliefs about the world and ourselves largely originate from that time.

We set most of our base tracts for how we filter reality when we are still at a pre-verbal stage. Do we feel that the universe is nurturing and supportive? Do we believe that we have a place in the world and that we belong? Do we believe that we are lovable? We frame the answers to these questions instinctively based on our primal experiences at an early age.

We believe that our environment and our caregivers are the universe and that everything that we experience is about us. We instinctively take responsibility and blame for our childhood circumstances. For survival purposes we must think of our parents as inherently good. Instead of realizing that our parents may lack the tools, emotional availability, or capacity to care for a child, we accept the blame for the circumstances; we might feel somehow wrong or we might alter our behavior considerably to survive.

We formulate our ideas about what the universe is and what it contains based on minimal contact with it. We carry these beliefs from childhood to adulthood and create a "base script" that organizes the entirety of our existence.

If our loops originate from severe trauma and pain, we lose sight of anything outside of it. People in a lot of pain, regardless of their age, cannot see outside of themselves enough to comprehend their impact on others, and cannot see qualities in people beyond their own projections, wants, and needs. This does not excuse their behavior, it is just helpful to acknowledge that someone drowning in pain cannot look beyond themselves.

People who are trapped in loops of great pain due to not receiving adequate nurturing as children remain locked in that child state: greedy, consuming, wanting of nurturing, as an infant deserves to be. They do not believe that their needs will be satisfied, having been shown that they cannot safely get what they want and need. As a result they believe that they must manipulate, violate, or harm others.

This is because they have a base script or an organizing reality centered around great want that was never satisfied, and they could not receive what was given at the age they wrote the script. They no longer believe that anyone could simply love them, offer them things, or relate to them in a healthy way. They do not believe that they are unconditionally lovable or worthy, but instead believe that they must relate transactionally in order to receive love and worth. This is a common pattern, and we do not need to admonish ourselves or others for it, but we can understand it as a "loop" that stems from a base need that was not met.

We may know that things are not working on some level, and that our loops come from pain rather than health. But our minds are too defended and caught in their programming to see our way out of it, or to even believe that there can be any other way of relating to others.

Completion of the Biological Process

We are hard-wired to desire completion, a satisfactory end to things. When we complete a process, we experience an initiation in which we pass through a doorway into a new way of being. This is the death-pause-rebirth process.

In trauma, we do not get what we truly need—love, acceptance, safety, and being seen and heard. We needed someone to help us process what happened so that we could understand that it wasn't our fault.

While it is easy to picture trauma as something large, like a sexual assault, picture something more mundane, like a pregnancy that was planned. The doctor was chosen, a timeline was established, the bags packed weeks prior. Now imagine that the baby is born three weeks early. The doctor is out of town, and the natural birth turns into a complicated cesarean section. Now the child is premature, and there are additional costs, days off work, extra time in the hospital.

As a result of this experience, the parents did not complete a biological process that they should have finished in a satisfactory manner. They did not get what they needed or wanted out of the situation. Yes, they ended up with a child, which is wonderful. But on a biological level, we are intended to pass through specific initiations to reach a satisfactory completion.

Some of our most common initiations are sexual encounters (especially our first, but also occasions like a wedding night), and passing through life stages—from infant to toddler, toddler to child, child to adolescent, adolescent to teen, teen to early adult, adult to elder, and elder to death. If any of these initiations do not "complete" like they should then we experience a feeling of being incomplete. Some of our energy stagnates at that age.

We require a sense of completion on all levels of self, including mental, emotional, physiological, psychological, and spiritual.

In daily life, this need for completion can cause issues in past relationships, careers, friendships, and educational opportunities. A lot of our energy and vitality gets stuck in events and life passages that are not "complete." Finding completion through inner child work allows us to move forward on many levels, to be reborn, and to bring more of our vitality into the present day.

Breaking Down Loops

Out of trauma come beliefs: beliefs about ourselves and beliefs about the nature of the world and other people. In a loop the wounded self replays the original circumstances or issues again and again accompanied by the same beliefs.

If we notice our chronic issues, or which scenarios repeat in our world again and again (for example, we keep making the same destructive choices, keep having the same relationship issues, etc.) we can begin to clearly see our own loops.

Then we can begin to break them down. For example, Edna has chronic migraines. Most of the time it is easiest to work backwards with loops as we already know the results all too well, in this case, the migraine.

- *But what happens before that?* She feels disassociated, like she is watching herself on TV.
- *What happens before that?* She feels anxious and panicked.
- *What happens before that?* She feels overwhelmed, as if the walls are closing in on her.
- *What happens before that?* She sees her "to-do" list with all the many tasks she must complete, and she starts to feel quite stressed about her ability to manage it all.

So now she has the full cycle of the loop. She knows the end result and she can notice and sit with the behaviors that make up the loop. Most of our loops will have three to five behaviors before the final result. The earlier in the process that Edna can make a different decision, rather than follow the same repetitive behaviors, the more likely she will be able to either partially or fully break the loop.

For example, when she feels overwhelmed and claustrophobic, she could go for a walk. Or even better, when she sees her "to-do" list, she could accept that she doesn't need to take care of it all today.

Once she reaches this level of awareness, she can then start the practice of healing her wounded self, by either sitting with her emotions or working with her inner child. By "breaking" a loop like this, or even by fully acknowledging the loop, we interrupt the unhealthy pattern.

Noticing the repetitive nature of our loops will either naturally begin a healing process, or will at least motivate us to desire a different outcome.

Let's look at another example. Brandon struggles with overeating, specifically sweets. He puts "overeating/sweets" as the end result of his loop. He then tracks backwards to find out what he does or feels before each step. He notices feeling grief before craving sugar, then loneliness before that. When he sits with it more, this loneliness feels like despair, and he realizes over time that the original catalyst for this loop are situations that leave him feeling like he isn't good enough.

He then asks, "Who doesn't feel good enough?" and discovers that it is his inner four-year-old seeking his neglectful mother's acceptance and not receiving it. What he does receive are chocolate chip cookies and Coca-Cola. This desire for "sweetness" is a result of wanting and needing the sweetness that he never received from his mother.

By doing both healing work and habitual work (noticing this loop and circumventing it) he was able to stop engaging in this loop, and it eventually disappeared. Now when he feels lonely, he calls or texts a friend instead.

Opposing Loops

Another type of loop is an opposing loop. While people can be complex or multi-faceted, we are also paradoxically quite simple in a lot of ways. We have similar ways of being and similar loops that we enact. Often the masks we wear, or the mythic selves that we create, show us the nature of our inner pain.

There is a reason why one of us visualizes winning a reality show, while another fantasizes about giving a successful speech in front of approving male figures. An opposing loop is the creation of a script or fantasy that centers around giving our wounded inner child what they need. This is often done in a mythic or dramatic way that highlights what is being compensated for.

For example, someone with an inner child who feels powerless will create a mythic self that is powerful or that even has "too much power." They also may spend their entire lives boasting about how nobody else is as powerful as they are or tearing down other individuals who do have power. Another person may feel inauthentic and fraudulent and so they spent their lives telling everyone how authentic they are and pointing out others who are not "real" like they are.

A wounded self that is stuck feeling powerless and disconnected from everything will create a compensatory persona of being deeply connected and powerful. The "mythic self" that we create will directly oppose the wounded self. For example, a woman who believes herself to be "popular" continually points out and deprecates anyone that she deems to be a loser or "unpopular," because to contend with her inner feelings of unworthiness would be too much for her. A man who lacks confidence is obnoxious and boastful about his achievements to anyone who will listen while inwardly feeling low self-worth.

We continually belittle the wounded parts of our own psyche in the outer world. Our shadows cannot rest until we make peace with all aspects of ourselves and notice the divides that we create.

The Rising of the Deep

What we are aware of regarding ourselves in our daily waking reality is like the surface waves of an ocean. This is our conscious mind. We also have the depths of the ocean, or the depths of our subconscious. Most of us don't really get to the bottom of the ocean, the subconscious. We tend to make it a bit below the waves or perhaps to mid-ocean.

In our most difficult loops whatever is at the depths of our subconscious, the bottom of the ocean, is attempting to rise up into our consciousness.

When something rises into our consciousness, we may simply repress it and shove it back down. We may deny it, acknowledge it, or decide to work on it. Many of these choices are subconscious; we are not consciously choosing to avoid an issue or numb ourselves from life. Whatever is too painful to see, we are simply unable to face.

Acknowledging whatever is arising in us allows our loops to change. When we see what is coming up in us clearly, even if we do not fully understand it, we can prepare ourselves to work with that material when we are ready to.

What typically arises is an awareness of a type of loop that we are engaging in or a recognition that a part of our lives simply isn't working for us. There is a reason why aspects of ourselves remain unresolved and cause us difficulty: it is because they require healing. They are frozen in time, repeating the same loops. They cause the same circumstances, the same roles. They often consolidate the same beliefs (which are proving their wounding and their need for defense mechanisms right).

For example, four-year-old Steven's parents divorce. He feels rejected, abandoned, and like it is all his fault. He feels that if he were enough— good enough, perfect enough, lovable enough—or more like his brother, his father wouldn't have left.

The realization of this is too painful for his mind, which will protect itself from feeling this level of rejection. Steven's mind then constructs a "mythic reality" to protect and distract itself from the original trauma. Steven is now secretly a superhero, and all superheroes have difficult origin stories. He may also believe that his father will return and the family will be reunited.

Steven's myth-making further separates him from grounded reality. It stops him from ever looking at the original pain that has caused this schism of mind. It is a protection to the extent that Steven will continue to create more illusions, never questioning why he needs such mythologies in the first place.

These myths do not stop the pain or prevent the loop from being acted out again and again. Denying or distracting himself from pain may have been the best way that he could survive as a four-year-old and make sense of challenging circumstances. But that means that Steven at fifty may still believe the myths of his child self and act them out because of how they shielded him, in order to survive, at age four.

We experience this type of split all the time—it is how we deal with pain, especially severe pain. Being abandoned, feeling unloved or rejected, is a painful reality.

When we are younger, we are much more inclined to need to survive by myth-making, because we can't go anywhere other than our family home or school. Also, at that age we are immersed in myths and stories, fairy tales, and superhero films.

When we are willing to look at our myths, we can see that they are false. Underneath them lies the true emotion that got buried in the deep. When we recognize those emotions and take steps to work with them, we can move beyond our mythic selves into our true selves.

Power Loss

There are common loops, and common reasons for developing loops that result in similar behaviors. If we look past a person to see their loops, we can begin to see the type of pain that has caused them to become who they are.

We can lose power through trauma, in which a part of us learns to shield, defend, or separate from ourselves and the world. We can also lose power by sectioning off aspects of ourselves that we are taught are "too much" or societally inappropriate. Intuition, joy, creativity, happiness, extroversion, and intellect can be hidden or denied because we have been taught that those gifts are wrong or are cause for shame. These are shadows of light, and they can create as much power loss as the darkest of traumas.

Any time we fracture from ourselves, for whatever reason, it is a form of power loss. Any time that we disconnect from ourselves, our bodies, the natural world, the supernatural world, or from other people, this creates power loss. We no longer have our full vitality or our full ability to connect to ourselves and the outer world.

We mainly lose power around issues surrounding money, sexuality, biological drives and impulses, and masculinity/femininity.

War, masculine oppression of the feminine (and subsequent feminine oppression of the feminine), enslavement, as well as cultural, racial, and religious divides, all lead to power loss at a systemic level. This lives within each one of us and separates us from our power.

What happens when we examine our loops is that we start to engage with the health of our system, instead of allowing our lives to be directed by loops that formed out of great pain and survival instincts.

We can create more open filters that allow us to consciously interface with new ideas and ways of being. Instead of seeing these things as threatening and reacting blindly or automatically rejecting the new, we can consciously decide what information is right for us. We can discern what leads us towards health and greater integrity of our systems, as opposed to what merely perpetuates and consolidates loops of pain.

We will naturally, in an untrained mind, move towards our imbalances and ingrained loops, defending them vigilantly. The pain-filled aspects of us feel the need to put up defenses simply to survive. This may have worked when we were three, or seventeen, but those defenses will no longer work in adulthood. They only lead to separation and pain.

When we grow older, it is typical that our tracts become more and more ingrained. Our universe shrinks as we age, and we become less tolerant of anything outside of our familiar tracts. The other tracts, even those that we formerly used on occasion, become dark with disuse.

Our brains do not have to work very hard with loops—they utilize the same tracts that they always do. This is why so many TV programs, newspapers, and books repeat the same things again and again (and again and again): because we like our loops. They provide us with comfort and the assuredness that our universe is known, controlled, and safe.

By examining our loops, we regain the power that we have lost and develop an open but discerning mind as we grow older. Breaking free of our loops allows us to feel more comfortable within ourselves, and less concerned about what others think about us.

The Rejection Loop

We experience many common loops out of pain. One of the most common, the rejection loop, has the following steps:

- We perceive rejection or abandonment.
- Our inner child or adult cannot face this, so we say, "I don't want this/you anyway" or "I am too good for you."
- In this process, a split occurs: we build walls to avoid seeing or feeling the rejection, and we escape to the "mythic" beliefs that shield us from experiencing the pain.
- We feel isolated and disconnected, both outwardly (from the situation) and inwardly (due to the split of mind).
- Disconnection loops back to feeling rejected or abandoned, and the cycle starts again.

Denial of Reality Loop

When things do not feel "quite real" to us, it is often a sign of a denial-based defense mechanism to prevent us from fully facing the facts.

A part of us can accept that something is happening while another part of us is stuck in self-delusion: we can know that something has happened or is happening, and deny it at the same time.

This especially happens with larger trauma. The sexual assault that you suffered may not feel "real" because there is a denial mechanism in place that prevents you from acknowledging it. Acknowledging it would mean facing the grief and the impact of the assault on your life and your selfhood. It would also mean feeling the terror, and understanding that such an experience did happen and could happen again.

But denial of reality can occur with smaller (or seemingly less traumatic) things as well. For example, graduating from college can feel unreal. Part of you may deny that you have a college degree because that would mean acknowledging and celebrating your achievements. Part of you may still feel puzzled that you are an adult with a mortgage.

Indifference, apathy, and numbing are typical defense mechanisms that we use to deny reality. If we truly desired something, it would be painful if we didn't get it, and so we cocoon ourselves in apathy. If we truly felt an essential need to receive something from another human being, it would be painful if they rejected us. If we are indifferent, or if we have zero expectations, we are shielded from disappointment.

By slowly coming to terms with what has happened to us in our lives, we can move out of delusion and fully process what has occurred. This allows us to set the experience behind us, rather than loop through it in our present-day reality.

The Superiority/Inferiority Loop

The most common loops arise from trauma in our intimate relationships, such as our inner child seeking the nurturing they never received from their parents. Beyond this kind of trauma, loops are also created out of societal and religious conditioning, as well as from biological impulses.

The most basic form of biological "looping" is the superiority/inferiority loop. We enact this loop in the outer world because we do not recognize that we are projecting our inferiority complexes onto others.

We can project our own competency, mastery, and beauty onto others. Many people are all too happy to accept projections onto them of specialness, enlightenment, beauty, or being chosen.

While some individuals certainly may be more conscious, competent, intelligent, or skilled in a specific area than we are, we can recognize this without projecting the idea of superiority onto them. We all have our gifts and talents; our light may just shine in a different way than another's.

When we are still playing out this loop, we need to maintain that we are "superior" or "special" or more important or "real" than others. We can then point to others that we feel are inferior to us. If we do not feel inferior, we do not need to convince others of our superiority. We can remove ourselves from this tiring play in which we dance with the shadow of our own inadequacy in the outer world.

If we can see this loop for what it is—a sick game that we play in which there are no winners—we can simply stop playing it. We can work on whatever is preventing us from feeling confident and happy within ourselves. We can stop externalizing our inadequacies in the form of contempt, arrogance, and shaming. Most importantly, we can take back our gifts that we have so readily given to others. Our light is meant to be shining from within ourselves. To see our own beauty, talent, intellect, and uniqueness in an embodied way means that we totally and completely own these qualities within ourselves. We no longer need to point to others as superior or inferior.

Chapter 15

Understanding Collective Shadows

*T*he healing from our individual shadow work ripples outwards. Our relationships change, and in some small or large way our family, ancestry, society, culture, and world change. Our healing may affect our relationship with our husband in a large way, and our culture in a smaller way. But each one of us impacts the collective.

Similarly, each one of us casts a shadow. The world is composed of the sum of all our individual shadows, and our shadows become a part of our family, society, culture, and world. Collectively, our individual wounds and unrealized parts of ourselves become the pain of the world.

Combined together, our shadows create a world stage. The stages of our family, culture, ancestry, society, and world, cast roles and follow scripts just like we do on our own individual stage. The world loops through its pain until some element of the script changes and until we are no longer willing to play the role in which we have been cast.

Our individual suffering, and the unhealed suffering of those who came before us create a collective shadow. Through shadow work, we begin to recognize that our pain is not just our own. Our pain is our neighbor's pain. Our pain is the pain of our community. Our pain is universal pain. Our shadows move from being wholly personal to being partially individual and partially collective.

The mirror that we use to see ourselves in one another in the outer world also reflects the outer world back to us. In the world we can see the faces that show us what we do not wish to see about ourselves: our self-hatred, disillusionment, and ignorance. We can also see what is happening in the world as a macrocosm of our inner divisions and our need for healing.

If our society is out of balance, if our community is sick, if people are becoming increasingly fractured and out of touch with reality, we also carry that within ourselves. Communal sickness is personal sickness. We are in no way separate from the issues that play out on the world stage: racial injustice, poverty, ill health, tragedy, violence, humanitarian disaster, war, apocalypse. Any type of conflict that plays out on the collective stage also exists within ourselves.

In doing individual shadow work, we begin to take back our contributions to the large collective shadows that populate our world. To heal our inner trauma, hatred and othering is an incredible act of service to the world. Conversely, when the wounds that keep repeating on the world stage are healed, we also find healing within ourselves.

One criticism that arises from doing any type of inner work is a belief that we cannot just sit on a mat, separate from society, and heal societal issues. This ignores the important spiritual principle that "what is within is without, and what is without is within." We carry the legacy of our family and other collective energies within us, and we can do our part to heal them within ourselves.

The more pragmatic answer to this critique is that when we do our own shadow work, we create space within ourselves to be able to think about more than our own pain. We are capable of doing more than looping through the same scripts, roles, and archetypes in our plays. To break free from these restrictions is to create significant emotional and personal energy. We rarely recognize how exhausting it is to be continually repeating our wounds until we break free from them.

If we were to simply break free from the superiority/inferiority loop we would find that our entire life would open up, unlocking a tremendous amount of energy for our own healing—and for assisting others.

Our own healing ripples outward to others. It also restores our natural vibrancy and ignites our desire to connect with and help others. We are typically too wounded and restricted in our victim role to consider that we can offer considerable gifts to the world. Our gifts are hidden in the shadows, desperately wanting to emerge.

If we break free from our reactivity to the world by doing inner work, we start to relate to the world differently. When we notice our reactivity and what we fixate on (the roles, scripts, and loops) we see how we have projected our own individual shadows onto our family, community, society, and the world.

As we work with our shadow, we create a small pinprick of light within us. Something has penetrated that darkness; it is only by sitting with our own darkness that we can access our light. That pinprick eventually becomes a small light, a torch, and then an opening into which we can see the goodness and beauty of the world.

Discerning Collective Energies

We carry the universe within ourselves. We are multi-layered beings, composed of stars and constellations. We are also composed of the stories and experiences of our family members and ancestors.

Robert Bly once stated that the "unabsorbed shadow can darken air around all human beings." While this has always been true, it has never been more apparent than in the modern world. We are drowning in the wounds that are now coming to the surface to be healed. Our subconscious depths have been coming up collectively for the past several years; subjects like terror, apocalypse, death, disease, violence, class, race, and sex/gender are now part of our daily reality.

These energies are difficult to handle, even for the most reasonable and healed of souls. It is in wars and anywhere that our culture or group creates divides that the collective shadow most reveals itself.

One of the significant tools that I offer to sensitives (or to anyone) is to ask, "Is this mine?" People typically start this exercise with emotions or even thoughts, but when it comes to world energies, it is helpful to understand the concept of contagion. Similar to a virus, we can succumb to the "mood" on social media, websites, and the news, or we can pick up what is going on in the world (even without our awareness).

If we consider that the world has a mood, or that our family (or household) has a mood, we can begin to discern what that mood is and how we react to it personally. Our household might be tired or angry on certain days. Or the world might be depressed, chaotic, or simply troubled for a week or more.

It is helpful to discern these moods because they are a part of us, and we react to them. Our reactions are rarely conscious, except in the most sensitive of individuals. Even then, they may not be aware that their depression is severe today because the mood of the world is depressed. We may not recognize that when something terrible happens in the world, we experience a personal reaction to that news within ourselves.

If we consider the world as a drama playing out on a larger stage, we can see that some acts of that play are quite violent, while others are peaceful. We expect the same scripts, the same responses, and the same actors (just with different faces and names, like in our own play). In our individual plays, we express moral outrage when we expect something other than what we receive. We may also feel angry when the script of the world changes, and desire to bring it back to the way that it was. Seeing the world, or our family, as an opportunity for shadow work can help us understand many of our responses to the world.

Seeing the world stage clearly can bring a sort of depressive realism, the type of understanding that occurs when we see the world repeating its suffering without changing the script. This depression is very real and derives from understanding that we cannot do much to change something so massive. We cannot singularly change the environment. We cannot change the course of a war or a tornado. Eventually it is easy to see our individual despair arising in sympathy with the despair of the world. It is important to feel whatever we are feeling and to validate it.

On the other hand, what we react to in the world can be seen as a macrocosm of what is happening inside of us. We react to a news story not only because it is unjust or tragic on its own, but also because the subject of that news story points to something within us that needs to be healed. If we are willing to accept responsibility for how we react to the world stage, we can take back considerable parts of our shadow from the collective. Thus we help heal some aspect of the collective shadows and divisions that play out on the world stage.

When we react to events in the world, we can remember to ask, "Is this mine?" This means inquiring if what you are feeling stems from inside yourself, or if it comes from a larger source such as your family, your town, the world, or other sources. While on rare occasion it is one or the other, it is often both.

Plenty of negative events occur around the world, but there is a reason why we gravitate towards particular stories and become personally invested in them. For example, Uma fixates on multiple allegations of sexual assault against a celebrity because it represents an aspect of her shadow.

In this case, Uma is fixated because she was once sexually assaulted by an authority figure. This story regarding the celebrity is bringing up not only her individual experiences, but also larger considerations of female/male archetypal schisms. Her inner hatred of both the feminine and the masculine parts of herself are playing out within her.

If she were to question why she fixates on these allegations, she would reach her "ocean floor" and access her personal and visceral response to the larger situation. She would hear an inner voice stating, "I hate men." To her confusion, she would also hear an inner voice saying, "I hate women." Uma, if up to the task, now would have the opportunity to consider her hatred towards men and women and start to heal her relationship with those archetypes within herself. This does not neces-sitate absolving men or women of the terrible things that they can do.

Just as the world is at war with itself, we are at war with ourselves. It is by seeing the outer wars of our reality that we find the largest divi-sions within the self. To heal these divides, we can move towards the Self, or unification. To heal does not require fully resolving the conflict, but accepting it. When we arrive at a place of radical acceptance of both sides of the inner conflict, we can accept reality for what it is, rather than for what we would like it to be.

We should feel fear, anger, confusion, and every other single emotion that arises in response to devastating occurrences in the world. We should give ourselves permission to feel those things. There is, however, a difference between allowing ourselves to feel empathy for others and sorrow at the state of the world, and letting ourselves become subsumed by these emotions.

For example, Katarina is horrified every time she hears news about an ongoing war. She lives in Canada, but some of her relatives as well as her ancestors come from the country where the war is taking place. She feels a deep connection as well as despair regarding the ongoing crisis.

It is totally normal for Katarina to feel this, and part of shadow work is to normalize such feelings. If we are not horrified by the world, then we are not paying attention. But when she discerns that some of the energies she feels are coming from the world, she can then sit with her personal feelings and differentiate these from what is happening on the world stage.

One simple tool is to use basic percentages to distinguish how much of what you are feeling is due to world energies, or the mood of the world, from your reaction on an individual level. Katarina might realize that ninety percent of what she is feeling is empathy for those suffering during wartime. In Uma's case, she might discern that ninety percent of what she is feeling is personal, while ten percent is about the celebrity rape trial. She feels empathy for the women involved, and disgusted that people in positions of authority can harm women in such a skewed power dynamic. She allows herself to feel that ten percent fully, and then she does her personal work on the rest of what she is feeling.

Having clarity about these percentages offers us space to categorize what we are feeling and make sense of it. We do not have control over the outer world, or the people in it, but we do have control over our own actions and reactions.

We can then consider why we are so reactive to what is happening in the world. Pick three reasons why you feel emotionally activated. Do the "bottom of the ocean" exercise to figure out what is the real, root reason for your reactivity. Often this is something terribly practical and simple. What is happening in the world, or in the life of a person we are focused on, is horrible or amoral, or we feel empathy for those who are suffering. Then we question why, out of all the things happening in the world, are we so focused on this particular "play" of horribleness?

Before looking within, however, consider whether the reason you are so obsessed is not a deep need for healing around the issue, but is instead due to "contagion." Our world, our country, our town, our family fixates on one topic for a day, or a week, or longer. It is possible that you are so absorbed in something on the world stage because it is the "play" of the day, and as such, it is omnipresent. Every time you watch the news, scroll through social media, or chat with friends, that topic is front and center. The more people discuss and share it, the more contagious it becomes. If we can recognize this principle of contagion, we can discern when we are being pulled into a topic because it is simply the "play" of the day and take a step back from being pulled in it.

When you sense the reason why you are so reactive to an issue or event, you can look internally, and see your personal shadow part that requires attention and healing. There is some essential conflict going on, some inner hatred or disgust occurring, that is easier to see on the world stage than within yourself. When you take back your most shadowy parts: your self-loathing, abandonment issues, hatred, racism, sexism, classism, and inner monsters, you can view the unfortunate happenings of the world with greater peace and equanimity.

This does not mean that such happenings are okay, or that people doing terrible things are anything but monsters. It means that we reach a state of radical acceptance in which we recognize that people do terrible, hurtful, and amoral things because that is who they are. We all, within ourselves, have terrible, hurtful, and amoral parts. Some of us choose to act on them. Some of us are so consumed by them that we cannot help but act out our inner monsters. If we understand this, we will move beyond moral outrage and into acceptance.

People are who they are, and they show us who they are through their actions. The history of the world repeats itself through loops until its pain can be seen and heard. Just as we experience individual healing, the world and its players require validation and reconciliation. They need a clear pathway out of the script they have been given and the roles that have been placed upon them.

When we notice a loop arising communally, that loop is "charged." It is rising to the surface like the crest of a wave. This crest presents the perfect opportunity for you to attend to it. If you notice these waves and what they are bringing up, your own healing will be supported by them. Deep personal and communal work can result.

When we see how our individual play mirrors what is in the world, we do our small part to heal the world. When we move beyond our own play, we find ourselves in a place of resilience and strength that allows us to assist others on a larger scale. The real question regarding our reactivity is discerning how to move into radical acceptance. Our outrage stems from expecting people to act differently, or wanting the world play to diverge from its script. When we let go of the hope and expectation for people to be anything other than what they show themselves to be, we can take back a considerable part of our shadow from the world.

Roles on the World Stage

The easiest way to see the "play" of the world is to look at politicians, celebrities, and public figures. We can see such individuals as people in their own right, with pain, wounds, and lives of their own. But from a different perspective, such people gained popularity because they were created by the combined shadows of many individuals. This does not mean that we have created the actor or politician, but this person would not play a role on the world stage if they were not propelled there by the collective shadows. What these figures say, how they act, the beliefs they espouse represent the combined shadows of a specific group of people.

We can gauge what is arising in the collective unconscious by viewing the news cycles and listening to what we talk about with others. Just as we experience topics that emerge from our depths into our individual consciousness, the world also experiences the deepest shadows of its ocean floor rising to the surface. There is so much rising from the ocean depths that public discourse has rapidly shifted. How we see ourselves individually and on the world stage has also changed. When rapid change occurs, the static principle attempts to become more rigid and fundamentalist in order to keep the status quo. We derive comfort from keeping things how they are; any type of change is scary. The world seeks stability, and there are always individuals who will play the role of the moralist to keep the world play how it is, rather than allowing the natural growth and evolution of the play to unfold.

The world itself can be in a liminal state, in between plays—a period of "disorganized reorganization" or a dark night of the soul. We no longer know what to expect and reality itself seems to lack the congruency and habitual patterning that once made us feel so safe.

In such a liminal state, we may feel so much emotion because all of our darkness and all of our wounds, personally and collectively, are coming to the surface. This is an excellent opportunity for growth. If we recognize what is happening in the collective, we can look at those same qualities or conflicts within ourselves and heal them. We grow the most during periods of darkness and disorganization, because we are not so stuck in our own routine play, or the plays on the world stage; thus more personal expansion is possible.

When we look at the world stage, we can consider how a popularized figure represents the shadows of many. That pop singer or social media sensation is popular for a reason. They are composed of the thoughts, wishes, ideologies, and inner divisions of a particular time and of a particular group. They express the shadow of their world.

Such projections of our shadows onto popular figures comes at a cost. It must be difficult for them to deal with these projections, for example, unexpressed sexuality projected onto a female TV star or inner hatred directed towards a political figure. Especially in the age of social media, the likes, comments, and displacement of emotional material onto a public figure can cause them significant mental health issues and distress.

On a collective level, our projection of our shadow parts onto a celebrity may seem insignificant, for example, displacing our inner machismo and physical health onto the male action star. But projecting our health and machismo onto that star keeps us from finding those qualities within ourselves. Those qualities become achievable only by him, and are therefore not available to us.

To take back our shadows from popularized figures, we can look within to see if we have access to that particular archetype within ourselves. If we do not, we can acknowledge it and take steps to expand our personal narrative to include that archetype. For Zeke, taking back his inner action star entails playing Frisbee outside with his dog. For Debra, taking back her inner vengeful actor means venting her frustrations in therapy and learning martial arts so that she can defend herself. There may be some popularized figures that we cannot see within ourselves. The figures that represent hatred, division, and opposing views can be difficult to claim as a part of ourselves. But we can start to see why that figure emerged. What are they giving voice to? If they represent a collective shadow of many, what is that shadow? Perhaps it is the unrevered masculine, the traditionalist, the fantasy-deluded, the hopeless romantic. By seeing clearly why this figure emerged, and what it says about our collective shadow at this time, we can move beyond individual reactivity and respond to the larger problems of our day.

Radically Accepting the World (and Public Figures)

When you fixate on a particular public figure or event, consider whether you need to sit with any emotions and fully feel them. Are there any inner children that require healing? Once you determine this, focus on embodying whatever archetypes are coming up within you. For example, if you notice on the world stage that the "dark feminine" is coming up, are you embodying that quality? What would that quality look like within you? How would your script change? Embodying the dark feminine will look quite different for each of us. The purpose in embodying her is not to become her, but to express that part of your shadow freely. She can now consciously come forward as she wishes, rather than remain separate from you, where she acts out without your awareness.

This may be more difficult for things that you are morally opposed to. Looking at our own hatred of the masculine or feminine, or our own racism or classism, is difficult when we see such large and explosive examples of hatred and intolerance. But we each have an inner part of ourselves that desires to be selfish, to destroy, to divide and dehumanize. By looking at those parts we can stop projecting so much energy onto the public figures that we hate. In large part, we hate these figures because they represent a small part of ourselves. If we take back our projection, and see that part within ourselves, we no longer feed the public figure our energy. They will wither and collapse in the collective, and a new character with a new script will emerge (or a slightly different character with a slightly different script).

Think of a conflict playing out on the world stage. How do you feel about that conflict? If you could see both sides clearly (a difficult thing to be sure, as we tend to take a side morally and get stuck in our righteousness) what would you see? If you could see the humanity in both sides, what would you see? Even if one side of the conflict is truly evil, or despicable, can you (and I know this is hard) see those qualities playing out within yourself?

The purpose here is not to absolve any sociopaths of their wrongdoings, but to stop ourselves from participating in their play. If we see an evil, narcissistic, misandrist (man-hating) psychopath, we can either react to her over and over, or we can stop engaging with her. Her role requires opposition and conflict. But we are not this versus that, us versus them; we are our own individual person and our lives should not be in reaction or opposition to any person. Our power lies in taking back control of our own narrative and our own play. We define our own role and we can move out of reactivity and stop giving them negative attention. They count on the vitality that accompanies our attention and we can deny them that.

On some level, those who express hatred, creating fear and division, and spreading ignorance, thrive on the negative shadows that we feed them. If we were to take those shadows back, they would no longer be figures on the world stage. If we give voice to the individual pain that makes up that public figure and seek a solution, instead of hating and scapegoating, that public figure would no longer need to act a role in the world play.

Collective Archetypes

Consider the politician, the actor, the social media personality, the comedian, the ingenue (female pop star and muse) as collective archetypes. They can exist as roles in our individual plays, but they are also players on the world stage: we project our shadows onto them, and they live them out.

Onto the ingenue we project our innocence, the somewhat odd mix of burgeoning sexuality, feminine objectification, and naivety that we so prize in American culture. She is the figure of the 1950's homemaker, the virginal slut; she takes on the shadow of our culture's fixation on young children as sexual creatures. She is the unique soul who inspires the songwriter, the musician, and the artist to create. To deconstruct such an archetypal figure, we need to question the entirety of our beliefs regarding the feminine in our society. Once she has aged, the ingenue is no longer valued. The muse is only utilized by the male, and cannot be her own being.

The comedian represents the voice of reason and the truth teller. He is lucid and sane in an insane world, the shaman who tells us stories so that we can also see. When we bring a dark topic into the light through laughter, its energy breaks up. It disperses. This was known by shamans and spiritual workers of old, and it is still understood on a subconscious level by many. Telling our stories, letting the truth of this world be known to one another, brings light into a world that is in desperate need of levity. The jester is the ultimate contrarian, moving beyond taboos, acting deliberately outlandish to point out the ridiculousness of societal beliefs and behaviors.

The politician may represent the greatest divides within ourselves. He is equally despised and celebrated. There is no greater arena for us versus them, "I" versus the "Other," than that of the politician. When we are sharply divided politically, we can no longer identify with the Other. We become tribal, feral, rooting for a politician with an allegiance that we usually reserve for a sports team, blind to the individual politician's humanity. There is no greater collective archetypal figure than the politician. This would classically be considered the archetypal "king," the ruler of a nation. He represents the health and power of the country that he rules. If the country is sick, the king will be sick. If the king is sick, the country will be sick. There is no greater barometer of health, vitality, and power of a nation than the functionality of its governing body.

The social media personality represents our collective tendency towards anti-intellectualism, our reverence of mediocrity, our fetishizing of materialism. While we have always suffered collectively from ignorance, to have it celebrated by reality television and social media has brought this archetype to the forefront. American writer Isaac Asimov said: "Anti-intellectualism has been a constant thread winding its way through our political and cultural life, nurtured by the false notion that democracy means that 'my ignorance is just as good as your knowledge." With the "death" of the movie star—a figure who was celebrated for their acting talent and excellence—has emerged the era of social media "influencers." These new celebrities represent our growing social media and internet addiction and our disconnection from reality and one another. They reflect our inability to read and to focus, and the spread of misinformation. With "authority" given to so many who have nothing but hatred, chaos, and ignorance to share, we pave the way for authoritarianism.

The superhero (or Superman) is our inner moralist. He is the arbiter of black and white thinking. He is the moral victor, superior in every way to the Other, who is immoral, evil, and inferior. This type of rigid thinking allows fundamentalism and nationalism to thrive. When we inhabit the grey areas that include both wrong and right, we become human. To suppose that we are singularly right while all others are wrong and to see ourselves as the moral victor is to participate in a child-like fantasy of simplistic division. As adults, we can embrace nuance, openness, and a welcoming curiosity regarding the Other.

Our archetypal figures require an opposing shadow side to come into being. The greatest example is our superhero, who requires a monstrous, evil force to reckon with. Another archetypal figure to see this shadow side through is the guru.

Classically, the guru has worked inwardly on themselves to the point where they can lead others down the same path. She is simply farther along and knows the terrain, so can share that knowledge. If the guru has achieved any self-realization, they will be able to access their light. They have worked with and through their darkness to the extent that they have uncovered what lies underneath it: love, light, and the oneness of humanity. Their role is to teach others to access their own light. Plenty of successful spiritual teachers have operated in this classical sense. However, the archetypal figure of the guru has become quite skewed in modern Western culture. It has morphed into an authority figure who requires followers to view them as a demi-god rather than as a human being. It has become a figure of separation, rather than connection.

Many wounded souls look towards their spiritual teacher in an attempt to find the connection and warmth that they did not receive from their parents or guardians. The archetypal follower wants the guru to provide the answers to life's questions. They do not desire to think for themselves, or to sit with the uncertainty of existence. They want to believe that the guru is special or chosen so that they can project all of their fear of the unknown, all of their parental abandonment, and all of their own light and power onto the guru.

While the classical guru will give back any light or power their followers attempt to give to them, the false guru relies on the follower to give them their light so that they can shine. If the archetypal false guru lost his followers, he would lose his light. We so readily give our light away to others when we are unable to claim it within ourselves.

It is not surprising that the "script" for the false guru is their eventual downfall. Power arises in accordance with character, and if we develop our own light, we have no reason to receive the light of others. If we have not done our own shadow work, we will take the power and light of others, and our shadow side will have no choice but to act out. Their persona—the mask the false guru wears in front of the world—and who he truly is have reached such a dividing point that the inner monster has no choice but to act.

Another figure in this play is the anti-guru. This is an archetype who spends their time denouncing gurus but who otherwise acts like an archetypal guru. They make fun of gurus, talk at length about their toxic qualities, or fixate on specific gurus who have abused or misled their followers, all the while doing the same things themselves. This person is so focused on the outer guru because they cannot claim this archetype within themselves.

The quest of the seeker is always founded on the premise that there is something wrong or missing within themselves. When the seeker heals such false notions, they can move on from being an archetypal seeker and become found. They find within themselves a sense of completion and stop looking outwards to fill themselves.

Monk Linji Yixuan once famously said, "If you meet the Buddha on the road, kill him." This mentality helps us to break the cycle of guru/anti-guru/follower. We need teachers who can help others find their own light and support others in taking personal responsibility for their lives. While it is normal to start by offering our light to a teacher, the teacher–student relationship should allow the student to reclaim that light back gradually until they can see that light within themselves. This can only happen if the archetypal guru is not reliant on the seeker offering the guru their light in order to propel the guru's self-created myths.

Collective Shadows in Groups

When we progress beyond our individual play, we can see how interconnected we are. We are, in some small way, our neighbor, our friend, and the stranger down the street. We believe that we exist as singular beings but we really exist in a state of interbeing, in which our relationships and connections make us who we are.

On a simple level, we may intersect with another individual because we are both interested in Buddhism, Korean barbecue, or travel. We may also share the same pain, or contain the same shadows; we either like them or hate them based on this fact.

We may have a small connection to the waiter serving us lunch, or a huge cord of connection to our best friend of thirty years. Our connections with each other form webs of relating, a vast web of interconnection with the world.

Our relationships with groups can form smaller or larger webs. For example, our relationship to our individual synagogue may be quite small, but our web connecting us to the entire Jewish faith will be quite a bit larger. We can get even more abstract and say that when you purchase a specific product you are in some way relating with that brand, and interacting as a part of their web.

A group, an organization, a workplace, and a business are all examples of webs that we interface with every day. We also interact with the web of a book, a painting, or the same group of people who ride the bus with us every day.

This concept is important because each of our webs have their own play, with their own script and roles. We act in our plays and assume roles that may be quite life-affirming, but other roles can cause us to make parts of ourselves shadow. We may not be fully ourselves because the web of our family, religion, or workplace insists that we act in specific ways.

In each of our plays, a group shadow develops. It is composed of its individual members as well as the history of that web: the players and roles that created and maintained that web in the past.

In these groups we may take on a specific role or act in a specific way because the group shadow requires it. Our behavior in a group is partially due to who we are as an individual and partially due to the energies of the group. For example, a member of a church may yell out spontaneously because that congregation requires someone to play that role. A person at a workplace may be overly strict and supervisory because that is her nature (she is a good fit for the role) but also because the company has placed her in such a role in order to balance the elements of the workplace play.

We may notice that certain aspects of our personality come forward when we are in a specific group, while they take a back seat when we interact with another group. At work our office is full of serious professionals and so we take on a serious and professional role. As a result our own productivity and intellect is challenged in a healthy way that allows us to thrive. At home we may be more free, joyfully playing with our children and relaxing on the front porch with friends and a beer.

We may also notice, particularly in large groups, that contagion and mass hysteria can occur. This explains the violence and tribalism that emerges at sporting events, and the anger that we may feel while driving alongside many other angry drivers during rush hour.

Being aware of who we are and how we change with each group can allow us to consciously participate in life, with the flow and enjoyment of a musical performance. It can also allow us to take a step back at a family event, for example recognizing that we do not need to take on a particular role or act in a specific way simply because the energy field requests it.

Our Family Energy Field

Consider your family as one organism, one person, with a variety of individuals composing its parts. Each family member contributes qualities and elements that combine together to form the collective family unit. It is typical for a family to cast roles. Some of these roles are understandable: mother, father, son, daughter, grandmother. In other cases, as mentioned in Chapter Ten, the roles are developed by the family play: golden child, black sheep, forgotten child.

In considering the family as a single organism, we can move from blaming the dysfunction of one individual in the family and see how the family unit as a whole created that individual. For example, an addict and his enabling mother and forgotten sister all create a system that fosters his addiction. Michael, a golden child, has the entire family revolve around his achievements, which is understandably a lot of pressure for him. Sara, the black sheep, is the "lightning rod" of the family; their blame, harassment, critiques, and lack of emotional intelligence all require Sara to absorb the issues of the family. Both Michael and Sara are fulcrums, or the figure around whom the family pivots.

If Michael were to pass away, the family would be lost. It would lose its center. Either the family would need to reorganize (in a similar way that the individual ego organizes around its wounds and stories), or the family would fall apart, lacking the cohesion to continue. To reorganize its wounds the family might make every gathering a memorial to Michael, invoking his name and sharing stories to attempt to keep the family system intact. Or the awkwardness of gathering without Michael would mean that the family would interact far less often.

When doing shadow work, it is typical for someone to reach a point where they no longer wish to heal, because it would mean leaving their family energy field. Their entire family is angry or unhealthy, and so on some primal level, they do not wish to abandon their family by becoming happy or healthy. This can also happen when a person gains higher education, financial wealth, or other opportunities denied the rest of the family. For example, Sandra was the first in her family to attend college. While her parents were proud, her siblings often made fun of her, shaming her in small ways, joking about what she was going to buy them now that she had a good job. They continued to shame her when she bought a new house and moved to a better neighborhood.

Sandra not only had to deal with her family and their subconscious desires to achieve normalcy and integrity of the field (to keep anyone from venturing too far outside of what was known) but also her own guilt at leaving the field, even if she was offering herself and her family members a better life. To release the family energy field is to move through the feelings of guilt and self-sabotage that naturally occur when we are subconsciously holding on to the childhood roles and household play that we once participated in. We need to recognize that, in a healthy family system, the family naturally reorganizes around any healing or change that occurs. In an unhealthy family system, it is no longer your job to play a role that does not allow you to thrive. Recognizing our tendency to remain within the family field and working through our emotions about breaking free can only result in greater health for all of the members of the field.

Spiritual Immunity

If you put crabs in a bucket, and one of those crabs tries to escape, it will be pulled down by its fellow crabs. Instead of helping one another climb out of the bucket, the crabs prevent each other from climbing out. With this type of behavior, no crab will get out of the bucket unless someone pulls one out to eat it.

Think of a group that you belong to, such as an organization or family. Just as you have a body, that organization or family also has a "body." It is composed of its group members, just as you on an individual level are composed of an arm and a leg and a spleen. On an individual level, our system seeks out anything "abnormal" so that our immune system can take care of it. Basically, anything perceived as "Other" or foreign to what it already knows.

This same immune system occurs in groups and organisms to ensure the survival of the group organism. Spiritual immunity ensures homeostasis, or a way of ensuring the health of the group by making sure that none of its parts stray too far from the group's "norms." Like crabs in a bucket, we will pull each other back to ensure that our group remains "healthy," with its sense of normalcy intact.

We live according to explicit and implicit rules of the groups that we belong to. To counter those rules results in shaming, a tactic used to bring others back into line with what the group believes is healthy or "normal."

We live in a world in which we as people, when threatened by something new, can act in primitive and violent ways in order to keep the "health" of the system intact. Recognizing this with clarity allows us to discern when and where it may be safe to be totally vulnerable and fully ourselves, or when it is better to act in accordance with the spoken or unspoken rules of the group so that we do not endanger ourselves.

On a primal level, we seek to belong. For much of human history, rejection or exclusion from the group meant death. In the modern world, being shamed or rejected does not usually mean death, but on a deep subconscious level we still harbor that primordial fear. We stop ourselves from thinking or behaving outside of the group "norms" because of it.

On a simple, physiological level, our immune system understands what is "mine" versus what is "not mine." Things that are "not mine" are treated like invaders and threats that activate the troops. On a spiritual level, our immune systems serve the same function. Beliefs and ideas that are the "same" as ours feel safe. Those that are "different" are viewed as threats, and we activate our inner defenses. This can mean feeling unsafe or threatened by other cultures, races, religions, lifestyles, sexuality, and many other things.

In spiritual immunity the homeostasis and cohesion of the group is considered more important than its growth or evolution. In an unhealthy system there is a rigid and static framework that resists any type of change. This is why a lot of clubs that people traditionally joined in the past are now struggling to recruit new members. These groups have not changed with the times and no longer appeal to younger members.

In a healthy system, however, evolution can occur and new rules can be explored. Innovation and growth arise from encountering irritating or conflicting energies. Most groups will drive out dissonant thoughts and ideas that challenge their homeostasis. A healthy system will have an outlier (such as the archetypal comedian or jester) as part of the group. This creates healthy conflict and ensures growth. This also allows community members to freely contribute their own thoughts and ideas, instead of modeling their suggestions on group thoughts and rules.

One of the ways that we can begin to see spiritual immunity is to read or watch book and movie reviews. First, read a book or watch a movie without looking at any reviews. Now, look at the reviews. Perhaps your opinion will not change but in most cases, if we love a movie but everybody else hated it, our own opinion of it will diminish. Or perhaps we might inhabit the role of contrarian and because everyone else loved a book we must now hate it. If we can observe spiritual immunity in small ways like this, we can start to consider the spiritual immunity of the groups and organizations that we are a part of in larger ways.

One of the most common examples of spiritual immunity is a child who thinks differently from other children and who doesn't fit in with the dynamics of their school. In this situation, a child could be shamed because there is safety in the child being energetically and behaviorally similar to the parent. A parent brings up their child in the style in which they were raised or how they felt they should have been raised. Parents also often adhere to the institutional "norms" of the day, what schools, governments, and medical establishments determine is normal and healthy.

To see these "norms" and to appreciate the differences between what society considers healthy and what is actually healthy for the individual child means to consider the needs of both the individual and the group.

The end result of spiritual immunity is a type of shut-down experienced by the individual, in which they feel ashamed of the parts of themselves that do not fit into the group system. Within our shame lies a deep vulnerability, due to being hurt or told we were wrong when we revealed ourselves and offered our voice in the past. Understanding shame as a mechanism pulling us back to the homeostasis of the group puts our experiences in a different perspective. We can choose to be vulnerable, to share our Self and our true voice, and recognize that inhabiting our inner outlier is necessary for the overall health of a system. We need unique individuals who question and see differently for us all to grow.

To love our uniqueness and to move beyond the layers of shame that we have collected regarding our true expressions, preferences, and identity can allow us to be ourselves despite the world.

If we view our differences and unique qualities as necessary and vital for the world as a whole, we can move beyond the shaming of our bodies and ourselves by a system engineered to accept only mediocrity and sameness, and we can move into being confidently and comfortably who we are.

Part 4

Embracing the Other
(Essays and Contradictions)

The candle is not lit
To give light, but to testify to the night.

Robert Bly

All the darkness in the world cannot extinguish
the light of a single candle.

St. Francis of Assisi

If you are in a spaceship that is traveling at the speed of light,
and you turn on the headlights, does anything happen?

Steven Wright

Chapter 16

Embracing Our Full Continuum

So the darkness shall be the light, and the stillness the dancing.

T.S. Eliot

*I*n Energy Work there is a model of the human being that is comprised of three bodies: physical, mental/emotional, and spiritual. As humans we tend to gravitate towards our strongest body and neglect our weakest. Put more simply, someone with natural athletic ability will likely choose to exercise during his spare time rather than pick up a book.

To achieve balance, we must tend to all three of these bodies, moving beyond our natural gravitation towards neglecting our weaker "body." For example, Kenya works in an office all day and comes home with an aching lower back and images from her computer oscillating in her brain. She decides to relax on the couch and play video games to alleviate stress. All of us know logically that Kenya would be much better off taking a walk or meditating to decompress from her day.

What we do not recognize is that our greater growth often depends on working on our weakest "body." Stefan has been a serious meditator for thirty years. He has reached a point where he feels quite stuck in his development. He has sought advice from his meditation teacher and others. Finally, when he gets off the cushion and begins volunteering, he finds that his spiritual block vanishes. His meditation practice is much more fruitful.

When evaluating which of your three bodies is strongest and weakest, you do not need to bully or shame yourself. Continue working on what is strong in you and what you naturally gravitate towards but also recognize that if you start developing your weakest "body," it will balance your whole system. If you are ever stuck in your shadow work, it may seem odd that taking up running, or painting, or going to church may get you out of that stuck place. We so naturally gravitate towards our imbalances, compounding them further. To truly grow, we need to evaluate our mind, body, and spirit and see where we need the most assistance. Then we can direct our efforts there.

Riding a Tractor

We are many things all at once, yet we rarely allow ourselves to experience anything outside of what we have already experienced. The confines of gender, culture, class, and family teach us who we are and who we are not. While we can reclaim our shadow by breaking through mental patterns, we can also reclaim large aspects of our shadow through trying new things.

Read the following list and see which activity feels most taboo to you. Read it again. Now decide what is within your sphere of possibility—you haven't done it, but you are willing to try it. Experiencing something once or a few times does not mean that it will become a dominant part of your personality. What this exercise does is allow the possibility of its expression through you. If you have done the activity but felt discomfort, you may want to do it again, this time feeling comfortable and confident in doing it. This is all about embracing our full continuum, trying things to see how they can become a part of us:

- Ride a tractor or other large piece of equipment
- Wear a dress or a skirt
- Put on eyeliner
- Do karaoke in front of others
- Do a home improvement project or build something
- Dig a hole

- Wear a bathing suit
- Cook yourself a full meal
- Hike somewhere high up (or take a helicopter or plane ride, skydive, or do anything else that can allow you to see the world from a high place)
- Walk around your home or room nude
- Eat food from a culture or cuisine that you have never tried. If you have tried the cuisine before, order something new
- Attend a church, temple, or ashram open house (call or visit website to see when they are open to visitors)
- Build a fire
- Read a book that is considered a "classic"
- Listen to a speech, blog, or podcast from someone who thinks quite differently from you; see where your ideas or interests intersect, rather than where they collide
- Travel to a place you have never visited
- Play a video game
- Join a gymnastics class
- Watch the waves of an ocean or other body of water until you feel it is a spiritual experience
- Wear a suit and tie
- Go to a place where you can sit in total silence for an hour or longer
- Sit and stare at a flower or landscape for fifteen minutes without distraction
- Help someone without expecting anything in return (even praise!)
- Watch a movie that you would never watch (e.g., horror, romance) and allow yourself to enjoy it
- Listen to music that you would never listen to and allow yourself to enjoy it
- Watch reality television or a show about people who live entirely differently from you; see how you connect with them in your shared humanity
- Dance
- Learn a new language, or at least a phrase in a new language
- Allow yourself to cry; allow yourself to cry in front of someone

This is by no means a comprehensive list. The point is to break through taboos—the areas of self that we cannot claim due to shame, fear, or hatred—and to reclaim them through action. The scariest thing for Marcia may be to put on eyeliner. For Josh it would be difficult to see himself in reality television stars. Each area in our lives where we can expand our ideas of who we are is ripe for allowing us to become more wholly ourselves.

To really grow, do something that opposes your character. Meek and quiet? Try boxing. Loud and extroverted? Try a quiet day reading a book. An atheist can respectfully visit a church, and an "alpha male" can wear a dress. If we have an open mind, our experiences can consolidate who we are and expand our view about what is possible for us. We can let go of ideas of the Other, releasing the latent hatred of the parts of ourselves that we have yet to explore and experience.

Being of Two Minds

When we do shadow work, we can recognize that we are many things simultaneously, and often paradoxically. For example, we can be soft and open but with an iron will to get things done.

The most fundamentalist aspects of self are harboring a cut-off opposite. For example, a politician who preaches about family values is found to be having an affair. A guru who preaches ethics is found to be unethical. It is in our hypocrisies—the space between who we believe ourselves to be and who we truly are—that we find the denied parts of our shadows.

If we are willing to explore any of our opposing parts, the more dominant aspects of ourselves will become more stable and we will become more confident in who we are.

For example, Craig is a workaholic who rarely spends time with his family. He feels a lot of pressure to provide. Over time, his work suffers because his stress creates overwhelm and sleep issues. His partner convinces him to take a vacation. When Craig returns to work after his first relaxing trip in years, he finds that he is more mentally clear and the quality of his work has improved.

Being of two minds about something reveals two different forces within us, two different selves, two different points of consciousness. As long as we are opposing something or someone, that opposite controls us. Embracing the gray area in which we truly live gives us a certain type of freedom. By exploring beyond strict binary divides we can move into a place of nuance.

Our ability to inhabit an opposing (and seemingly paradoxical) point of view will only strengthen and solidify that original quality within ourselves. When we see our point of view from a different perspective, our viewpoint may change. We may also gain helpful information regarding our already established viewpoint.

We can fully inhabit the entire continuum of self, from masculine to feminine, to androgyny—embracing both at the same time. We can attune to the feminine and still dislike romantic comedies. We can see how others enjoy these films, and see a small part of ourselves reflected in the person who enjoys those movies.

When we are of two minds, two different parts of ourselves may be wanting two different things. If we avoid imagining our incongruities as dueling forces, but simply think of them as aspects of ourselves desiring different things, we can tend to both sides of our inner conflict. For example, a part of you may want to go hiking and another may want to take a bath. They are not opposing, they simply both want to be a part of you. A part of you may want a diet of all candy and another, healthy food. You can look towards the part that wants all candy and see if it needs healing, perhaps an inner child craving sweetness, or if there are any emotions to attend to that would heal the conflict.

In this way we can tend to the multitude of selves within us, ease conflict, and integrate expanded notions regarding who we are.

Chapter 17

The Power of Being Ordinary

The idea of the "chosen one," an ordinary child or adult who is seen for their extraordinary unrealized power, is a common archetypal story. We crave being seen in our individuality, we need our unique qualities to be appreciated. We want the world to be in no doubt that we are special.

Internally we feel a push-pull between standing out and fitting in; the parts of ourselves that wish to be seen in their specialness and the parts of ourselves that wish to belong in our community.

This essential conflict plays out in all of us, even those who have no desire for fame, or those whose inner child no longer yearns for the love and attention that it did not receive. There is a basic primary conflict between the parts of us that feel Other and the parts of us that belong. We all have both alien and human within; it is by accepting all our parts that we see that even the most remote aspects of our being do belong.

There is a power in being ordinary. Large parts of us resist this notion as we wish to be large, special, and noticed. To be small and ordinary would deny us the attention and affection we so deeply desire. We are so accustomed to transactional love, in which we need to act a specific way in order to gain affection or approval, that we do not feel deserving of unconditional love simply because we exist.

This part believes that it will receive validation only if we stand out from the group. We do not feel worthwhile otherwise. It is only through our achievements, through being "extra-ordinary," that we can prove to the world, and to ourselves, that we deserve to exist. We can take up space only if we are exceptional enough to be deemed valuable.

The desire to be special comes at a steep price. There is immense pressure to achieve, to prove ourselves, to have others validate our worth. Yet we will never be special or worthy enough or receive enough validation. If we let go of this pressure, we can find our own inner validation. We are worthy of existing whether we are doing extraordinary things or whether we are not doing anything at all. When we realize that the desire to be special and to prove ourselves to the outer world is a trap, we can stop seeking what we will never find.

We can begin to revel in our ordinariness. We can find a self stripped of pretension, of masks, of needing to be anything or anyone in particular. When we reach this state, we settle into our bodies, knowing that we are home, perhaps for the first time.

We can recognize that beauty lies in the simplicity of life—the sound of rain, a simple breeze, and the feeling of our breath moving in and out of our rib cage. Cooking dinner for our family, watching a movie, and laughing at our cat chasing a crumpled-up piece of paper teach us what really matters in life. The simplest states of being constantly offer us meaning and purpose. We just need to learn how to look, how to experience, and how to be present with them.

If we release the pressure of doing, of becoming, we can simply be who we are. The ordinary part of us can emerge. It is in the ordinariness of our lives that we find salvation. By accepting the ordinary and very human aspects of ourselves, we see how the light is already present in our lives. We are just too busy and too distracted to notice it dance through our existence. As we get older, our most indelible memories are often the simplest and most joyful moments. A child opening a present, a smile from a loved one, a connection we feel when talking with a friend. Attuning to the simplest aspects of existence allows us to revel in their innate bliss.

Chapter 18

The Myth of Perfection

One of my teachers used to say, "The only perfect human is a dead human." A bit of dark humor, but it reveals an essential truth: as humans we will always be imperfect. We will never be complete, and our quest for an illusory finish line only ends in frustration as another finish line simply arises in the distance.

There is no enlightenment, there are only those who have given up the quest.

We are sold this idea that we can be perfect if only we tried hard enough. A huge industry repeatedly sells us the idea that if we only dedicated more effort, were strong enough, or thought more positively, we would have it all. We would be healthy, wealthy, and happy if only we wanted it badly enough.

This same industry denies death. We get sick or die because in some way we are guilty of a moral failing. Millions of people give over their money in exchange for the myth that the right vitamin, juice, exercise, or mantra will make us well. We will be vindicated in our hero's quest against aging, disease, stress, and unhappiness.

To confront reality is to release the myth that we will become perfected. If we are sick, we may become well. We may also need to accept whatever our physical and emotional limitations are and live our lives despite them.

We understand that we cannot have it all because we do not have the time or capacity to have it all. We cannot work, manage our households, our children, our physical and mental well-being, and navigate the onslaught of societal upheaval all at once. The greatest gift that we can offer ourselves is understanding that we feel depleted for a reason: our lives are exhausting.

Part of releasing this myth is to recognize that millions struggle against systemic inequities over which they have little control. While some do achieve great things despite this, to see reality clearly is to see that some of us face a small wave coming at us in our quest for better physical, emotional, financial, and spiritual health, while others face a tsunami.

The myth of perfection is a myth of control. It is the belief that we can control every facet of our lives. To let go of this myth is to be able to engage with the uncertainty of existence.

As long as we are human, we are imperfect. We become enlightened by digging deep within ourselves and realizing our perfectly imperfect humanity. Paradoxically, it is by sitting with our humanity and really embodying it that we can transcend it. We can move beyond the fear that underlies so many of our existences, to accept the uncertainty and chaos that are omnipresent in our lives, and to accept the pain and suffering that comes our way. It is by becoming deeply human that we, rather ironically, "transcend" what the typical experience of human life is. We cannot become "lightworkers" unless we have created space for that light; we do this by digging in the dirt of ourselves, by sitting with our darkness.

We can become "love" by deeply accepting and loving all aspects of ourselves. This is not by forcing things to become love, but by loving every vicious, atavistic, ugly, dirty, ashamed, wounded, and grotesque aspect of ourselves for exactly who they are.

We can only learn if we are willing to contend with the limitations of our knowledge. We can only progress if we are able to see how much further we can go. We can only leave behind illusion if we contend with the inner suffering that causes for us to create fantasies of power, attainment, achievement, and perfection.

We are not, nor will we ever be, static beings. Even bliss is full of nuance and darkness, and it will flow into something else. Our sorrow reveals our joy, our darkness our light, our imperfections our utter perfection.

Perfection is a self-made cage until we break free. We desire to become perfect out of self-loathing. We cannot accept ourselves as we are, and we have constructed a series of rigid and inhumane rules that we cannot live up to, nor can anybody else. By these standards we will never be good enough, perfected enough. Once we realize that we will never live up to our own illusory standards of perfection, we break free from the need to be anything other than who we are. We recognize that it is okay if we do not live up to the morals and judgments that we so harshly place on ourselves and others. We fully accept ourselves for who we are in the present moment, rather than who we desire to be or who we are planning to become.

It is by grounding deeply in the forces of chaos and uncertainty that we ride the waves of life. It is by welcoming even the darkest and most imperfect aspects of ourselves that we truly love ourselves. It is by deeply loving our human imperfections that we experience our perfection.

Chapter 19

Moving beyond Forgiveness

*I*n 1974, Yugoslavian artist Marina Abromavic presented a six-hour performance art piece in which she stood still and invited people to do what they wished to with her.

A table with 72 objects that she had arranged was in front of her, ranging from feathers and roses to razors and a loaded gun. Over the course of her performance, visitors who began with light and curious touch moved on to ripping off her clothes, cutting her with razors, and assaulting her physically and sexually. The piece ended when a fight broke out because someone had put a gun in her hand and placed her finger on the trigger.

This piece has become something of a legend, varying in interpretation based on the storyteller. In all of the stories the contradictions of human nature, of compassion, destruction, and violence, are in the forefront of the narrative.

Our ideas regarding compassion come from societal conditioning. They are wounded ideals, stemming from the notion that we are better people than we truly are. We understandably wish to think the best of ourselves and of one another. There is a true beauty in seeing the best parts of our nature and the light in one another. But often we do not wish to see the darkest parts of our own nature; we are willingly naive regarding our basest inclinations. Each one of us is capable of harming, abusing, and even killing. This may be out of necessity, circumstance, job (such as soldier), or out of psychological darkness like greed, fear, ignorance, intolerance, or hatred.

We separate ourselves from these aspects of our nature because truly acknowledging them means reckoning with them. We are fine seeing them in movies or on television. This maintains a safe distance from the darker aspects of our nature. The horrors of the world are "out there," beyond the bubble we have created around ourselves and our lives.

We like to think of ourselves as morally good, when we are more ambiguous in nature. We maintain a paradoxical tension of being both better than our inner critic tells us, and worse than our inner moralist cares to think of ourselves.

Even those with ideologies and theologies where they see themselves as doing no harm, create harm simply by their presence on earth. We create physical, emotional, and spiritual harm through our thoughts, actions, and our projections into the world. We cannot be fully compassionate until we reclaim the parts of ourselves that create harm, that think ourselves superior or different, or that believe that darkness is something that populates the world rather than ourselves.

Each one of us has bullied, harmed, or violated others in small and large ways. To heal that part of us is an inside job. To be willing to see that we have harmed others is a task that only those of us willing to see the darkest aspects of ourselves can do. There is too much denial and too much identification with victimhood that needs to be worked through prior to seeing how we too have harmed.

People are complex, and part of contending with our shadows is to see our nuance. Someone can be suffering immense pain and still feel love in their heart for another human being (though it may not be you). Someone can volunteer at an animal shelter and also be abusive to their spouse. Someone can be in a terrible mood and you leave your brief interaction thinking that they are the most horrible person on Earth, but you just happen to run into them on the exact day that their child died four years ago. You caught them in the midst of their suffering, on a day in which it was too overwhelming for them to bear.

To be grounded in reality is to understand that we have been both a victim and an abuser at different points in our lives. We often identify with victimhood because the parts of us that have been victimized need to come to terms with the full extent of how we have been wronged.

Then we can move forward, recognizing that life offers bad fortune and uncertainty to us all. We have all been victimized, but we are not powerless. We can reclaim our power and enter into adulthood, and no longer identify as a victim. The darkness of the world simply becomes a part of us, rather than something that eclipses the entirety of our identity.

We often desire to offer forgiveness and compassion to our abusers because it allows us to skip over the hard work of truly feeling. As I describe to many of my clients, what they are attempting to do by offering forgiveness and understanding is like calculating A + B = C but skipping B and moving from A to C.

We do not heal if we skip B, the pain and emotions that require unearthing, the stories that require telling. The parts of us that have truly suffered require being seen, validated, and justified in their pain. Often another person needs to see our pain and truly empathize with it for us to heal. We are not alone in our suffering. No matter what kind of pain or circumstances we have endured, someone else has suffered similarly. There is a certain grace in connecting to others who have known the same kind of suffering. When we realize that someone else has suffered the way we have, we can move out of alienation and into a place of connection. That is where healing takes place, where the lonely parts of ourselves find relief.

Shadow work is not about forgiveness. We do not need to forgive in order to heal. The pain and violence and brutality within the heart of someone else do not require your absolution. It is not your job to heal the pain of someone who has hurt you, or to provide them with closure.

I often work with incredibly empathetic people and they so often forget their own needs. Instead, they worry about everyone else around them. They understand the circumstances that can lead someone to experience enough pain to create suffering for others. Some have met those without souls, without human feeling, who simply seek to harm because they can.

They truly and meaningfully feel sorry for those who have harmed them, but this empathy prevents them from feeling their own pain. We can deny the full reality of what has happened to us by wielding forgiveness as a shield. We can utilize compassion towards others as a way to bypass our own pain. It is only by clearly seeing and by fully feeling what has happened that we can complete the process.

The end goal of shadow work is not forgiveness, it is acceptance. Acceptance of what has happened to us is far more important than any compassion or forgiveness that we can feel for another. If forgiveness and compassion arise after our own pain has been met, that is wonderful. But it is not necessary. Some acts cannot be forgiven, they can only be seen for exactly what they are.

The goal of shadow work is to see with adult clarity and to respond to life from a place of initiated adulthood. With the clarity of adult eyes, we can fully validate the pain that we carry and heal it in an embodied way. So often, we intellectually know what we have experienced, but our bodies have not yet processed and released the emotions and reactions to those experiences.

When we fully feel, we release the legacy of what has happened to us and move forward with our lives. What has happened will always be a part of us. However, it will move from something that still reverberates in our present reality into something unfortunate that happened to us in the past.

Suffering Is Not a Gift

Not all things that we experience are gifts. Sometimes we can become broken in a way that marks us and takes our life in a different direction. All of our experiences shape us, both good and bad. We intersect with time, place, circumstance, and people, and these experiences change what we know, who we are, and what we believe.

We can suffer deeply at the hands of another, but beliefs such as "everything is a gift" are naïve. The wounded aspects of ourselves are not gifts. The violent, atavistic aspects of ourselves arise within us individually and collectively and we live out their devastation. Some traumas in this world simply need to be experienced. There is no gift, no lesson; there is only a slow and intensive process of healing from being broken.

Look into the eyes of someone whose ALS is causing their throat muscles to slowly seize up on them, and tell them that this is a gift.

Or a parent whose six-year-old is dying of cancer, or someone who was severely neglected and abused as a child. It would be entirely appropriate for the recipient of this comment to rage at your ignorance.

To treat suffering as if it were a gift is to deny the pain of living. The human condition is one in which we suffer mightily. Not only that, but to truly accept our humanity is to recognize that each one of us is capable of committing the most depraved and inhuman of acts. To turn a blind eye to this is to mythologize suffering, to live it out on our televisions and online but to think it separate from anything that we could ever experience.

Even if such people "grew spiritually" or deepened their perspective due to their suffering, they still need to deal with its effect on their lives. A child who grew up in a household with severe neglect and abuse, who develops a nervous system that is wired to understand fear and violence at an early age, is at a distinct disadvantage. A soldier returning from war is not gifted with night terrors or panic attacks. Someone who has been sexually assaulted is not gifted with a pelvic floor that has emotionally and physically closed itself off from intimacy.

I have many clients who were traumatized, brutalized, or assaulted and told that it was a gift, that they attracted it (or "pulled it" to them), or that it is was an "initiation." This places the blame directly on the victim: that person deserved it because they acted, thought, or otherwise were morally inferior. The person saying this is separating themselves from the notions of darkness, disease, death, sickness, and the randomness that accompanies living in human bodies. To treat everything as a gift or an initiation is to neglect the parts of ourselves that were severely betrayed by life and by people.

We can learn to meet suffering with the healing qualities of softness and empathy. When we stop attempting to create meaning out of our suffering, we can sit with it as it is, instead of pretending that we are okay or that the situation is somehow beneficial.

When we can see the full continuum of dark to light within ourselves, we can see it within one another. This does not make hatred, violence, ignorance, or intolerance okay. It means that we no longer willfully blind ourselves to the realities of the world.

In our desire to see the best in one another, we blind ourselves to the darkness. In our pain we blind ourselves to the light, support, and connection that is already around us.

When we break free from ideologies like this we can truly sit with the suffering of humanity, rather than separating ourselves from the pain of the world out of fear. It is to meet death as an understood eventuality no matter how good or bad we are. In accepting the uncertainty of life there is no separation between ourselves and a person who randomly got hit by lightning, or who was sexually assaulted, or who has early onset Alzheimer's.

My friend Sara is the most loving person that I know. She is the one who comes to mind when I think of a truly open heart. Everyone in her presence simply feels better. She offered her children a household of love and safety and she was truly interested in who each of them was as a person. In fact she has this energy with everyone she meets—she is truly fascinated by them. She let her children feel the unconditional love of being truly accepted for who they were as individuals. She is older now, with grandchildren, and her children and grandchildren are some of the most stable, loving individuals that I have ever met.

Her children's stability and loving kindness is the result of having a childhood filled with positive regard and unconditional love. I meet so many people who feel so wrong and broken and harmed by not experiencing a childhood like this. The deepest healing those individuals can experience is to recognize that they may have not been loved or cared for to the depths that they needed by their parents, but that they can open to receiving it from other sources. Our adult self can offer it to our inner child. Our partner, spouse, or friends can offer us the love and connection that our parents were not able to offer. It is not too late for any of us. The fear and pain and insecurity that comes from not being loved can be healed, but it requires significant time, awareness, and effort.

To our parents we can bring the adult perspective that they are human, and they did the best that they could. However, this may have been a terrible job. More than likely it is more complicated than that—they could not deeply love us because they did not receive that love themselves. They could not emotionally connect because they never learned how. They lacked the basic tools and emotional intelligence to be able to offer a healthy, secure environment in your childhood. They were suffering, and passed on that cycle of harm. The end result of shadow work is not to forgive, or to forget; it is to see our parents as human. In doing so, we can move on from our childhood pain and blame; our inner child can finally grow up. Empathy for our parents develops as we recognize their suffering and limitations through an adult perspective.

The deepest healing that we can offer to anyone in pain is human empathy and connection. To witness without judgment, no matter our pain or history. When we are accepted, we feel it. When we fully accept even the darkest and most wrong and broken parts of ourselves, the person suffering knows that they no longer need to hide. They can be who they are, how they are, broken parts and all.

The Light in the Dark

There is a crack in everything, that's how the light gets in.

Leonard Cohen

Kintsugi is a Japanese art in which an artist repairs broken pottery by using gold, silver, or platinum epoxy. The result is often more beautiful or interesting than the original piece.

Those who have known the depths of human suffering and darkness are people who contain the greatest light. There is no need to romanticize suffering, but when we see our darkness clearly, we recognize it as the awakening force that it is. Out of suffering, a depth of soul, lived experience, and empathy emerges that does not typically arise in those who have not experienced the darkest aspects of humanity.

When we have truly known suffering, we can feel the empathetic mirror between ourselves and another shine more brightly. We are more likely to forgive them their trespasses, because we know how painful life can be. This is what it means to truly sit with our suffering, to truly know it.

If we face our suffering, we meet the entirety of our being. This is soul-making work. When we confront the fear and divisions within, we see that each one of us suffers in our own way. Out of the hardness of life comes the softness of knowing.

In the depths of suffering we find grace. Out of the darkest place arises the light of wisdom and acceptance. We each have a choice in our suffering and brokenness. It can make us hard, deadened to the world. It can also make us softer to ourselves and to others. Both can happen simultaneously. We can feel broken and shielded and guarded; in seeing that in another, we recognize ourselves. We feel a softness in our shared reality.

To accept the new shape of our lives due to our experiences and traumas is one of the most difficult things to do. We often seek to wage war against our mental and physical health issues and to fix the parts of ourselves that we see as broken. This warring against ourselves is never helpful. It simply keeps us in a loop of self-hatred.

To accept what is, including what we believe to be the broken and imperfect parts of ourselves, is the deepest form of compassion that we can offer ourselves. It is a hard acceptance, knowing that our bodies fail, and that our minds get overwhelmed with neuroses. But eventually, this acceptance leads to peace. We heal by repairing ourselves with gold and silver. We are not what we once were, but we are something new—a platter or a cup whose brokenness and emptiness has been filled with the golden light of compassion and acceptance.

Chapter 20

Rediscovering the Child Self

When we rediscover our child self, we may laugh at ourselves, even our worst qualities. Our shame and faults become humorous, rather than cause for self-hatred. We are all deeply human. By accepting that, we move beyond self-hatred into loving self-acceptance. We may even laugh at our imperfect humanness.

When we begin shadow work, our inner child is fragmented. Due to trauma or life circumstance, our inner child has moved out of wholeness. With healing, our inner child embodies the play and light of existence.

By loving our inner child in their totality, we can once again become like a child. We carry the wisdom of being an adult with our considerable life experience but we allow the joy, curiosity, and openness of the child self to emerge.

We become enchanted by the way a dandelion swings in the wind, we sit still and watch the rain stream down our windows, we take delight in eating a small treat. Once we have voyaged deeply into our darkness, the light of life emerges. We can embody joy, stillness, and the simplicity of just being: full of wonder, possibility, and hope.

This is the cycle of life and of self-realization. We begin as children, go through life experiences—including suffering and trauma—which lead to individuation. Then, through shadow work, we move beyond even that into a place of being all things: simultaneously child, parent to the inner child, and fully functioning adult.

When we can find the dark humor in the circumstances of our suffering, our humanity no longer weighs so heavily on us. Our faults are not a reason to feel shame, nor the self-deprecation of apology. We can accept our inadequacies just as fully as we embrace the ways in which we are perfect. To release the yoke of perfection is to gain the ability to laugh at ourselves in all of our human imperfection. To grapple with our darkness is to dance with our shadow and to experience it as a fount of creativity. This moves us far beyond thinking of the shadow as something to transform into light, but rather as something that we have distanced ourselves from and failed to integrate for far too long.

One of the most rewarding results of shadow work is the ability to recapture the positive aspects of the inner child. Our inner child is filled with the humor, innocence, and naivety that so many of us have lost in adulthood.

There is a healthy selfishness that is often absent from our adult lives. We must consider ourselves first, lest our work and personal lives and shadows and families deplete us until we become walking zombies.

In spite of cultural notions that it is narcissistic to do so, a healthy selfishness allows us to build the energy and fortitude to help others. Without it, we will continually be depleted by the world. When we tend to ourselves first, from a solid basis of self-love we can assist others. Our energy becomes so radiant from tending to ourselves first that helping others no longer depletes us; rather it is an extension of our energy. At this point, someone in our presence can simply feel better—how often are we given an opportunity to be around someone who has done consistent self-work so that they can offer love?

The most realized souls are those who no longer take life seriously. Life is a serious thing, but it is also terribly funny. If we can see the humor in life, even in tragedy, we gain an inner resilience that serves us well.

Those who seek to regain their inner child can develop a sense of play again. Playing as a child and as an adult serve entirely different purposes. As an adult, play can become strict and centered around rules and winning. As a child, play is about imagination, creation, and enjoyment. Developing a healthy sense of play can help us rediscover our inner child and make her a part of us again.

Chapter 21

Releasing the Shame of the Body

Those who would preserve the spirit must also look after the body to which it is attached.

Albert Einstein

Our bodies are the present moment. If we are at home in our bodies, we are at home in our lives. Our physical forms are mirrors to the physical world. We can move freely in the world when we are at ease within ourselves. We must feel to become.

There is so much preventing us from realizing the natural body and its truths. There is a wisdom of our primal body, hidden beneath cultural manners and masks of habit. We are taught to hate our physical bodies and to feel shame regarding our natural eroticism.

We become heads without bodies, thoughts divided from feelings. Philosophy, religion, and spirituality perpetuate this divide. When we believe that we are superior to our bodies and their animalistic instincts, we separate ourselves not only from every other species on Earth but also from our human nature.

Our bodies are the physical world, and we can see our disgust and separation from our own physical forms mirrored in our collective attitudes toward the natural world.

We are taught to enact certain mannerisms, assume specific shapes to be appealing to our culture. For many of us, a conflict emerges between the romanticized archetypal physical form and our own real body. We love and lust after the perfection that we see outwardly, but we disconnect, or loathe, the physicality of our own bodies.

When we remove the social body, we can appreciate the beauty of the physical form and its innate intelligence: our body has a consciousness, an intelligence, all its own. We are composed of trillions of cells, tissues, organs, and a nervous system that all coordinate to keep us alive despite ourselves. There is magnificence in our physiology, in the way that nerve cells resemble the outer reaches of the universe, and in the way that the waters of our body compose their rhythms like the tides of the ocean.

Through connecting to the body, we access our intuition and our emotions; we hear the subtle language of what our body has to say. If we only learn to listen, we can forge a deep and sustaining connection between mind, body, and spirit.

Our bodies hold on to so much pain. They are repositories for the stories and emotions that got stuck and require unearthing. Beyond these are the impulses that we were never able to express. I was once in a car accident as a passenger, with my legs up on the dashboard. When healing this injury, my body moved into the same position that I had been in during the car accident in order to release the thwarted impulse. As my body spontaneously acted out its original injury, along with the subsequent energetic movements and emotions that it never got a chance to fully express at the time of the accident, both the injury and lingering impulse were released. It is not unusual in my work with clients for static postures, spontaneous shaking, and sporadic movements to arise as the body releases stuck impulses and emotions.

So many of us sublimated our desires to walk, run, flee, shout, or play when we were children. We were afraid to move our bodies in the ways we wanted to. We could not dance or shout or be dirty as it would mean punishment. We could not flee, as we had nowhere to go. Now as adults we can set a specific intention to let go of what the body holds— not only the emotions but also the denied impulses and movements. Many people undergo decades of therapy but miss out on this piece. The trauma of our lives cannot be fully processed without moving it out of our nervous system in a bodily way. Until we do so, it remains stored and unresolved.

When we do shadow work, we take back the projections we have cast onto others. We do this until our play unravels, and after that we can totally and truly connect with the world. That connection is also developed within—what is within is without, and vice versa—so we can reach a point where we are truly home within ourselves. Our defenses have released, our emotions flow through us, and we radically accept the world (and the people in it) for what they are.

It is at this point that we can totally reclaim our shadow. While once we saw the shadow as an accumulation of our own pain, we can now understand that within the depths of our darkness is the light. Every moment of ecstasy and inspiration comes from the shadow. It is through our darkness, not our light, that we experience passion, bliss, ingenuity, and creativity. When we remove the blockages to accessing these gifts, we feel their darkness shining through us, through our body.

Our shadow is our bodily, innate, wild twin. When we allow this wildness, this darkness, to fully express itself through us, we can dance, make love, experience intimacy, and be one with the flows of existence.

Every bit of work we have done, every examination of our shadow and of our own reactions to the outer world, leads us to a fully realized shadow. This shadow can run and jump and move and respond to life in the instinctual way that it has always desired. This movement is free, regardless of how others will respond. This does not mean that we disregard societal conventions and rules. The feral aspects of the self do not need to scratch and pull and destroy simply because they can. They can act in a way that is both fully expressive and yet considerate of others. This does not destroy the fun, but it allows us to express our primal parts in safe and life-affirming ways, with regard for those around us.

The way to express our shadow is through movement. While routine movements prescribed by others can help, it is in spontaneity that our shadow expresses itself fully. How would you like to move, shake, or stretch? Tune into your body and allow it to move as it wishes—without strain but following the guidelines of feeling good. Give permission for your shadow, your body consciousness, to express itself however it would like through movement. This may be taking a pause or even resting in complete stillness. It may also be dynamic, jumping or shaking your whole body, or it may just be tiny micro-movements of a finger or a toe discovering that it can move.

When we allow our shadow to fully emerge through our physical form, we break the bonds that tie us to civility and severe us from our bodies. We release the shame that has been heaped upon us to prevent us from discovering our power. In our bodies lies our latent power, just waiting to rise up.

Chapter 22

Recapturing Voice

$\mathcal{F}$or many of us, having a voice that expresses our truth feels next to impossible. We must please others, or at least speak within the confines of societal and familial scripts.

We have severed off our voices, separating our heads from our bodies, so that our real voice does not emerge. Chinese medicine teaches that there is a channel of energy—an internal aspect of the Heart channel—that travels from our heart through the tip of our tongue. If this channel is connected, vibrant, and healthy, then we speak what is true in our hearts. But most of us are closed down and armored, cutting off the voice of the heart, blocking that clear passage of energy.

This passageway was shut down for a very good reason: speaking up in certain situations, including the childhood home, or even the adult workplace, can have consequences. The mind and body determined that those consequences were too dire, and so it decided to shut down, so that it wouldn't accidentally speak out and find itself in an unsafe place for the entire being and body.

Many of us remain invisible because we believe that being seen and heard means that we will experience pain and harm. We hold deep shame about being vulnerable, about expressing who we truly are, because we have been told so many times that who we are and what we have to say is wrong.

It is important to understand that this fear is totally correct. Having a voice means that others can say that you are wrong or misguided. They may hate you for having a voice when they do not. They may resent you for being willing to be seen and heard in a world in which so many hide themselves and their light away.

The throat and mouth are considered the avenue of expression, and it is typical for individuals to experience a lockdown of this area due to a backlog of things that they didn't express when they wanted or needed to. Examples of this include thinking of a response a day after we are asked a question, or realizing an essential truth about a relationship, friendship, or work situation but not knowing how to communicate it. Many of my clients have known that they needed to leave a job or relationship months or even years before they physically left. Even more common is choking back conversations that need to be had or not being able to admit unmet needs.

As an adult, we can acknowledge that while there are consequences for using our voices (and in some cases, incredibly valid safety concerns) we no longer live in a restrictive childhood home in which utilizing our voice may have led to ridicule, shame, or punishment. We can see how society expects passivity and a closed mouth. We can understand that aligning with our soul, our heart, and our voice, goes against considerable conditioning that seeks to keep us silent.

We can also recognize that whatever we have closed down, disassociated from or rejected is out of our control. It is shadow. We then project this shadow onto others so that we do not own it. We have angry outbursts because we have not claimed our anger (or we passive-aggressively try to swallow our anger or be "nice" instead of express it). Our voice speaks in ways that we may regret later; it may say things that come more from unprocessed emotion and trauma than from any sort of clarity.

By reclaiming the voice, the tongue, the throat, and the heart, we can not only heal prior trauma (and our voices) but we can also wield our voice in a way that is under our control.

We can consciously decide when, where, and how to utilize our voice.

We can have full access to our voice and decide when to use it. When our voices are "offline" or when we are disassociated from them, we cannot make that decision. It is made for us.

Having a voice does not mean saying whatever we want despite the consequences. It means accepting that utilizing our voice does have consequences—which may include anything from receiving disapproval, feeling pain, forging a great connection, or crying tears of joy.

We may recognize when we are going to waste our breath, when our voice may not be appreciated, heard, or respected. To not speak in such situations is an option we can choose, instead of being the only choice that we have. It is also critical to recognize when our voice can mean a lack of safety and consciously decide whether to use it or not. This is much different from shutting it down entirely.

To reclaim your voice is about consciously expressing all that you wish to. You can argue, speak calmly, or remain silent. You can punch someone in the mouth with your words or acknowledge that who you are speaking to is not worth your voice.

Using your voice can mean facing opposition from mediocre minds who simply wish to hear their own thoughts, dogmas, and fears repeated back to them. Realize this and use your voice anyway.

Having a voice means expressing your truth and your light, as well as hearing from other voices who wish to connect with you. In the process you might receive plenty of blessings. We cannot fully connect unless we share who we are—our voice—in some way with one another. Our voice does not need to be expressed through speech, we can share through singing, drawing, writing, dancing, or any other creative pursuit. We can "speak" through offering excellent tax returns. Our voice can radiate out into the world, showing everyone exactly who we are by our presence.

Having a voice means having access to your heart, to your truth, to your soul, in a way that a lot of people hunger for, but few have access to.

It is possible that your voice is misguided, wobbly, the voice of a six-year-old or a teenager, rather than an adult. It may be a voice full of pain or a voice that lacks reason. It might also be a voice unwilling to examine itself, so locked into trauma that its expressions are clouded over with pain from an earlier age. It may be an attempt to process that pain, for an inner child to be noticed and heard, in order for that pain to be seen and rectified by the world. When we can finally be heard, we can close chapters of our lives and move forward.

The great voices in history did not speak in the same ways as everybody else. They brought new ideas into the world; utilizing the voice through literature, architecture, poetry, singing, and other ways that are not immediately appreciated or understood. These unique voices propel our culture, as a whole, forward. Our voices pass knowledge down through the generations that come after us, changing the world for the better.

Chapter 23

Engaging the Deep Wild

*W*hen we first begin shadow work, we consider the shadow to be composed of the traumatized parts of ourselves that we needed to shut off in order to survive. Many view the shadow as being strictly composed of negative parts, the emotions and traumas that we could not process at the time because they were too overwhelming, or because we lacked the tools to contend with them.

As we do shadow work, we find our shadows in other people. By examining our reactivity, we have an opportunity to resolve inner conflict. We can reach a point where we are grateful for others triggering us, as they are showing us something unhealed within ourselves.

We define the behaviors and ways of being that arise out of trauma as pathological, but they are in fact natural and appropriate reactions to that experience. By understanding and feeling compassion for these survival mechanisms we can heal our relationship with them much more readily than if we were to categorize them as pathological or wrong.

Nothing about trauma is pathological. There is nothing wrong with you, or anyone else, for enacting survival mechanisms, such as denying, repressing, or sectioning off energy/vitality as a result of great pain. For being incredibly afraid of an experience that rightfully induced fear.

When we can fully appreciate our survival mechanisms, we can convert them from permanent fixtures in our lives to useable tools, available when ready, in our toolkit. We know perfectly well how to be invisible or to flee and we can use such tools consciously if we need to. This mentality can allow us to see that our defenses and tools do not need to be overcome or "fixed" but simply put in their right place. Rather than denying our rightful responses to trauma and to life, we can fully appreciate them. We did the best we could at the time.

Finding forgiveness for our past selves can bring us through the grief of realization and recognition. It is a part of growth to see that we could have acted differently before, or have clarity regarding how our protective mechanisms and emotions previously separated us from others. The ability to see this indicates significant growth. Rather than grieving for time lost, we can recognize that we can act differently in the present and future.

When we begin to reclaim our shadows, we discover that shadow work is just as much about reclaiming our light as it is our darkness. In our Otherness lie our gifts, and when we embrace them, we find that what is different about us is what we have to bring into the world.

There is a layered path to shadow work. Beyond working on trauma or reactivity, or even the reclamation of individual gifts, comes the intelligence of our innate responses. At this point we can see our shadow directly, and it takes on a different definition. The shadow is now our instinctual self, which brings us into contact with our intuition and the magical possibilities of reality.

Austin Osman Spare (1886–1956) was an English painter and occultist who defined "atavistic resurgence" as the magical part of human consciousness that lies buried deeply within us. It is that which rises in symbols, dreams, and passions. When we have cut off considerable parts of our shadow, we divorce ourselves from the magical, sensory, and existential aspects of living. The more of our shadow we have cut off, the greater the distance between ourselves and this magic.

When we reclaim our shadow, the magic returns, accompanied by passion for living and a deep curiosity for the unknown. Instead of fearing the dark, we welcome it. All of our innate responses, and even our defense mechanisms against reality, can simply be seen as tools that helped us to trek through difficult terrain. We may learn better tools, or wield prior tools more consciously. But at this point we can see our biological impulses and our reactivity to our experiences in life laid bare before us.

We no longer act it out, but consciously participate as a viewer of our own play. When we do this, we step beyond our play and recapture the spontaneity, passion, and creativity that make up the foundation of our being. This is flow, which can now move through us freely.

It is the tendency of our culture to mistake what is dark within ourselves for what is wounded, rather than seeing darkness as its own kingdom that carries its own beauty. When we move beyond dark, meaning "bad," or the impulse to transmute any darkness into "light," we revel in the shadows. We embrace the unknown and love our darkness as fiercely as we love the socially and morally acceptable parts of ourselves.

Then we see that our darkness and light cannot be separated, they create and interweave with one another. Thus our self-realization process is complete. We are no longer dark versus light, good versus bad, body versus mind. We are all things at once.

The yin-yang symbol reveals a balance between darkness and light. Within darkness there is light; within light there is darkness. This primordial symbol of creation shows us that neither darkness nor light is inseparable; if we are able to move beyond binary thinking—this versus that—we can move into paradoxical thinking, where opposites are no longer in conflict but emerge from the same source.

Our inner perfectionist loves the binary of dark/light and wants to hold on to it. Within the light it places perfection and order, and within the shadow it puts everything messy and chaotic and animalistic. Many individuals who are interested in spirituality still keep the Other at bay; they block their own self-realization because the spirit realms, the natural realms, and our daily lives, do not fit into tidy transcendentalist (light-based) paradigms.

Monsters and darkness hide underneath our social morality and our ideas of human superiority. There are inner tyrants and swamp monsters and mermaids who wish to drown us (for sheer pleasure) and they can remain exactly who they are. It is the work of a lifetime to integrate them. They will not be introduced to polite society or know which fork to eat with during the salad course, but these creatures lurking within allow us to recapture our vitality and power.

The wild twin connects us to the natural and spiritual realms. Our shadows are the entry point, a doorway, that takes us beyond the binary that teaches us to put light on one side and dark on the other, forever battling each other, and into a place of recognizing the beauty and inherent worth of the dark. Our lives are mostly composed of grey. To reclaim our shadow in its totality is to move beyond this or that, shadow or light, and to embrace being all things at once.

Personal power is simply the ability to make conscious choices. To decide for ourselves what we do with our lives is terrifying—we are used to delegating an outer authoritarian archetype to do it for us. We like having our answers given to us; we get upset at the idea of searching and finding out that the world is not so simple, that our queries might not receive answers. Our mind is designed to crave control and knowing.

Our shadows, our darkness, can become vital aspects of our being, transmuting not from "dark" to "light" but from feeling dissociated and castigated to feeling the fuel of creative energies and impulses.

We fear these primal parts of ourselves; our instincts whisper fantasies of harm, destruction, and revenge in our ears. All of these feelings and desires are exactly right, and we are human for feeling them. Do not deny them or stuff them back into a box. Recognize that every human being feels this way because we have thousands of years of biological impulses that have been denied and bottled up.

The important caveat is to acknowledge the distinct divide between fantasy and reality. A part of you may wish to be Godzilla destroying a whole city. A part of you may wish to stab someone who has caused you immense pain. These fantasies are understandable. Most people, if asked, recognize that they do not actually wish to enact this in reality.

We are so afraid of our violent impulses that we do not have the tools to bring them into the daylight for examination. Even if you are one of the few people who desires to actualize your fantasy, you can recognize that your fantasy is coming from a place of wounding, or you can enact it in a safe, life-affirming way. For example, our inner caveman may love throwing axes, or building a fire.

Know that it is normal to want to hurt someone who has hurt you. The difference is in the choices we make in the daylight, understanding that we do not need to bestow our pain upon others. We can take responsibility for it, even in cases where we desire retribution. To do this is to have real power.

English author Neil Gaiman writes, "If you are protected from dark things then you have no protection of, knowledge of, or understanding of dark things when they show up." Children like dark fairy tales and frightening ghost stories. They need to experience powerful emotions. The character who turns up most often in fairy tales is death, who often takes away the beloved. If we shield ourselves from the dark, we experience a primary split from that part of ourselves and project it outward.

We lack interface and healthy expression of our darkest instincts. We project them onto the archetypal prisoner, drug kingpin, or serial killer. Part of the darkness is the cast of villainous archetypes onto whom we displace our basest instincts. We place the alien, the psychotic, and the archetypes of evil onto the most inhuman objects we can find. Our horror movies, alien conspiracies, and societal shaming of mental health issues show this inability to reclaim our own inner darkness.

It is typical for people who feel separated from others or displaced from reality to create myths regarding their circumstances. It is simply too painful for a child to contend with sexual abuse from a parent, and so he projects that evil onto the figure of an alien. It is painful to not belong in a friend group at school, and so she creates a myth that she is special or magical.

Onto the psychotic or mad woman we place the pain of living. The psychotic cannot abide by the rules of society and so he acts out, receiving punishment for his expressed pain. Scottish psychiatrist R.D. Laing thought that psychosis was the birth–death process—the disorganized reorganization period that we all go through—gone awry. The expression of psychosis allows passive, taciturn people to stand up for themselves and act out the role of villain, asking for what they could never request in their normal role. After psychosis, the mind can reorganize around a healthier system.

It is common for us to project every fear of death, disease, and disability onto those who are different. Any person who strays too far from what is considered normal is shunned, castigated, dismissed, out of our own fear of ourselves.

The further we stray from nature, and our own human nature, the more that we invent an Other to fear. We suffer from an incorrect assumption that our environment is set and that we must adapt to it. Instead, we affect and change our environment. If we separate from our inner human nature, the natural world suffers for it. If we do not connect to the natural world outwardly, we disconnect from it both within and without, and it becomes neglected. We become out of sync, and both we and the natural world suffer. We are a part of the world, and have a reciprocal relationship with it. Our presence in it matters.

The largest stories in mythology and religion relate to the nature of good and evil. Marie Louise Von Franz, a Swiss Jungian psychologist, explains that evil is something beyond human nature. When a murderer is killing another he is performing something god-like. That person loses his humanity in the process of performing such an act. Jung said that, "Good does not become better by being exaggerated, but worse, and a small evil becomes a big one through being disregarded and repressed."

Within humans lie darkness, deception, and the capacity to enslave, demean, control, and commit great violence against one another. It is easy to project this capability onto a mythical Other, or to not see ourselves in the eyes of a serial killer. Indian sage Ramana Maharshi famously said: "I am the person I hate. I am the evil archon. I am the darkness I seek to deny or cast onto the Other. I am the beliefs that have been created out of trauma. There are no others."

When we fully reclaim our shadow, we can recognize that evil is not an archaic or primitive Other that confounds humans into harming one another, but rather something that lives within each one of us. Our basest thoughts may take on a mythic scope, but our decision to act on them is a very human one. We all have instincts, even violent or evil ones, and it is a question of whether we consciously choose to harm another or not.

The demons that we see outwardly are a result of our personal and collective shadow. They stem from the greed, lust, harm, and trauma that we inflict on one another. They are the collective shadows that have formed through our own denied impulses. Any primitive impulses that originate from beyond the human community are still enacted in the hearts and lives of humans. We may or may not fully understand such forces, but when they become a part of us, we can accept them as a part of our individual shadow.

When we accept the darkest aspects of ourselves, we let the light in. We can honor our sexual and animalistic selves and invite them to live through us, giving us access to our power. When we can feel our anger in all of its magnificence, when we can see that sex, meditation, death, and trauma are portals to profound surrender and awakening, our darkness transitions to light.

As W.B. Yeats wrote, "The World is full of magical things, patiently waiting for our senses to grow sharper." To accept the existence of magic in the world instantly puts us at odds with today's society. But the alternative—a world in which normality means that the light in our eyes has grown—is untenable.

To gain access to the darkest, wildest aspects of ourselves is to access the grace, forgiveness, and love that we long for. We cannot love ourselves, or one another, if we deny our darkness.

Chapter 24

Our Online Shadows

*W*e are experiencing a breakdown of reality. In this time of disorganization, chaos, and crisis we are coming face to face with our shadows. Our relationship with authority has shifted such that those with no knowledge become arbiters of truth. Increasing tribalism is dividing us so that any identity, label, thought, idea, or person that does not fit with our "tribe" is considered a threat. They are "canceled," shamed, harmed, hated.

While anti-intellectualism has always been a pervasive trend, the nature of the internet means that this tendency has grown stronger. There are definitely benefits to everyone having a voice or a platform, but in the process we have moved away from trusting and listening to those who truly have knowledge, experience, and authority. We harm ourselves through disinformation. In our online spaces we celebrate those we want to hear, rather than those who have helpful or informed viewpoints. There has long been a need to release the doctor archetype as an authoritarian role, but too large of a swing in the other direction means that we have recast this role with ignorant authoritarians.

As we increase our dependence on the metaverse and the internet as our place of communal gathering, we become further unmoored from reality. Our ability to focus lessens as the world turns into sound bites, video clips, and information at our fingertips. We no longer need to memorize, recall, or bring ourselves out of our distracted, disassociated states.

When we connect to our physical bodies and the natural world, we are much more likely to see our shared humanity. We are also more likely to adhere to cultural and societal norms, considering "truth" as well as "goodness." We can look outside of our personal bubble and see other perspectives and consider other people.

The internet is one of the easiest places for us to project our shadows: our unhealed life, problematic elements of reality, and difficult emotions that we are not yet ready or able to reconcile within ourselves. It is a place where we can readily dehumanize others and perpetuate suffering that distracts us from our own lives.

While we have always been able to place a bubble between ourselves and reality, the ease of doing this online ensures that we do not need to interact with any information that we do not want to see. We can change our preferences to the point that all we receive are reflections and magnifications of our own thoughts. Thanks to the algorithms used by social media platforms, personally and collectively we are creating online spaces of darkness and fear. We are casting larger shadows than ever before onto our public figures: politicians, celebrities, and social media personalities.

We all desire community, and every shadow has its light. For those unable to participate fully in reality, or for those who have a unique path in this world or a specialized interest, finding others who share that interest has never been easier. We can connect and find friends, romantic partners, or simply another person to chat with to combat the loneliness.

Yet the internet induces a dissociative state. This means that we can move beyond physicality and find ourselves sharing on a much deeper level with others than we would if we had met in person. Because of the anonymity as well as the separation from the physical world and our bodies, there is an immediate depth when we engage online. This can be deeply healing, as we voice our pain for many others to witness. This pseudo intimacy can also allow for us to skip over the "steps" of socialization in which we gradually grow closer to someone until we disclose our deepest truths and most vulnerable of states. We fast forward to that place right away online.

Due to the nature of the internet, we can find our shadows mingling and joining with the shadows of others. Similarly disconnected and wounded souls can find themselves in groups where their collective worldview consolidates, fractured from the webs of reality.

Such consolidation occurs by surrounding ourselves with others in the "tribe" who espouse the same beliefs, while any other ideology or "tribe" is met with contempt, shaming, hatred. The more time we spend with groups who do this, the more fractured we become.

The split that occurs when we are online causes our shadows to feel free to fully emerge. Our basic hatred and unhealed wounds can fixate on someone and our shadows of light can find someone else on social media to project onto. We can view examples of the darkness of the world at lightning speed and in such immense quantities that we have words like "doom scrolling" to describe the depravity that is constantly available to us.

We can bring our basic wounds of wanting to be liked and accepted and loved into social media. Our ability to receive "strokes" in transactional relationships has changed dramatically; we can receive transactional love and approval online from a worldwide audience. The nature of the internet creates parasocial relationships, in which our fixation on a celebrity, social media personality, or someone we have simply interacted with online, becomes entirely one-sided. In the loneliness and separation of the internet, we have so much information about one another at our fingertips, and we can use that information to create whole relationships that are unmoored from reality. This results in suffering, because our emotional energy is not met by the person we are fixated on. We are not in a real relationship, and the shadow relationship leads only to more isolation and delusion.

We have created large shadows online that loom over us like large clouds collectively enveloping us. These energies can on some days feel so incredibly raw, full of the type of pain that creates immense (and understandable) existential distress in all of us.

With any clarity, one can see that the world is a difficult place to be in. It is full of suffering, pain, ignorance, and misuse of power. It is unfair, unjust, and out of touch with human emotions. If you feel that the world is filled with pain and suffering and darkness, recognize that you are completely and totally right.

But it is easy to lose our way in this darkness. Listen to music, learn a new recipe, look at art, watch the birds, do something to bring beauty into this world. Remind yourself of the beauty and love present in the world underneath all of the pain.

We have a choice regarding how we spend our time online. Question how you feel when you visit specific websites (before and after, this will show you why you may be drawn to a specific website in the first place). Begin in this small way to take back your energy and emotions from the collective shadow.

Use technology for its light side. Multiple clients over the years have shared that someone simply texting them to say "hello" has reminded them that they are not alone. Acts of service do not need to be large, and we never know how much they can mean to someone.

When we clearly see how our shadows play out collectively online, we naturally want to step back from our addictions and tendencies. We can reclaim the shadow energy we have put into the internet and find life-affirming ways to connect with each other instead.

To become an individual, who can think freely and see reality with nuance, without taking part in this form of online tribalism, is a remarkable thing.

Chapter 25

Fear of Death, Fear of Life

*Be like water making its way through cracks. Do not be
assertive, but adjust to the object, and you shall find a way
around or through it. If nothing within you stays rigid,
outward things will disclose themselves.*

Bruce Lee

Let come what comes, let go what goes, see what remains.

Ramana Maharshi

*I*n my sessions I often ask my client if we can sit and feel together whatever heaviness they carry. Together in this heaviness we experience the loneliness and isolation that so frequently accompanies pain, trauma, and sickness.

A deep transformation can occur when someone who has felt completely separate and alone in their suffering recognizes that another person is willing to sit with them in that suffering. They can feel that no part of them is wrong, and that all parts of them are worthy of being seen. They do not have to change, to become more whole or healed, they can be seen and loved and cared for exactly as they are.

No words are necessary, simple presence and humanity is enough. What we ultimately want, what we so desperately need, is someone to be present with us.

What people feel about us and how they treat us rarely has anything to do with us. We can recognize that they have struggled and due to their own suffering they have built walls around themselves which they now carefully guard so that no one can enter. They can no longer feel love, or be loved, because they must defend themselves.

Most of us live our whole lives afraid, carefully encaged behind the walls we have erected to protect ourselves. We defend ourselves against being hurt again, we protect ourselves from feeling. We stop ourselves from considering the larger existential realities that create havoc in our lives. We end up in a prison of our own making, too afraid to free ourselves.

To accept that uncertainty and chaos rule our lives much more than order ever will is to reclaim the shadow. Every part of ourselves that we have pushed out of the light because we didn't see it as worthy or lovable is a part of us. We can open up and welcome back those parts with loving kindness.

Our greatest shadow is fear of death. Most of us ignore death until it becomes an unavoidable presence in our lives. To alleviate this, we can take care of the practicalities of death: medical directives, wills, speaking to our loved ones about how we wish to die and what to do with our belongings. No matter our age, death can visit us at any time. Attending to practicalities allows us to understand that death at some point will visit us personally.

When we greet death as a friend, we accept that we will one day die. Death is simply a door that we pass through, an initiation. It is likely that within our lifetimes we have already experienced many deaths and renewals that resemble the physical death process.

So many of us remain stuck because we have a fear of change. This is rooted in a primal fear of death, as our instinctual selves know that any change can mean death. We have had a whole life to show us that change can mean bad things happening, so we cling to the ways that life has denied us or created pain for us. We stop ourselves from receiving. By accepting our own death, we accept that change and flow and impermanence are the very ground our lives are built upon. In this acceptance, we come into contact with our own vitality and enthusiasm for living again.

We can allow life to flow through us, if we let go of the parts of us stuck in death. Death means stuckness, stagnancy, and control. If we let go of this control (and realize that we never had control in the first place) we can embrace life, instead of living our lives in fear of death.

One of the largest shadows in the modern world is the denial of death. When we fear death, we deny it. The more we deny it, the larger that fear grows, and we attempt to alleviate it by creating myths of control. We then regard sickness and death as moral failings, rather than a part of life that simply visits us all, no matter how perfect or imperfect we are.

Our minds seek to control our external reality to such an extent that they cling to the idea that the world is just. Believing that bad things can happen unfairly or randomly is simply too frightening, and so we believe that victims must have done something wrong to deserve their fate. New Age ideologies that there are no victims or that you create your own reality seek to exert a type of control over life that simply doesn't exist. There is a thought form in Western culture that you are to blame for your misfortune and all you have to do is "pull yourself up by your bootstraps."

We can learn to accept death, disease, discomfort, pain, and ill health of all kinds. In this acceptance, we recognize that many things can contribute to ill health, including our own habits and personal history. When we can sit with the darkness of others with compassion instead of defending ourselves, we find love. We find life. Until that point we will push our fears of uncertainty and death onto others.

Within this shadow of unacknowledged death is the death wish, the desire for non-being that visits many of us as suicidal ideation. It longs for the bliss of the womb, and harbors the wish for suffering to end. In my suicidal clients, their sincere wish is rarely to die, or to cause themselves harm. It is simply to no longer exist.

In such a dark place our essential loneliness is revealed. We are each lonely souls, and the disconnected parts of ourselves that are mired in darkness will see the light only when they recognize that they are not the only ones who suffer. Yet we can sit in our loneliness together, and in that find healing.

The desire for death is a desire for change. If we recognize that our lives are not working, we can change them. On a mythic level, our fantasies of death—the latent death wish—arise in us because we may be transitioning into a new phase of our lives. If we can see that we desire death because a part of us is dying, we can pivot towards renewal and rebirth, instead of remaining in misery.

It is through suffering and the greatest depths of darkness that we find the light of our being. We know what it is to suffer, and in that utter darkness, the light of the soul eventually shines. Suffering is soul-creating, soul-making, and those who survive the worst of circumstances develop something beyond the fear that drives our lives—love.

When we move beyond this fear, we discover that our greatest fear is not death, it is life. It is much easier to see our death wish than to see our fear of life—how we hold ourselves back and do not fully live. We rarely take advantage of the opportunities that life affords us in the brief time that we are alive.

In doing shadow work myself and with so many clients and students, I find that we reach a point where we start to experience the vital energy that was stuck under piles of trauma and fear; that's where we truly begin to feel our own power. We offer so much of our own light to others while remaining unable to recognize it within ourselves. The thought of reclaiming that light is truly terrifying.

We associate having any energy at all with feeling fear. This is understandable in a physiological sense because we are not used to experiencing states like bliss and ecstasy. We confuse such things with fear and anxiety—we are familiar with those states. The idea that we can experience both darkness and light, meaning that we also contain multitudes of light, is a wonderful concept. But to actually embody it can be terrifying.

We are afraid of the infinite possibilities of life. If life is a wide open space, and we are able to ride the waves of an uncertain existence, what do we have to live for? What happens when our quest to resolve our childhoods is behind us and we can truly assume an adult role in which we get to decide for ourselves what provides meaning and purpose in our lives? When we move beyond the script, the roles, and the play, the blank space is initially frightening. We are so lost and lonely, so assured that we are worthless, that moving past our ideologies of separation is rightfully difficult.

Underneath all of this is life. It is the state of being that is love. We can be wildly passionate about life, feel genuinely curious about its possibilities, and still clearly see the darkness of the world. When we have an unrealized shadow, we focus on the negative. We are not good enough, and the world is a dark and negative place filled with hatred.

When we radically accept the darkness of the world, we also accept that darkness within ourselves. We encounter all aspects of ourselves, and at our core, we access the atavistic instincts and deep feelings of love and self-worth that we have longed for.

When we truly know that we deserve love simply because we are human, we can move beyond the bounds of transactional love. We can recognize that others may not love us, not because we are not inherently worthy of love, but because they are simply not able or willing to offer it. They have their own barriers to love—both giving and receiving—just as we did.

In seeing this, we begin to accept life on its own terms. We can release the ideals of perfectionism and control. Instead, we flow with our existence, whatever its darkness, light, and shades in between.

The final phase of shadow work is opening up to the simplicity of being love. It is who we are once we have let go of all the rest. At the base layer of our being, we desire to love. We can be love while being loved in return, but we can also be love in and of itself. We can move beyond desiring love from another because we have accepted that they may not have love to give back. When we realize how good it feels to offer love without expecting anything in return, we can love unconditionally. We can be love.

When we accept that we are going to die, that we are impermanent creatures, we realize that underneath is the fear of life. When we recognize this fear of life, we can accept this fear too. We can also move beyond it, and fully grasp that beyond this fear of truly living is the opportunity to live. We can be without a script, a narrative, a role, an archetype, or a play. We can also embody all scripts, narratives, plays, roles, and archetypes. We can see ourselves reflected in everything and everyone in the world. Instead of feeling fear and division, we can see shared humanity. In this seeing, unconditional love arises.

Afterword

Seeing the Beauty in the Dark

*M*ost of shadow work involves bringing what is shadow into the light. We hear what has been unheard in us and we see the patterns that have prevented us from truly living. We face the beliefs and problems that limit us as individuals. We see the beauty in life continually break us until our hearts lie bare.

Shadow work is known as one of the most direct routes to self-realization because it allows us to look towards the outer world to see our own inner pain. What we have made shadow within us, what lacks realization within us, will always populate the outer world. How we react towards it shows us what still needs inner resolution.

Over time, an interesting thing happens with shadow work. You get over your shit. You no longer are a child repeating the traumas and patterns that were ingrained in you from an early age. You are no longer a storehouse of repressed emotions. You welcome embodiment, feeling, and the experience of truly living. Each part of ourselves that we have cut off has also stolen a bit of our vitality, a bit of who we truly are. When we welcome more and more of ourselves back, we realize that how we think of ourselves is of the utmost importance. We can determine our own self-worth and our own motivations for being. We can let go of what others think we should be and discover who we truly are.

This work dissolves barriers within the self until we see humanity in each person that we meet. Beliefs fall away and patterns and ingrained behaviors that we thought were simply a part of our personality reveal themselves to be wounds. We are left with a blank slate and a new ability to decide what creates meaning in our lives.

When we get over ourselves, we find that the enormous amount of time and energy that we spent trying to be worthy, lovable, and approved by the outer world can be better utilized. Likewise, we bring an end to the endless egoic competitions that we once engaged in to prove our superiority—or inferiority. We no longer need to fight against those deemed Other; we discover the essential humanity and simplicity that lie within each one of us. Instead of seeing our differences, we see our humanity mirrored in each person we meet.

We are worthy because we always have been worthy. We are inherently worthy and lovable. We all have the spark of divinity within us. That light has simply been dimmed, bit by bit, until we associate ourselves with the negativity and darkness that we have experienced.

There is an incredible irony in that shadow work creates individuals who embody light and who can be loving in a world that is so often cruel and merciless. When we get over ourselves, we find that we naturally gravitate towards being of service in the world. We have the energy and capacity to offer our unique abilities and skills when we no longer spend all of our time and energy fighting against ourselves.

The final phase of shadow work is to come into stillness—into a place of essential being. When we can be still, so many things with which we identify ourselves fall away. This includes the endless quest to improve ourselves and the desire to bring our shadows into the light.

We can simply feel. We can simply live.

In the end, shadow work leads to the ability to sit with darkness, to sit with intuition and feeling and uncertainty and change and to find comfort in them. It is in our comfort with that chaos, with the darkness within ourselves, that we become embodied. There we find our essential humanity, as we let go of the need to be perfect or to reach a specific goal. We do not need to be anything other than who and what we are right now.

It is yet another irony that when we become comfortable with chaos and uncertainty, we feel the deep stillness that many of us seek.

At this juncture we find the deep and abiding self-love that has been lacking for so long. We come out of the state of isolation and alienation that kept us in a fractured darkness, and we find connection. We were never alone, we just thought that we were.

Each one of us is a lonely soul, desperately seeking connection. It is by releasing the idea of separation, the false competitions, the desire for outer approval that we deeply connect with others. When we de-armor ourselves, our vulnerability opens us to the love and beauty of the world. The world can reflect all its beauty back to us, yet we see it only if we journey through the pain. We can reach out to each lonely aspect of ourselves reflected in the outside world and offer simple human empathy. We deepen our self-compassion by seeing ourselves in each person that we meet.

As we explore the very depths of our wrongness, our alienation, and our feelings of not being good enough, we find the golden light of realization.

May you find that light within yourself . . . and in the world.

Further Reading

Resources that have inspired my understanding of the shadow

Berne, Eric. *Games People Play.* New York NY: Ballantine Books, 1996.

Bly, Robert. *A Little Book on the Human Shadow.* San Francisco CA: HarperOne, 1988.

Brown, Norman. *Life Against Death.* Middletown CT: Wesleyan University Press, 1985.

Edinger, Edward. *Archetype of the Apocalypse.* Chicago IL: Open Court, 1999.

Frankl, Viktor. *Man's Search for Meaning.* Boston MA: Beacon Press, 2006.

von Franz, Marie-Louise. *Shadow and Evil in Fairy Tales.* Boulder CO: Shambhala, 1995.

Fromm, Erich. *The Anatomy of Human Destructiveness.* New York NY: Owl Books, Henry Holt and Company, 1973.

Hillman, James. *The Dream and the Underworld.* New York NY: Harper & Row, 1979.

Joiner, Thomas. *Myths about Suicide.* Cambridge MA: Harvard University Press, 2010.

Joy, W. Brugh. *Avalanche.* New York NY: Ballantine Books, 1990.

Kalsched, Donald. *The Inner World of Trauma.* Abingdon-on-Thames, UK: Routledge, 1996.

Kristeva, Julia. *Black Sun.* New York NY: Columbia University Press, 1989.

———. *Powers of Horror.* New York NY: Columbia University Press, 1982.

Lacan, Jacques. *Anxiety*. Malden, MA: Polity Press, 2016.

Lowen, Alexander. *Fear of Life*. Alachua FL: Bioenergetics Press, 2003.

Marlan, Stanton. *The Black Sun*. College Station TX: Texas A & M Press, 2005.

Maté, Gabor. *When the Body Says No*. Toronto: Vintage Canada, 2004.

Paul, Marla. 2014, February 4. How Your Memory Rewrites the Past; https://news.northwestern.edu/stories/2014/02/how-your-memory-rewrites-the-past

Rogers, Carl. *On Becoming a Person*. Boston MA: Mariner Books, 2012.

Wilson, Robert Anton. *Prometheus Rising*. Grand Junction CO: Hilaritas Press, 2016.

Winnicott, D.W. *Playing and Reality*. Abingdon-on-Thames, UK: Routledge, 1982.

Woodman, Marion. *Addiction to Perfection*. Toronto: Inner City Books, 1982.

———. *Leaving My Father's House*. Boulder CO: Shambhala, 1993.

Yalom, Irvin. *Staring at the Sun*. Hoboken NJ: Jossey-Bass, 2008.

———. *Existential Psychotherapy*. New York NY: BasicBooks, 1980.

About the Author

Mary Mueller Shutan is a spiritual healer and teacher with an extensive background in Chinese medicine, energy work, and somatic bodywork. She is the author of several books, including *The Spiritual Awakening Guide*, *Managing Psychic Abilities*, *The Complete Cord Course*, *The Shamanic Workbook*, and *The Body Deva*. Mary lives near Chicago, Illinois.

For more information on her work please visit her website:
maryshutan.com